食とクッキング
英語小事典（第2版）

重要語句・基本英会話・食ミニ情報

中島恵子
藤平英一

共編者

A. D. ローゼン
栄沢啓子

協力

JN009221

開文社出版

まえがき

　食に関する英語は、すでに日本語化されているものを含め日常会話の中でもかなり重要な部分を占めています。

　食は、世界中どこでどんな生活をしていても、営みの中心になっています。日本では食材もありとあらゆるものが、世界中から輸入されていて、すでに国際化されています。現在日本の食糧輸入依存率は供給熱量ベースで58％、穀物重量ベースでは71％に達しています。調理方法や料理作法も、国際化と共に大きな影響を受けて一段と多様化してきています。

　誰もが気楽に海外へ行ける今日、外国の料理を食べる機会も多く、それが大きな楽しみのひとつにもなっています。また、食を通して異文化を体験し理解することもますます大切になってきています。

　日本に滞在する外国人登録者数は、1997年末現在148万人にも達し、1996年末に比べて4.8％も増加しています。その中には、日本料理の研修にさまざまな国から来た多くの外国人がいます。日本人もまた、たくさんの料理人が海外で研修を積んでいます。

　本書は、膨大な食の世界からみればささやかな小事典ですが「小道具の玉手箱」として、ナイフやフォークや包丁と同じように、いつでも身近に持って、有効に活用していただけましたら幸いです。

編著者

☆食物は生命の糧なり
　Bread is the staff of life.

目　次

PART 14

食とクッキング英語小事典 (第2版)

A Little Dictionary of Food & Cooking
(second edition)

PART 1

レストランのメニューなどに関する重要語句 （和英）

あ	赤出し	dark brown *miso* soup
	揚げ出し豆腐	deep-fried *tofu* with amber sauce
	揚げ物	fried dishes
	あさりの酒蒸し	*sake*-steamed clams
	あじのたたき	horse mackerel *tataki*
	厚焼き卵	thick omelet
	網焼き	cooked over a wire grill
	炒め物	fried food
	一品料理	a-la-carte dish
	稲荷寿司	*sushi* rice in fried *tofu*
	いり卵	scrambled eggs
	いわしの薩摩揚げ	deep-fried sardine ball
	うどん	*udon*; whitewheat noodles
	うな重	grilled eel "piled" over rice
	うな丼	bowl of eel and rice
	梅（定食・ランチ）	*ume*; regular quality
	Ａランチ	"A" lunch special
	海老グラタン	macaroni gratin with shrimp
	海老ドリア	shrimp doria
	海老ピラフ	shrimp pilaf
	大ざる	large portion of *zaru soba*
	大とろ	fattest meat of tuna
	大盛り	large helping [serving]
	お子様ランチ	children's lunch
	お好み焼き	Japanese-style savory pancakes
	お新香	Japanese-style pickled vegetables
	おでん	*oden*; fishcakes and vegetables in broth

レストランのメニューなどに関する重要語句 （英和）

A	à-la-carte dish	一品料理
	"A" lunch special	A ランチ
	appetizers	前菜
	a set menu selected food served on an individual tray	会席料理
	assortment	盛り合わせ
	assortment of stewed seasonal vegetables	季節の炊き合わせ，旬の煮物
	au gratin	グラタン
B	bacon and eggs	ベーコンエッグ
	barbecue	バーベキュー
	bean curd baked and coated with *miso*	田楽
	beaten egg soup	かき卵汁
	beef bowl	牛丼
	beef curry	ビーフカレー
	beef cutlet	ビーフカツレツ
	beef steak	ビーフステーキ
	beef stew	ビーフシチュー
	beef *teriyaki*	牛肉の照り焼き
	beer (*bière*〈仏〉; *birra*〈伊〉)	ビール
	black tea	紅茶
	blowfish and vegetable pot	ふぐちり
	boiled fish	煮魚
	boiled rice	ご飯
	bowl of cooked egg and rice	玉子丼
	bowl of cooked meat, vegetables and rice	中華丼
	bowl of eel and rice	うな丼
	bowl of pork cutlet and rice	かつ丼
	bowl of raw tuna and rice	鉄火丼

落とし卵	poached eggs
オードブル	hors d'oeuvre; *antipasti*〈伊〉
オニオンスープ	onion soup
オムレツ	omelet
親子丼	chicken and egg over rice
か 会席料理	*kaiseki*; a set menu selected food served on an individual tray
海草サラダ	seaweed salad
かき卵	scrambled eggs
かき卵汁	beaten egg soup
かきフライ	deep-fried oyster
かけ	plain noodles in hot broth
かつおたたき	slightly broiled bonito
かつ丼	bowl of pork cutlet and rice
かっぱ巻	cucumber-filled rolled *sushi*
かに酢	vinegared crab and cucumber
かに雑炊	crab risotto
かに肉のソテー	crabmeat saute
釜飯	steamed rice with various ingredients
蒲焼(かばやき)	broiled eel
鴨南蛮そば	duck *nanban soba* noodles
鴨のロースト	roasted duck
かゆ	gruel
カルパッチョ	carpaccio〈伊〉
カルビ	Korean-style beef rib meat
かれいのから揚げ	deep-fried flounder boat
カレーライス	rice with curry sauce
季節の炊き合わせ	assortment of stewed seasonal vegetables
キッシュ	quiche〈仏〉
牛丼	beef bowl
牛肉の照り焼き	beef *teriyaki*
餃子	Chinese-style pork dumplings
魚介類料理	seafood platter
具入りオムレツ	Western omelet

breakfast (*petit déjeuner* 〈仏〉; *prima colazione* 〈伊〉)	朝食
broiled dishes	焼物
broiled eel	蒲焼(かばやき)
broiled fish	照り焼き
broiled [roast] fish	焼魚
broiled sword fish	めかじきのあぶり焼き
broiled [roast] fish	焼魚
buckwheat noodles	そば

C

cake	ケーキ
carpaccio	カルパッチョ
charcoal grilled salmon	鮭の炭火焼
cheese (*fromage* 〈仏〉; *formaggio* 〈伊〉)	チーズ
chef's selection of *tempura* pieces	天ぷら盛り合わせ
chicken and egg over rice	親子丼
chicken au gratin	チキングラタン
chicken cutlet	チキンかつ
chicken fricassee	チキンフリカッセ
chicken pilaf	チキンピラフ
chicken pot	水炊き
children's lunch	お子様ランチ
chilled *somen* noodles	冷しそうめん
chilled thin wheat noodles	冷麦
chilled *tofu* cut into blocks	冷奴
Chinese food	中華料理
Chinese noodles in *miso* broth	味噌ラーメン
Chinese noodles in soup	ラーメン
Chinese noodles in soup with barbecued pork	チャーシュウ麺
Chinese noodles in white soup	タンメン
Chinese-style barbecued pork	チャーシュウ
Chinese-style pork dumplings	餃子
***chirashi sushi*; assorted raw fish over rice**	ちらし寿司
chop suey	八宝菜
clear soup	コンソメスープ

串揚げ	deep-fried meat, seafood and vegetables on skewers
クッパ	Korean-style steamed rice in soup
グラタン	au gratin
軽食	light meal
ケーキ	cake
紅茶	black tea
ご飯	boiled rice
御飯物	rice dishes
コーヒー	coffee
コーヒーケーキ	coffee cake
小料理屋	small restaurant
コロッケ	croquette
コンソメスープ	consommé; clear soup
さ 魚料理	fish dishes; *poissons*〈仏〉; *pesce*〈伊〉
鮭の炭火焼	charcoal grilled salmon
刺身	sliced raw fish
刺身盛り合わせ	platter of assorted raw fish
サテ	satay
サラダ	salad; *salade*〈仏〉; *insalata*〈伊〉
ざる(そば)	*mori* with dried seaweed strips
サーロインステーキ	sirloin steak
シチュー	stew
シーフードカレー	seafood curry
シーフードグラタン	seafood gratin
シーフードサラダ	seafood salad
シーフードピラフ	seafood pilaf
しゃぶしゃぶ	*shabu-shabu*; thinly sliced beef quickcooked in boiling broth
しゅうまい	steamed Chinese-style pork dumplings
旬(の)	seasonal
旬の煮物	assortment of stewed seasonal vegetables
上	*jyo*; special quality
しょうが焼き	ginger pork sauté

	codfish steak	たらのステーキ
	coffee	コーヒー
	coffee cake	コーヒーケーキ
	cold Chinese-style noodles	冷し中華
	consommé	コンソメスープ
	cooked over a wire grill	網焼き
	crabmeat egg	芙蓉蟹
	crabmeat saute	かに肉のソテー
	crab risotto	かに雑炊
	croquette	コロッケ
	cucumber-filled rolled *sushi*	かっぱ巻
	cucumber with *miso* paste	もろきゅう
	curried pilaf	ドライカレー
D	dark brown *miso* soup	赤出し
	deep-fried assortment of fish or meat	ミックスフライ
	deep-fried flounder boat	かれいのから揚げ
	deep-fried ground-meat patty	メンチかつ
	deep-fried marinated chicken	鶏の竜田揚げ
	deep-fried meat, seafood and vegetables on skewers	串揚げ
	deep-fried oyster	かきフライ
	deep-fried sardine ball	いわしの薩摩揚げ
	deep-fried *tofu* with amber sauce	揚げ出し豆腐
	dessert (*desserts*〈仏〉; *dolce*〈伊〉)	デザート
	dinner (*dîner*〈仏〉; *cena*〈伊〉)	夕食
	duck *nanban soba* noodles	鴨南蛮そば
E	egg rolls	春巻
	entrée	中心になる料理
	everyday (household) dish	総菜, 惣菜
	extra-special quality	特上, 松
F	fat liver of goose or duck	フォア・グラ
	fattest meat of tuna	大とろ
	fermented beans	納豆
	fine wheat noodles	そうめん
	fish and vegetable stew	ちり鍋

上ちらし	special quality of *chirashi-zushi*
食堂	restaurant
すき焼き	*sukiyaki*; thinly sliced beef and vegetables
寿司	*sushi*; rice and raw fish dish
酢だこ	vinegared boiled octopus
酢の物	vinegared dish
スパゲティ	spaghetti
スープ	soup; *potage et soupes*〈仏〉; *zuppe*〈伊〉
酢豚	sweet and sour pork
ゼリー	jelly; flavored gelatin
前菜	appetizers; hors d'oeuvres
ぜんざい	sweet red bean soup with rice cakes
総菜，物菜	everyday (household) dish
そうめん	fine wheat noodles
そば	*soba*; buckwheat noodles
た 竹	*take*; special quality
タコス	taco; Mexican pancakes
だし巻き卵	rolled omelet
玉子丼	bowl of cooked egg and rice
たらのステーキ	codfish steak
タンドリー・チキン	tandoori chicken
タンメン	Chinese noodles in white soup
チキンかつ	chicken cutlet
チキングラタン	chicken au gratin
チキンピラフ	chicken pilaf
チキンフリカッセ	chicken fricassee
チゲ	spicy Korean-style stew
チーズ	cheese; *fromage*〈仏〉; *formaggio*〈伊〉
チャーシュウ	Chinese-style barbecued pork
チャーシュウ麺	Chinese noodles in soup with barbecued pork
チャーハン	fried rice
茶碗蒸し	savory custard cup

	fishcakes and vegetables in broth	おでん
	fish dishes (*poissons*〈仏〉; *pesce*〈伊〉)	魚料理
	flavored gelatin	ゼリー
	French-style fish stew	ブイヤベース
	fresh oyster	生がき
	fried bean-curd	生揚げ
	fried chicken	鶏のから揚げ
	fried Chinese noodles	焼そば
	fried dishes	揚げ物
	fried egg	目玉焼き
	fried food	炒め物
	fried rice	チャーハン，焼飯
	fried seafood and vegetables	天ぷら
G	garnish	つま(料理用)
	ginger pork sauté	豚肉のしょうが焼き
	grilled chicken on skewers	焼鳥
	grilled eel "piled" over rice	うな重
	grilled steaks and other foods	鉄板焼
	gruel	かゆ
H	ham and eggs	ハムエッグ
	hamburger	ハンバーグ
	homemade dish	手料理
	hors d'oeuvre *antipasti*〈伊〉	オードブル，つき出し，前菜
	horse mackerel *tataki*	あじのたたき
	hotchpotch-style stew	寄せ鍋
	hotpot (cooked at the table)	鍋物
I	Indian flat bread	ナン
	Indonesian-style fried rice	ナシゴレン
J	Japanese food	和食
	Japanese ginger	みょうが
	Japanese-style barbecue cooked in front of customers	炉ばた焼
	Japanese-style pickled vegetables	お新香；和風ピクルス
	Japanese-style salad	和風サラダ

ちゃんこ鍋	seafood and vegetable stew often eaten by *sumo* wreslers
中華サラダ	salad with spicy Chinese-style dressing
中華丼	bowl of cooked meat, vegetables and rice
中華料理	Chinese food
昼食	lunch; *déjeuner* 〈仏〉; *seconda colazione* 〈伊〉
中心になる料理	main dish, main coure; entrée
朝食	breakfast; *petit déjeuner* 〈仏〉; *prima colazione* 〈伊〉
ちらし寿司	*chirashi sushi*; assorted raw fish over rice
ちり鍋	fish and vegetable stew
つき出し	hors d'oeuvre
ツナサラダ	tuna salad
つま（料理用）	garnish
詰め物	stuffing
定食	set meal; table d'hôte
デザート	dessert; *desserts* 〈仏〉; *dolce* 〈伊〉
鉄火丼	bowl of raw tuna and rice
鉄火巻	tunny slices rolled in rice
鉄板焼	grilled steaks and other foods
テリーヌ	terrine
照り焼き	broiled fish
手料理	homemade dish
田楽	bean curd baked and coated with *miso*
天重	*tempura*-fried prawns on rice in a box
天丼	*tempura*-fried prawns over rice
天ぷら	*tempura*; fried seafood and vegetables
天ぷらそば	*soba* noodles with *tempura*-fried prawns topping
天ぷら定食	pieces of *tempura* with rice, soup, and pickles

	Japanese-style savory pancakes	お好み焼き
	Japanese-style set meal	和定食
K	Korean-style assorted vegetable platter	ナムル
	Korean-style barbecue	焼肉
	Korean-style beef rib meat	カルビ
	Korean-style steamed rice	ビビンバ
	Korean-style steamed rice in soup	クッパ
L	large helping [serving]	大盛り
	large portion of *zaru soba*	大ざる
	light meal	軽食
	lunch (*déjeuner* 〈仏〉; *seconda colazione* 〈伊〉)	昼食
M	macaroni gratin	マカロニグラタン
	macaroni gratin with shrimp	海老グラタン
	main course	中心になる料理
	main dish	中心になる料理
	maple syrup	メープルシロップ
	meat dishes (*viandes*〈仏〉; *carni*〈伊〉)	肉料理
	meat pot	肉鍋
	menu (*carte* 〈仏〉; *lista* 〈伊〉)	メニュー
	Mexican pancakes	タコス
	miso soup	味噌汁
	miso soup with pork and vegetables	豚汁
	mori with dried seaweed strips	ざる(そば)
N	noodles	めん類
	noodles piled on a bamboo screen	もり(そば)
O	omelet	オムレツ
	onion soup	オニオンスープ
	Osaka-style molded *sushi*	バッテラ寿司
	our specialty	当店自慢の料理
P	pasta	パスタ

天ぷら盛り合わせ		chef's selection of *tempura* pieces
当店自慢の料理		our specialty
特上		extra-special quality
トム・ヤム・クン		spicy shrimp soup
ドライカレー		curried pilaf
鶏のから揚げ		fried chicken
鶏の竜田揚げ		deep-fried marinated chicken
豚かつ		pork cutlet
豚汁		*miso* soup with pork and vegetables
な	ナシゴレン	Indonesian-style fried rice
	納豆	fermented beans
	生うに	raw sea-urchin roe
	鍋物	hotpot (cooked at the table)
	鍋焼うどん	*udon* noodles in clay pots
	生揚げ	fried bean-curd
	生がき	fresh oyster
	生卵	raw egg
	ナポリタン	tomato sauce with vegetables
	並	*nami*; regular quality
	ナムル	Korean-style assorted vegetable platter
	ナン	Indian flat bread
	にぎり寿司	*nigiri sushi*; raw fish pieces over rice fingers
	肉鍋	meat pot
	肉料理	meat dishes; *viandes*〈仏〉; *carni*〈伊〉
	煮込み	slowly stewed foods
	煮魚	boiled fish
	煮物	stewed foods
	ねぎとろ巻	scallion-and-tuna roll *sushi*
は	パエリア	Spanish saffron rice
	パスタ	pasta
	バッテラ寿司	Osaka-style molded *sushi*
	八宝菜	chop suey

	pieces of *tempura* with rice, soup, and pickles	天ぷら定食
	plain noodles in hot broth	かけ
	platter of assorted raw fish	刺身盛り合わせ
	poached eggs	落とし卵
	pork curry	ポークカレー
	pork cutlet	豚かつ
	potage	ポタージュ
	pot of loaches, eggs and burdock	柳川鍋
	preserved egg	ピータン
	pudding	プリン
Q	quiche	キッシュ
R	raw blowfish thinly sliced	ふぐ刺
	raw egg	生卵
	raw fish pieces over rice fingers	にぎり寿司
	raw sea-urchin roe	生うに
	regular quality	並, 梅
	restaurant	食堂, レストラン
	rice and raw fish dish	寿司
	rice dishes	御飯物
	rice with curry sauce	カレーライス
	rice with hashed meat	ハヤシライス
	roast	ロースト
	roast beef	ローストビーフ
	roasted duck	鴨のロースト
	rolled omelet	だし巻き卵
	rolled *sushi*	巻き寿司
S	*sake*-steamed clams	あさりの酒蒸し
	salad (*salade*〈仏〉; *insalata*〈伊〉)	サラダ
	salad with spicy Chinese-style dressing	中華サラダ
	satay	サテ
	savory custard cup	茶碗蒸し
	savory paste of liver, meat, or fish	パテ
	scallion-and-tuna roll *sushi*	ねぎとろ巻

パテ	savory paste of liver, meat, or fish
バーベキュー	barbecue
ハムエッグ	ham and eggs
ハヤシライス	rice with hashed meat
春巻	egg rolls; spring rolls
半熟卵	soft-boiled egg
ハンバーグ	hamburger
ビジネスランチ	working lunch
ピータン	preserved egg
ビビンバ	Korean-style steamed rice
ビーフカツレツ	beef cutlet
ビーフカレー	beef curry
ビーフシチュー	beef stew
ビーフステーキ	beef steak
冷しそうめん	chilled *somen* noodles
冷し中華	cold Chinese-style noodles
冷麦	chilled thin wheat noodles
冷奴	chilled *tofu* cut into blocks
ビール	beer; *bière*〈仏〉; *birra*〈伊〉
ブイヤベース	French-style fish stew
フォア・グラ	fat liver of goose or duck
ふぐ刺	raw blowfish thinly sliced
ふぐちり	blowfish and vegetable pot
豚肉のしょうが焼き	ginger pork sauté
太巻き寿司	thick-rolled *sushi*
芙蓉蟹	crabmeat egg
ぶりの照り焼き	yellowtail *teriyaki*
プリン	pudding
ベーコンエッグ	bacon and eggs
ポークカレー	pork curry
ポタージュ	thick soup; potage
ま 麻婆豆腐	spicy bean curd and pork
マカロニグラタン	macaroni gratin
巻き寿司	rolled *sushi*
幕の内弁当	"special of the house" boxed lunch
松	*matsu*; extra-special quality

scrambled eggs	いり卵, かき卵
seafood and vegetable stew often eaten by *sumo* wrestlers	ちゃんこ鍋
seafood curry	シーフードカレー
seafood gratin	シーフードグラタン
seafood pilaf	シーフードピラフ
seafood platter	魚介類料理
seafood salad	シーフードサラダ
seasonal	旬(の)
seaweed salad	海草サラダ
set meal	定食
shabu-shabu	しゃぶしゃぶ
shrimp doria	海老ドリア
shrimp pilaf	海老ピラフ
sirloin steak	サーロインステーキ
sliced raw fish	刺身
sliced raw tuna dressed with grated yam	山かけ
slightly broiled bonito	かつおたたき
slowly stewed foods	煮込み
small restaurant	小料理屋
soba noodles with *tempura*-fried prawns topping	天ぷらそば
soft-boiled egg	半熟卵
soup (*potage et soupes*〈仏〉; *zuppe*〈伊〉)	スープ
spaghetti	スパゲティ
Spanish saffron rice	パエリア
"special of the house" boxed lunch	幕の内弁当
special quality	竹, 上
special quality of *chirashi-zushi*	上ちらし
spicy bean curd and pork	麻婆豆腐
spicy Korean-style stew	チゲ
spicy shrimp soup	トム・ヤム・クン
spring rolls	春巻

水	water; *eau*〈仏〉; *acqua*〈伊〉
水炊き	*mizutaki*; chicken pot
味噌汁	*miso* soup
味噌ラーメン	Chinese noodles in *miso* broth
ミックスフライ	deep-fried assortment of fish or meat
みょうが	*myoga*; Japanese ginger
めかじきのあぶり焼き	broiled sword fish
目玉焼き	fried egg; sunnyside up
メニュー	menu; *carte* 〈仏〉; *lista* 〈伊〉
メープルシロップ	maple syrup
メンチかつ	deep-fried ground-meat patty
めん類	noodles
もり(そば)	*mori*; noodles piled on a bamboo screen
盛り合わせ	assortment
もろきゅう	cucumber with *miso* paste
や 焼魚	broiled [roast] fish
焼そば	fried Chinese noodles
焼鳥	*yakitori*; grilled chicken on skewers
焼肉	Korean-style barbecue
焼飯(チャーハン)	fried rice
焼物	broiled dishes
柳川鍋	*yanagawa nabe*; pot of loaches, eggs and burdock
山かけ	*yamakake*; sliced raw tuna dressed with grated yam
夕食	dinner; *dîner*〈仏〉; *cena*〈伊〉
湯豆腐	warmed *tofu* blocks in pot
洋食	Western dishes
寄せ鍋	hotchpotch-style stew
ら ラーメン	*lamen*; Chinese noodles in soup
レストラン	restaurant
ロースト	roast
ローストビーフ	roast beef

	steamed Chinese-style pork dumplings	しゅうまい
	steamed rice with various ingredients	釜飯
	stew	シチュー
	stewed foods	煮物
	stuffing	詰め物
	sunnyside up	目玉焼き
	sushi rice in fried *tofu*	稲荷寿司
	sweet and sour pork	酢豚
	sweet red bean soup with rice cakes	ぜんざい
T	table d'hôte	定食
	taco	タコス
	tandoori chicken	タンドリー・チキン
	tempura-fried prawns on rice in a box	天重
	tempura-fried prawns over rice	天丼
	terrine	テリーヌ
	thick omelet	厚焼き卵
	thick-rolled *sushi*	太巻き寿司
	thick soup	ポタージュ
	thinly sliced beef and vegetables	すき焼き
	thinly sliced beef quickcooked in boiling broth	しゃぶしゃぶ
	tomato sauce with vegetables	ナポリタン
	tuna salad	ツナサラダ
	tunny slices rolled in rice	鉄火巻
U	*udon* noodles in clay pots	鍋焼うどん
V	vinegared boiled octopus	酢だこ
	vinegared crab and cucumber	かに酢
	vinegared dish	酢の物
W	warmed *tofu* blocks in pot	湯豆腐
	water (*eau*〈仏〉; *acqua*〈伊〉)	水
	Western dishes	洋食
	Western omelet	具入りオムレツ

炉ばた焼	Japanese-style barbecue cooked in front of customers
わ ワイン	wine; *vin*〈仏〉; *vino*〈伊〉
和食	Japanese food
和定食	Japanese-style set meal
和風サラダ	Japanese-style salad
和風ピクルス	Japanese-style pickled vegetables
ワンタン	wonton

whitewheat noodles	うどん
wine (*vin*〈仏〉; *vino*〈伊〉)	ワイン
wonton	ワンタン
working lunch	ビジネスランチ
Y yellowtail *teriyaki*	ぶりの照り焼き

スープ（Soups）

ヴィソシワーズ	vichyssoise 〈仏〉
オックステイル・スープ	oxtail soup
オニオン・スープ	onion soup
粕汁	*sake* lees soup
ガスパチョ	gaspacho 〈西〉
カルビ・スープ	soup with beef-rib meat
牛肉のスープ	beef broth（料理用）
クリーム・スープ	cream soup
コンソメ・スープ	consommé
魚のスープ	fish broth（料理用）
スコッチ・ブロス	Scotch broth
澄まし汁	Japanese-style clear soup
卵スープ	egg soup
チキンクリーム・スープ	cream of chicken soup
テグタン・スープ	Korean-style rib soup
トマト・スープ	tomato soup
トム・ヤム・クン	spicy shrimp soup
鶏肉のスープ	chicken broth（料理用）
豚（とん）汁	*miso* soup with pork and vegetables
なめこ汁	Japanese-style soup with tiny mushrooms
ヌードル・スープ	noodle soup
日替りスープ	soup of the day
ビスク	bisque 〈仏〉
ブイヤベース	bouillabaisse
ふかヒレ・スープ	Chinese-style shark fin soup
ポタージュ	potage
ボルシチ	beetroot soup
豆のスープ	pea soup
ミネストローネ	minestrone 〈伊〉
野菜スープ	vegetable soup

Soups （スープ）

beef broth	牛肉のスープ（料理用）
beetroot soup	ボルシチ
bisque	〈仏〉ビスク
bouillabaisse	ブイヤベース
chicken broth	鶏肉のスープ（料理用）
Chinese-style shark fin soup	ふかヒレ・スープ
consommé	コンソメ・スープ
cream of chicken soup	チキンクリーム・スープ
cream soup	クリーム・スープ
egg soup	卵スープ
fish broth	魚のスープ（料理用）
gaspacho	〈西〉ガスパチョ
Japanese-style clear soup	澄まし汁
Japanese-style soup with tiny mushrooms	なめこ汁
Korean-style rib soup	テグタン・スープ
minestrone	〈伊〉ミネストローネ
miso soup with pork and vegetables	豚(とん)汁
noodle soup	ヌードル・スープ
onion soup	オニオン・スープ
oxtail soup	オックステイル・スープ
pea soup	豆のスープ
potage	ポタージュ
sake lees soup	粕汁
Scotch broth	スコッチ・ブロス
soup of the day	日替りスープ
soup with beef-rib meat	カルビ・スープ
spicy shrimp soup	トム・ヤム・クン
tomato soup	トマト・スープ
vegetable soup	野菜スープ
vichyssoise	〈仏〉ヴィソソワーズ

PART 2

飲み物などに関する重要語句 (和英)

あ アイスコーヒー　　　　　　　iced coffee
アイスティー　　　　　　　　iced tea
アイスミルク　　　　　　　　iced milk
アイリッシュ・コーヒー　　　Irish coffee
上がり　　　　　　　　　　　tea (*sushi* shop lingo)
赤ワイン　　　　　　　　　　red wine
アクアヴィット(じゃがいもが　aquavit
　原料)
甘酒　　　　　　　　　　　　*amazake*; sweet drink made
　　　　　　　　　　　　　　　from fermented rice
アメリカンコーヒー　　　　　weak "American-style" coffee
アルマニャック　　　　　　　armagnac
インスタントコーヒー　　　　instant coffee
飲料　　　　　　　　　　　　drinks
飲料水　　　　　　　　　　　drinking water
ウイスキー　　　　　　　　　whiskey
ウィンナコーヒー　　　　　　Vienna coffee
ウオッカ　　　　　　　　　　vodka
烏龍茶(ウーロンチャ)　　　　Chinese oolong tea
エスプレッソ　　　　　　　　espresso
エッグノッグ　　　　　　　　egg nog
オレンジジュース　　　　　　orange juice
か カクテル　　　　　　　　　　cocktail
果汁　　　　　　　　　　　　fruit juice
カフェインレスコーヒー　　　decaffeinated coffee
カフェオレ　　　　　　　　　café au lait
カフェロワイヤル　　　　　　café royal
カプチーノ　　　　　　　　　cappuccino
カルバドス(アップルブランデ　calvados
　ー)
牛乳(ミルク)　　　　　　　　milk

飲み物などに関する重要語句（英和）

A	a glass of wine	グラスワイン
	apple juice	りんごジュース
	aquavit	アクアヴィット（じゃがいもが原料）
	armagnac	アルマニャック
B	banana juice	バナナジュース
	barley tea	麦茶
	beer	ビール
	beverage	飲み物（水以外）
	bitter	ビター
	black coffee	ブラックコーヒー
	black tea	紅茶
	black tea with lemon	レモンティー
	black tea with milk	ミルクティー
	bottle (usually a "keep" bottle of whiskey)	ボトル
	bourbon	バーボン
	brandy	ブランデー
C	café au lait	カフェオレ
	café royal	カフェロワイヤル
	calvados	カルバドス（アップルブランデー）
	cappuccino	カプチーノ
	champagne	シャンパン
	Chinese oolong tea	烏龍茶（ウーロンチャ）
	Chinese tea	中国茶
	chocolate	チョコレート
	cider	りんご酒，シードル（りんごが原料）
	coarse green tea	番茶
	Coca-cola	コカコーラ

玉露	high-quality green tea
キルシュ(さくらんぼが原料)	kirsch
グラスワイン	a glass of wine
クリームソーダ	green colored soda with vanilla ice cream
グレープフルーツジュース	grapefruit juice
黒ビール	stout〈米〉; porter〈英〉
玄米茶	tea mixed with rice kernels
紅茶	black tea
氷	ice
コカコーラ	Coca-cola
コーク	Coke
ココア	cocoa
粉茶(こな)	powdered green tea; dust tea
コニャック	cognac
コーヒー	coffee
コーヒーフロート	coffee float
昆布茶	*kombu* (seaweed) tea
さ サイダー	pop
酒	Japanese *sake*; rice wine
サングリア	sangria
シェイク	shake
シェリー	sherry
地酒	local *sake*
シードル(りんごが原料)	cider
シャンパン	champagne
ジュース	juice
シュナップス	schnapps
紹興酒	shao-hing Chinese wine
焼酎	*shochu*; Japanese grain liquor
白酒(しろざけ)	white *sake*
シロップ	syrup
白ワイン	white wine
ジン	gin
ジンジャエール	ginger ale
新酒	new *sake*
新茶	the first tea of the season
ジントニック	gin and tonic

	cocktail	カクテル
	cocoa	ココア
	coffee	コーヒー
	coffee float	コーヒーフロート
	cognac	コニャック
	Coke	コーク
	cold *sake*	冷酒(れいしゅ・ひやざけ)
	cold water	冷水
	concentrated juice	濃縮ジュース
D	decaffeinated coffee	カフェインレスコーヒー
	draft beer	生ビール
	drinking water	飲料水
	drinks	飲み物, 飲料
	dust tea	粉茶(こちゃ)
E	egg nog	エッグノッグ
	espresso	エスプレッソ
	evening drink	晩酌
F	fruit cocktail	フルーツカクテル
	fruit juice	フルーツジュース, 果汁
G	gin	ジン
	gin and tonic	ジントニック
	ginger ale	ジンジャエール
	grapefruit juice	グレープフルーツジュース
	green colored soda with vanilla ice cream	クリームソーダ
	green tea	緑茶
H	highball	ハイボール
	high-quality green tea	玉露
	hot milk	ホットミルク
I	ice	氷
	iced coffee	アイスコーヒー
	iced milk	アイスミルク
	iced tea	アイスティー
	instant coffee	インスタントコーヒー
	Irish coffee	アイリッシュ・コーヒー
J	Japanese grain liquor	焼酎
	Japanese *sake*	酒
	juice	ジュース

	スコッチ	Scotch whisky
	ストロベリージュース	strawberry juice
	スピリッツ	spirit
	ソーダ	soda
	ソーダ水	soda pop
	ソーダ割り	Scotch and soda
た	炭酸	soda
	茶	tea
	中国茶	Chinese tea
	酎ハイ	*shochu* cocktail
	チョコレート	chocolate
	ティーバッグ	tea-bag
	テキーラ（メキシコ特産の酒）	tequila
	豆乳	soy milk
	とそ	spiced New Year's *sake*
	トニックウォーター	tonic water
	どぶろく（濁酒）	unrefined *sake*
	トマトジュース	tomato juice
	トルココーヒー	Turkish coffee
な	生ビール	draft beer
	生水	unboiled water; tap water
	日本酒	*sake*
	濃縮ジュース	concentrated juice
	飲み物	drinks; beverage（水以外）
は	ハイボール	highball
	パインジュース	pineapple juice
	発泡（ぶどう）酒	sparkling wine
	バナナジュース	banana juice
	バーボン	bourbon
	晩酌	evening drink
	番茶	coarse green tea
	ビター	bitter
	冷水（ひやみず）	cold water
	ピュア・モルト	pure malt
	ビール	beer
	ひれ酒	toasted blowfish fins in hot *sake*
	ぶどう酒	wine
	ブラックコーヒー	black coffee

K	kirsch	キルシュ（さくらんぼが原料）
	kombu (seaweed) tea	昆布茶
L	lager	ラガー
	lemonade	レモネード
	lemon squash	レモンスカッシュ
	liqueur	リキュール
	local *sake*	地酒
M	melon juice	メロンジュース
	milk	ミルク，牛乳
	mineral water	ミネラルウォーター
	mixed juice	ミックスジュース
	mocha blend	モカ
N	new *sake*	新酒
O	orange juice	オレンジジュース
P	perrier mineral water	ペリエ
	pineapple juice	パインジュース
	pop	サイダー
	port	ポートワイン
	porter	〈英〉黒ビール
	powdered green (ground) tea	抹茶（まっちゃ）
	powdered green tea	粉茶（こちゃ）
	pure malt	ピュア・モルト
R	red wine	赤ワイン
	rice wine	酒
	roasted tea	ほうじ茶
	root beer	ルートビアー
	rosé	ロゼ（ワイン）
	rum	ラム
S	*sake*	日本酒
	sangria	サングリア
	schnapps	シュナップス（穀物の蒸留酒）
	Scotch and soda	ソーダ割り
	Scotch whisky	スコッチ
	shake	シェイク
	shao-hing Chinese wine	紹興酒
	sherry	シェリー
	shochu cocktail	酎ハイ
	soda	ソーダ，炭酸

	ブランデー	brandy
	フルーツカクテル	fruit cocktail
	フルーツジュース	fruit juice
	ブレンドコーヒー	strong "blend" coffee
	ペリエ	perrier mineral water
	ベルモット	vermouth
	ほうじ茶	roasted tea
	ホットミルク	hot milk
	ボトル	bottle (usually a "keep" bottle of whiskey)
	ポートワイン	port
ま	抹茶(まっちゃ)	powdered green (ground) tea
	水	water
	水割り	whiskey and water
	ミックスジュース	mixed juice
	ミネラルウォーター	mineral water
	ミルク	milk
	ミルクティー	black tea with milk
	麦茶	barley tea
	メロンジュース	melon juice
	モカ	mocha blend
ら	ラガー	lager
	ラム	rum
	ラムネ	soda pop
	リキュール	liqueur
	緑茶	green tea
	りんご酒	cider
	りんごジュース	apple juice
	ルートビアー	root beer
	冷酒(れいしゅ・ひやざけ)	cold *sake*
	冷水	cold water
	レモネード	lemonade
	レモンスカッシュ	lemon squash
	レモンティー	black tea with lemon
	ロゼ(ワイン)	rosé
わ	ワイン	wine

	soda pop	ラムネ；ソーダ水
	soy milk	豆乳
	sparkling wine	発泡(ぶどう)酒
	spiced New Year's *sake*	とそ
	spirit	スピリッツ
	stout	〈米〉黒ビール
	strawberry juice	ストロベリージュース
	strong "blend" coffee	ブレンドコーヒー
	sweet drink made from fermented rice	甘酒
	syrup	シロップ
T	tap water	生水
	tea	茶，上がり
	tea-bag	ティーバッグ
	tea mixed with rice kernels	玄米茶
	tequila	テキーラ(メキシコ特産の酒)
	the first tea of the season	新茶
	toasted blowfish fins in hot *sake*	ひれ酒
	tomato juice	トマトジュース
	tonic water	トニックウォーター
	Turkish coffee	トルココーヒー
U	unboiled water	生水
	unrefined *sake*	どぶろく(濁酒)
V	vermouth	ベルモット
	Vienna coffee	ウィンナコーヒー
	vodka	ウオッカ
W	water	水
	weak "American-style" coffee	アメリカンコーヒー
	whiskey	ウイスキー
	whiskey and water	水割り
	white *sake*	白酒(しろざけ)
	white wine	白ワイン
	wine	ぶどう酒，ワイン

カクテル (Cocktails)

アレキサンダー	Alexander
ウイスキー・サワー	whiskey sour
オールド・ファッションド	old fashioned
カンパリ・ソーダ	Campari-soda
ギムレット	gimlet
サイド・カー	side car
サングリア	sangria
シンガポール・スリング	Singapore sling
ジン・トニック	gin and tonic
ジン・フィズ	gin fizz
スクリュー・ドライバー	screwdriver
ソルティ・ドッグ	salty dog
ダイキリ	daiquiri
トム・コリンズ	Tom collins
ピンクレディー	pink lady
ブラディ・メアリー	bloody Mary
マティーニ	martini
マルガリータ	margarita
マンハッタン	Manhattan

ブランデー (brandy)

V.O. (very old)
　ブランデーの貯蔵年数の少ないもの。10〜12年もの。

VSO (very superior old)
　ブランデーの貯蔵年数が12〜20年のもの。

VSOP (very superior old pale)
　ブランデーの貯蔵年数が20〜30年のもの。

Cocktails （カクテル）

Alexander	アレキサンダー
bloody Mary	ブラディ・メアリー
Campari-soda	カンパリ・ソーダ
daiquiri	ダイキリ
gimlet	ギムレット
gin and tonic	ジン・トニック
gin fizz	ジン・フィズ
Manhattan	マンハッタン
margarita	マルガリータ
martini	マティーニ
old fashioned	オールド・ファッションド
pink lady	ピンクレディー
salty dog	ソルティ・ドック
sangria	サングリア
screwdriver	スクリュー・ドライバー
side car	サイド・カー
Singapore sling	シンガポール・スリング
Tom collins	トム・コリンズ
whiskey sour	ウイスキー・サワー

補 遺 （カクテル和英）

アラウンド・ザ・ワールド	Around the World
スティンガー	Stinger
ドライ・マンハッタン	Dry Manhattan
ビトウィーン・ザ・シーツ	Between the Sheets
ホワイト・レディー	White Lady
モスコミュール	Moscomule
ラスティー・ネイル	Rusty Nail

飲み物などに関する重要語句　31

PART 3

日常の食べ物などに関する重要語句（和英）

あ	アイスクリーム	ice-cream
	和え物	foods dressed with sauce
	揚げ菓子	fritter
	浅漬け	vegetables lightly preserved in salt or rice bran
	鯵(あじ)たたき	chopped raw horse mackerel
	味付海苔	flavored laver
	味付ハム	spiced ham
	厚揚げ	thick deep-fried bean curd
	アップルパイ	apple pie
	油揚げ	deep-fried bean curd
	甘味のないチョコレート	unsweetened chocolate
	あられ(おかき)	rice-flour crackers
	あんまん	red bean-filled steamed bun
	いか丸焼き	whole grilled squid
	一夜漬け	pickles salted overnight
	稲荷鮨	rice wrapped in a bag of fried bean curd
	インスタント・ラーメン	instant Chinese noodles
	ウィンナソーセージ	Vienna sausage
	うずら卵	quail egg
	うどん	*udon*; fat wheat noodles
	梅干	pickled plum
	エクレア	éclair
	枝豆	boiled green soybeans
	エバミルク	evaporated milk
	大とろ	fatty portion of tuna belly
	大盛り	large portion
	お菓子	sweets; desserts
	おかず	side dish
	お好み焼き	Japanese-style pancake

日常の食べ物などに関する重要語句（英和）

|A| afternoon tea　　　　　　　　　　午後のお茶
　 apple pie　　　　　　　　　　　　アップルパイ
　 assortment of *oden* items　　　おでん盛り合わせ
|B| bacon　　　　　　　　　　　　　　ベーコン
　 baked goods　　　　　　　　　　　パン類
　 barbecued pork　　　　　　　　　焼豚
　 bean curd　　　　　　　　　　　　豆腐（とう）
　 bean curd baked and coated　　　田楽
　　　with *miso*
　 biscuits　　　　　　　　　　　　　ビスケット，クッキー
　 boild rice mixed with meat　　　混ぜご飯
　　　and other ingridients
　 boiled eggs　　　　　　　　　　　ゆで卵
　 boiled green soybeans　　　　　　枝豆
　 boiled rice ball　　　　　　　　　おにぎり
　 boiled rice with *matsutake*　　　松茸ご飯
　　　mushroom
　 boiled spinach　　　　　　　　　　ほうれん草のお浸し
　 boilled beans　　　　　　　　　　煮豆
　 boxed lunch　　　　　　　　　　　弁当
　 braised *hijiki* seaweed　　　　　ひじきのいため煮
　 bread　　　　　　　　　　　　　　パン
　 boiled fish paste　　　　　　　　かまぼこ
　 brown algae　　　　　　　　　　　ひじき
　 brown bread　　　　　　　　　　ブラウンブレッド
　 bun with filling　　　　　　　　　饅頭（まんじゅう）
　 butter　　　　　　　　　　　　　　バター
|C| cake of pounded fish　　　　　　はんぺん
　 camembert　　　　　　　　　　　カマンベール
　 canape　　　　　　　　　　　　　カナッペ
　 candy　　　　　　　　　　　　　　キャンデー

お汁粉		sweet mashed red bean soup with rice cakes
お澄まし		clear soup
おだまき		spool
お茶漬		rice in a bowl of green tea
おつまみ		snack dish
おつゆ		soup
おでん盛り合わせ		assortment of *oden* items
オニオンフレークス		onion flakes
鬼殻焼(おにがらやき)		roast lobster
おにぎり		boiled rice ball
オープン・サンドイッチ		open sandwich
おやつ		snack
か かき揚げ		fritters
かけ汁		sauce
菓子パン		sweetened bun
カステラ		castella
かつおぶし		dried bonito flakes
カナッペ		canape
かにコロッケ		crab croquette
かぶと煮		stewed head of fish
かまぼこ		*kamaboko*; boiled fish paste
カマンベール		camembert
かやくご飯		rice with chicken and vegetables
から揚げ		deep-fried
がり		slices of pickled ginger
カルパッチョ		carpaccio〈伊〉
カレーうどん		*udon* noodles in curry sauce
カレー料理		curried foods
乾燥マッシュポテト		dehydrated mashed potatoes
缶詰		canned food
缶詰スープ		canned soup
かんぴょう		dried gourd shavings
キッシュ		quiche
きな粉		soybean flour
絹ごし豆腐		very delicate *tofu*

	canned food	缶詰
	canned soup	缶詰スープ
	caramel	キャラメル
	carpaccio	カルパッチョ
	castella	カステラ
	cheap cakes	駄菓子
	cheese	チーズ
	chestnut rice	栗ご飯
	chicken meatballs	つくね
	chicken *mizutaki* in pot	水炊き
	chilled sliced tomato	冷しトマト
	chilled *tofu*	冷奴(ひゃやっこ)
	Chinese-style dumpling	餃子
	Chinese-style egg ［spring］ roll	春巻
	chocolate	チョコレート
	chopped raw horse mackerel	鯵(あじ)たたき
	clear soup	お澄まし，澄まし汁
	cod roe	たらこ
	condensed milk	コンデンスミルク
	cooked dried strips of radish	切り干し大根
	cooked with egg	卵とじ
	cookies	クッキー
	corned beef hash	コーンビーフ
	corn flakes	コーンフレーク
	crab croquette	かにコロッケ
	crackers	クラッカー
	cream	クリーム
	cream puff	シュークリーム
	crepe	クレープ
	croissant	クロワッサン
	croquette	コロッケ
	curried foods	カレー料理
D	deep-fried	から揚げ
	deep-fried bean curd	油揚げ
	deep-fried meat patty	メンチかつ
	dehydrated mashed potatoes	乾燥マッシュポテト
	dense *tofu*	木綿豆腐

キムチ	*kim chee*; spicy Korean-style pickled Chinese cabbage
キャラメル	caramel
キャンデー	candy; sweets
牛肉と野菜のうま煮	simmered beef with vegetables
牛肉のアスパラガス巻	rolled beef and asparagus
牛乳	milk
餃子	Chinese-style dumpling
切り干し大根	cooked dried strips of radish
きんぴらごぼう	*kimpira gobou*; sautéed burdock
草餅（くさもち）	mugwort rice cake
クッキー	cookies; biscuits
クラッカー	crackers
栗ご飯	chestnut rice
クリーム	cream
クレープ	crepe
クロワッサン	croissant
くん製(肉)	smoked (meat)
けんちん汁	*tofu*, pork, and vegetable soup, *kenchin*-style
高野豆腐	freeze-dried *tofu*
固形スープ	soup cube
午後のお茶	afternoon tea
昆布巻	rolled kelp with dried fish in it
胡麻	sesame seeds
胡麻豆腐	*tofu*-like of powdered arrowroot and sesame
五目ご飯	rice with vegetables and meat
コロッケ	croquette
コンデンスミルク	condensed milk
こんにゃく	*konnyaku*; devil's tongue jelly
コーンビーフ	corned beef hash
コーンフレーク	corn flakes
さ 魚の煮つけ	fish stewed in soy sauce
鮭の混ぜご飯	salmon and pickle rice
刺身	sliced raw fish
薩摩揚げ	fried fish cakes

	dessert	デザート，お菓子
	devil's tongue jelly	こんにゃく
	dog	ホットドッグ
	do-it-yourself *sushi* roll	手巻寿司
	doughnut	ドーナツ
	dried bean curd	湯葉(ゆば)
	dried bonito flakes	かつおぶし
	dried cuttlefish	するめ
	dried gourd shavings	かんぴょう
	dumpling	団子(だんご)
E	éclair	エクレア
	egg	卵
	egg cake	錦卵
	egg white	卵白(らんぱく)
	egg yolk	卵黄(らんおう)
	evaporated milk	エバミルク
F	fatty meat of tuna	とろ
	fatty portion of tuna belly	大とろ
	fat wheat noodles	うどん
	fermented soybeans	納豆
	fish and vegetable salad with vinegar and *miso*	ぬた
	fish paste dumpling	つみれ
	fish stewed in soy sauce	魚の煮つけ
	flavored laver	味付海苔
	food boiled down with soy sauce	佃煮(つくだに)
	foods dressed with sauce	和え物
	food served hot in the pot	鍋物
	freeze-dried *tofu*	高野豆腐
	French bread	フランスパン
	French fries	フレンチフライ
	fresh cream	生クリーム
	fried egg	目玉焼き
	fried fish cakes	薩摩揚げ
	fritter	揚げ菓子
	fritters	かき揚げ
G	gelidium jelly	ところてん

鯖のみそ煮	simmered mackerel in *miso*
サラミ（ソーセージ）	salami
サンドイッチ	sandwich
塩辛	salted fish guts
塩漬	salt pickling
シチュー	stew
シャーベット	sherbet
ジャム	jam; preserves
しゅうまい	steamed Chinese-style dumpling
シュークリーム	cream puff
精進揚げ	vegetable *tempura*
精進料理	temple-style vegetarian cuisine
食パン	sliced bread
しらたき	root starch noodles
白身	white meat
スキムミルク	skim milk
スコーン	scone
筋子(すじこ)	salmon roe
スナックフード	snack food
酢の物	pickled dishes
スープ	soup
スポンジケーキ	sponge cake
澄まし汁	clear soup
スライスチーズ	sliced cheese
するめ	dried cuttlefish
赤飯(せきはん)	rice boiled with red beans
せんべい	rice crackers
雑炊	rice gruel
雑煮(ぞうに)	soup with rice cakes
ソーセージ	sausage
ソテー	sauté
た 大根おろし	grated radish
大福	soft round rice cake stuffed with sweet bean jam
駄菓子	cheap cakes
たくあん	yellow pickled radish
たこ焼き	*takoyaki* ball with octopus in it

	glucose	水あめ
	glutinous rice cakes	餅(もち)
	grated radish	大根おろし
	grated yam	とろろ
	gravy	肉汁
	green pea rice	豆ご飯
	green tea poured over a bowl of rice	茶漬
	grilled chicken on skewers	焼鳥
	grilled clams	焼きはまぐり
	grilled eggplant	焼きなす
	ground meat rolled in cabbage leaves	ロールキャベツ
H	ham	ハム
	hamburger	ハンバーガー，ハンバーグ
	Hamburg steak	ハンバーグ
	honey	蜂蜜
	hot dog	ホットドッグ
I	ice-cream	アイスクリーム
	instant Chinese noodles	インスタント・ラーメン
J	jam	ジャム
	Japanese cake	和菓子
	Japanese soup stock	だし
	Japanese-style pancake	お好み焼き
	Japanese unbaked sweets	生菓子
L	large portion	大盛り
	laver	海苔(のり)
M	macaroni	マカロニ
	margarine	マーガリン
	marinade	マリネ
	marmalade	マーマレード
	meat and vegetable stew	煮込み
	meat ball	肉だんご
	meat-filled steamed bun	肉まん
	meat loaf	ミートローフ
	meat roasted on a hot plate	鉄板焼
	meunière〈仏〉	ムニエル
	milk	牛乳

だし	Japanese soup stock
だし巻卵	rolled omelet
伊達巻(だてまき)	rolled fish omelet
卵	egg
卵雑炊	rice gruel with egg
卵とじ	cooked with egg
玉子焼	omelet
たらこ	cod roe
団子(だん)	dumpling
ちくわ	tube-shaped fish cake
チーズ	cheese
茶粥(ちゃがゆ)	tea-mash
茶漬	green tea poured over a bowl of rice
茶碗蒸し	steamed egg custard
チョコレート	chocolate
佃煮(つくだに)	food boiled down with soy sauce
つくね	chicken meatballs
つけあわせ	relish
漬物(つけもの)	pickled vegetables
つぼ焼き	shellfish cooked in their shells
つみれ	fish paste dumpling
デザート	dessert
鉄板焼	meat roasted on a hot plate
手巻寿司	do-it-yourself *sushi* roll
テリーヌ	terrine〈仏〉
田楽	bean curd baked and coated with *miso*
豆腐(とうふ)	*tofu*; bean curd
豆腐とわかめのみそ汁	*tofu* and *wakame* seaweed *miso* soup
ところてん	gelidium jelly
トースト	toast
ドーナツ	doughnut
とろ	fatty meat of tuna
とろろ	grated yam
とろろ昆布	shavings of langle

	mousse	ムース
	muffin	マフィン
	mugwort rice cake	草餅(くさもち)
O	omelet	玉子焼
	onion flakes	オニオンフレークス
	open sandwich	オープン・サンドイッチ
P	pancake	ホットケーキ
	pasta	パスタ
	pâté	パテ
	peanuts	ピーナッツ
	pickled dishes	酢の物
	pickled plum	梅干
	pickled vegetables	漬物(つけもの)
	pickles	ピクルス
	pickles salted overnight	一夜漬け
	pie	パイ
	pizza	ピザ
	pork chop	ポークチョップ
	potato chips	ポテトチップ
	potatoes stewed with pork	肉じゃが
	preserves	ジャム
Q	quail egg	うずら卵
	quiche	キッシュ
R	red bean-filled steamed bun	あんまん
	red pickled ginger root	紅しょうが
	relish	つけあわせ
	rice boiled with red beans	赤飯(せきはん)
	rice crackers	せんべい
	rice-flour crackers	あられ(おかき)
	rice gruel	雑炊
	rice gruel with egg	卵雑炊
	rice in a bowl of green tea	お茶漬
	rice with chicken and vegetables	かやくご飯
	rice with vegetables and meat	五目ご飯
	rice wrapped in a bag of fried bean curd	稲荷鮨
	risotto	リゾット

な	納豆	fermented soybeans
	鍋物	*nabemono*; food served hot in the pot
	生菓子	Japanese unbaked sweets
	生クリーム	fresh cream; whipped cream
	煮いか	simmered squid
	肉じゃが	potatoes stewed with pork
	肉汁	gravy
	肉だんご	meat ball
	肉豆腐	*tofu* simmered with pork
	肉まん	meat-filled steamed bun
	煮込み	meat and vegetable stew
	煮魚	stewed fish
	錦卵	egg cake
	煮干し	small dried fish
	煮豆	boiled beans
	ぬかみそ漬	vegetables pickeled in rice bran paste
	ぬた	fish and vegetable salad with vinegar and *miso*
	ネタ	seafood for *sushi* topping
	海苔(⁇)	laver
	海苔巻	*norimaki*; vinegared rice rolled in laver
は	パイ	pie
	パスタ	pasta
	バター	butter
	蜂蜜	honey
	パテ	pâté
	ハム	ham
	春巻	Chinese-style egg [spring] roll
	ハンバーガー	hamburger
	ハンバーグ	Hamburg steak; hamburger
	パン	bread
	はんぺん	*hampen*; cake of pounded fish
	パン類	baked goods
	ピクルス	pickles
	ピザ	pizza

roast bean curd	焼豆腐
roast chestnut	焼栗(やきぐり)
roast lobster	鬼殻焼(おにがらやき)
roll	ロールパン
rolled beef and asparagus	牛肉のアスパラガス巻
rolled fish omelet	伊達巻(だてまき)
rolled kelp with dried fish in it	昆布巻
rolled omelet	だし巻卵
root starch noodles	しらたき
S salami	サラミ(ソーセージ)
salmon and pickle rice	鮭の混ぜご飯
salmon roe	筋子(すじこ)，イクラ
salted fish guts	塩辛
salt pickling	塩漬
sandwich	サンドイッチ
sauce	かけ汁
sausage	ソーセージ
sauté	ソテー
sautéed burdock	きんぴらごぼう
scone	スコーン
seafood for *sushi* topping	ネタ
sesame seeds	胡麻
shavings of langle	とろろ昆布
shellfish cooked in their shells	つぼ焼き
sherbet	シャーベット
side dish	おかず
simmered beef with vegeta-bles	牛肉と野菜のうま煮
simmered mackerel in *miso*	鯖のみそ煮
simmered squid	煮いか
skim milk	スキムミルク
sliced bread	食パン
sliced cheese	スライスチーズ
sliced raw fish	刺身
slices of pickled ginger	がり
small dried fish	煮干し
smoked (meat)	くん製(肉)
snack	おやつ

ひじき	*hijiki*; brown algae
ひじきのいため煮	braised *hijiki* seaweed
ビスケット	biscuits
ピーナッツ	peanuts
冷しトマト	chilled sliced tomato
冷奴（ひややっこ）	chilled *tofu*
麩（ふ）	wheat gluten
ブラウンブレッド	brown bread
フランスパン	French bread
フレンチフライ	French fries
ふろふき大根	stewed Japanese radish
ベーコン	bacon
紅しょうが	red pickled ginger root
弁当	boxed lunch
ほうれん草のお浸し	boiled spinach
ほうれん草の胡麻あえ	spinach with sesame dressing
ポークチョップ	pork chop
ホットケーキ	pancake
ホットドッグ	hot dog; dog
ポテトチップ	potato chips
ま マーガリン	margarine
マカロニ	macaroni
混ぜご飯	boild rice mixed with meat and other ingridients
松茸ご飯	boiled rice with *matsutake* mushroom
マーマレード	marmalade
マフィン	muffin
豆ご飯	green pea rice
マリネ	marinade
饅頭（まんじゅう）	bun with filling
水あめ	glucose
水炊き	chicken *mizutaki* in pot
ミートローフ	meat loaf
ムース	mousse
ムニエル	meunière〈仏〉
目玉焼き	fried egg; sunny side up
明太子	spiced cod roe

snack dish	おつまみ
snack food	スナックフード
soft round rice cake stuffed with sweet bean jam	大福
soup	スープ, おつゆ
soup cube	固形スープ
soup with rice cakes	雑煮(ぞう)
soybean flour	きな粉
soysauce seasoned with *wasabi*	わさびじょう油
spiced cod roe	明太子
spiced ham	味付ハム
spicy Korean-style pickled Chinese cabbage	キムチ
spinach with sesame dressing	ほうれん草の胡麻あえ
sponge cake	スポンジケーキ
spool	おだまき
steamed Chinese-style dumpling	しゅうまい
steamed egg custard	茶碗蒸し
stew	シチュー
stewed fish	煮魚
stewed head of fish	かぶと煮
stewed Japanese radish	ふろふき大根
sunnyside up	目玉焼き
sweetened bun	菓子パン
sweet mashed red bean soup with rice cakes	お汁粉
sweet red bean jelly	ようかん
sweets	お菓子, キャンディー
T *takoyaki* ball with octopus in it	たこ焼き
tea-mash	茶粥(ちゃ/がゆ)
temple-style vegetarian cuisine	精進料理
terrine	テリーヌ
thick deep-fried bean curd	厚揚げ
toast	トースト

	メンチかつ	deep-fried meat patty
	餅(もち)	glutinous rice cakes
	木綿豆腐	dense *tofu*
や	焼栗(やきぐり)	roast chestnut
	焼豆腐	roast bean curd
	焼鳥	grilled chicken on skewers
	焼きなす	grilled eggplant
	焼海苔	unflavored laver
	焼きはまぐり	grilled clams
	焼豚	barbecued pork
	野菜スティック	vegetable sticks
	ゆで卵	boiled eggs
	湯豆腐	*tofu* warmed in hot water
	湯葉(ゆば)	dried bean curd
	洋菓子	Western cake [pastry]
	ようかん	sweet red bean jelly
	ヨーグルト	yoghurt
ら	卵黄(らんおう)	egg yolk
	卵白(らんぱく)	egg white
	リゾット	risotto
	ロールキャベツ	ground meat rolled in cabbage leaves
	ロールパン	roll
わ	和菓子	Japanese cake
	わさびじょう油	soysauce seasoned with *wasabi*
	わさび漬け	*wasabi* preserved in *sake* lees

	tofu and *wakame* seaweed *miso* soup	豆腐とわかめのみそ汁
	tofu-like of powdered arrow-root and sesame	胡麻豆腐
	tofu, pork, and vegetable soup, *kenchin*-style	けんちん汁
	tofu simmered with pork	肉豆腐
	tofu warmed in hot water	湯豆腐
	tube-shaped fish cake	ちくわ
U	*udon* noodles in curry sauce	カレーうどん
	unflavored laver	焼海苔
	unsweetened chocolate	甘味のないチョコレート
V	vegetables lightly preserved in salt or rice bran	浅漬け
	vegetables pickeled in rice bran paste	ぬかみそ漬
	vegetable sticks	野菜スティック
	vegetable *tempura*	精進揚げ
	very delicate *tofu*	絹ごし豆腐
	Vienna sausage	ウィンナソーセージ
	vinegared rice rolled in laver	海苔巻
W	*wasabi* preserved in *sake* lees	わさび漬け
	Western cake [pastry]	洋菓子
	wheat gluten	麩(ふ)
	whipped cream	生クリーム
	white meat	白身
	whole grilled squid	いか丸焼き
Y	yellow pickled radish	たくあん
	yoghurt	ヨーグルト

デザート (Desserts)

アップルパイ	apple pie
アーモンド・クリスプ	almond crisps
泡雪かん	snow white jelly
いちごのスポンジケーキ	strawberry sponge
お汁粉	sweet red bean soup
カスタード・プディング	caramel pudding
キャラメル・ババロア	caramel bavarian cream
クッキー	cookies
クレープ・オ・シュークル	crêpe au sucre 〈仏〉
クレープ・シュゼット	crêpe suzette 〈仏〉
コーンブレッド	corn bread
ザバイオーネ	zabaione 〈伊〉
シフォンケーキ	chiffon cake
シュークリーム	cream puff
杏仁豆腐	Chinese-style almond jelly
タルト	tart
チョコレート・ケーキ	chocolate cake
チョコレート・スフレ	chocolate soufflé 〈仏〉
チョコレート・パイ	chocolate tart
チョコレート・ムース	chocolate mousse
ティラミス	tiramisu
バナナブレッド	banana bread
ピーチメルバ	peach melba
フルーツケーキ	fruits cake
フルーツコンポート	compote
ベイクド・チーズケーキ	baked cheesecake
ホットケーキ	pancake
マフィン	muffin
マンゴー・プリン	mango pudding
ライス・プディング	rice pudding
ラズベリー・チーズケーキ	raspberry cream cheesecake
りんごのタルトレット	apple turnover
レア・チーズケーキ	cream cheesecake
ワッフル	waffle

Desserts （デザート）

almond crisps	アーモンド・クリスプ
apple pie	アップルパイ
apple turnover	りんごのタルトレット
baked cheesecake	ベイクド・チーズケーキ
banana bread	バナナブレッド
caramel bavarian cream	キャラメル・ババロア
caramel pudding	カスタード・プディング
chiffon cake	シフォンケーキ
Chinese-style almond jelly	杏仁豆腐
chocolate cake	チョコレート・ケーキ
chocolate mousse	チョコレート・ムース
chocolate soufflé 〈仏〉	チョコレート・スフレ
chocolate tart	チョコレート・パイ
cookies	クッキー
compote	フルーツコンポート
corn bread	コーンブレッド
cream cheesecake	レア・チーズケーキ
cream puff	シュークリーム
crêpe au sucre 〈仏〉	クレープ・オ・シュークル
crêpe suzette 〈仏〉	クレープ・シュゼット
fruits cake	フルーツケーキ
mango pudding	マンゴー・プリン
muffin	マフィン
pancake	ホットケーキ
peach melba	ピーチメルバ
raspberry cream cheesecake	ラズベリー・チーズケーキ
rice pudding	ライス・プディング
snow white jelly	泡雪かん
strawberry sponge	いちごのスポンジケーキ
sweet red bean soup	お汁粉
tart	タルト
tiramisu	ティラミス
waffle	ワッフル
zabaione 〈伊〉	ザバイオーネ

PART 4

穀類・肉類などに関する重要語句 （和英）

あ	合鴨	duck
	合びき肉	ground beaf and pork
	小豆（あずき）	*azuki;* red bean
	あひる	duck
	あわ	fortail millet
	いのしし	wild boar
	うさぎ	rabbit（家うさぎ）；hare（野うさぎ）
	牛のあばら骨肉	rib
	牛の肩肉	chuck
	牛のくび肉	neck
	牛の腰肉	loin
	牛の尻肉	rump
	牛の胃腸 （シロ）	stomach and intestines
	牛のすね肉	shank
	牛の心臓 （ハツ）	heart
	牛のバラ肉	plate
	牛の腎臓 （マメ）	kidney
	牛の胸肉	brisket
	牛のわき腹肉	flank
	うずら	quail
	えん麦	oat
	大麦	barley
	オートミール	oatmeal
か	家きん	domestic fowl
	片栗粉	cornstarch
	がちょう	goose
	鴨（かも）	wild duck
	カラス麦（オート麦）	oat
	寒天	agar-agar
	乾麺	dried noodle
	黄粉（きなこ）	soybean flour

穀類・肉類などに関する重要語句（英和）

|A| agar-agar | 寒天
|B| bacon | 豚の腹肉
| barley | 大麦
| bean | 豆
| bean flour | 豆粉
| beef | 牛肉，ビーフ
| boned chicken | 骨抜き鶏肉
| bone in | 骨付き
| bran | ふすま
| bread crumbs | パン粉
| bread wheat | パン用小麦
| brisket | 牛の胸肉
| broken rice | 粉米（こごめ）
| buckwheat flour | そば粉
|C| cake flour | 薄力粉
| cereal | シリアル，穀物
| chicken | 鶏肉
| chicken breast | 鶏の胸肉
| chicken leg | 鶏のもも肉
| Chinese thin rice noodles | ビーフン
| chops | 切り身
| chuck | 牛の肩肉
| cock | にわとり（雄）
| cold meat | 冷肉
| common millet | キビ
| common rye | ライ麦
| corn | とうもろこし
| cornflakes | コーンフレーク
| cornmeal | ひきわりとうもろこし
| cornstarch | 片栗粉，コーンスターチ
|D| dairy products | 乳製品

	絹ごし豆腐	"silken" *tofu*
	キビ	common millet
	肝(きも)	liver
	牛肉	beef
	強力粉	strong flour
	切り身	chops; slices
	くじら	whales
	玄米	unpolished (brown) rice
	子牛の肉	veal
	極上あばら肉	prime rib
	穀物(こくもつ)	grain; cereals
	粉米(こごめ)	broken rice
	子羊肉	lamb
	子羊のもも肉	leg of lamb
	小麦	wheat
	小麦粉	wheat flour
	米	rice
	米ぬか	rice bran
	コーンスターチ	cornstarch
	コーンフレーク	cornflakes
さ	サーロイン	sirloin
	鹿(肉)	venison
	舌 (タン)	tongue
	七面鳥	turkey
	霜降牛肉	marbled beef
	食用蛙	edible frog
	白玉粉	glutinous rice flour
	シリアル	cereal
	新米	the first crop of rice for the year
	雀	tree sparrow
	すっぽん	soft-shelled turtle
	ステーキ(肉)	steak
	スペアリブ	spare rib
	ソーセージ	sausage
	そば粉	buckwheat flour
た	大豆	soybean; soya bean
	タピオカ	tapioca

	dark meat	鳥のもも肉
	domestic fowl	家きん
	dried noodle	乾麺
	duck	あひる，合鴨
	durum wheat	マカロニ用小麦
E	edible frog	食用蛙
F	fat back	豚の背ロース
	fillet	ヒレ肉
	flank	牛のわき腹肉
	foie gras〈仏〉	フォアグラ
	fore and hind loins	〈英〉豚のロース（背肉）
	fortail millet	あわ
	frozen meat	冷凍肉
G	gizzard	鶏の砂肝
	glutinous rice	もち米
	glutinous rice flour	白玉粉
	goose	がちょう
	grain	穀物(ふこっ)
	gravy	肉汁
	ground beaf and pork	合びき肉
	ground meat	ひき肉，ミンチ肉
	guinea fowl	ホロホロ鳥
H	ham	ハム，豚のもも肉
	hare	（野）うさぎ
	heart	牛の心臓（ハツ）
	hen	にわとり（雌）
	horse meat	馬肉
	hybrid rice	ハイブリッド米
J	Job's tears	ハトムギ
K	kidney	牛の腎臓（マメ）
L	lamb	子羊肉
	leg of lamb	子羊のもも肉
	liver	レバー（肝臓），肝(きも)
	loin	牛の腰肉
	lower wing	鶏の手羽先
M	macaroni	マカロニ
	mallard	真鴨(まがも)
	marbled beef	霜降牛肉

	澱粉(でんぷん)	starch
	豆粉	bean flour
	鳥肉	poultry
	鶏肉(チキン)	chicken
	鶏のささみ	white meat
	鶏の砂肝	gizzard
	鶏の手羽先	lower wing
	鶏の手羽もと	upper wing
	鶏の胸肉	chicken breast
	鶏のもも肉	chicken leg
	T-ボーン	T-bone (steak)
	テンダーロイン	tenderloin
	とうもろこし	corn
な	生米(なまごめ)	raw rice
	肉(獣肉)	meat
	肉汁	gravy
	乳製品	dairy products
	にわとり	cock(雄); hen(雌)
	ぬか	rice bran
は	ハイブリッド米	hybrid rice
	白米	polished (white) rice
	薄力粉	cake flour
	パスタ	pasta
	鳩	pigeon
	ハトムギ	Job's tears
	馬肉	horse meat
	春雨(はるさめ)	sticks of bean jelly
	春巻の皮	spring roll wrapper
	パン用小麦	bread wheat
	ひき肉	minced [ground] meat
	ひきわりとうもろこし	cornmeal
	羊肉	mutton
	ビーフ	beef
	ビーフン	Chinese thin rice noodles
	パンケーキ粉	pancake flour
	パン粉	bread crumbs
	ヒレ肉	fillet; tenderloin
	フォアグラ	foie gras〈仏〉

	meat	肉(獣肉)
	minced meat	ひき肉，ミンチ肉
	mutton	羊肉
N	neck	牛のくび肉
	noodles	麺(めん)
O	oat	カラス麦(オート麦)，えん麦
	oatmeal	オートミール
P	pancake flour	パンケーキ粉
	pasta	パスタ
	picnic shoulder	豚の肩肉
	pigeon	鳩
	plate	牛のバラ肉
	polished (white) rice	白米
	pork	豚肉
	pork loin	豚のロース(背肉)
	poultry	鳥肉
	prime rib	極上あばら肉
Q	quail	うずら
R	rabbit	(家)うさぎ
	raw rice	生米(なまごめ)
	red bean	小豆(あずき)
	rib	牛のあばら骨肉
	rice	米
	rice bran	ぬか，米ぬか
	round	牛のもも肉
	rump	牛の尻肉
	rye flour	ライ麦粉
S	sausage	ソーセージ
	shank	牛のすね肉
	shoulder butt	豚の肩ロース
	"silken" *tofu*	絹ごし豆腐
	sirloin	サーロイン
	slices	切り身
	soft-shelled turtle	すっぽん
	soya bean	大豆
	soybean flour	黄粉(きな)
	soybean	大豆
	spare rib	スペアリブ

	ふすま	bran
	豚肉	pork
	豚の肩肉	picnic shoulder
	豚の肩ロース	shoulder butt
	豚の背ロース	fat back
	豚の腹肉	bacon
	豚のロース(背肉)	pork loin；loin 〈米〉; fore and hind loins 〈英〉
	骨付き	bone in
	骨抜き鶏肉	boned chicken
	ホロホロ鳥	guinea fowl
ま	真鴨(まがも)	mallard
	マカロニ	macaroni
	マカロニ用小麦	durum wheat
	豆	bean
	ミンチ肉	minced [ground] meat
	麺(めん)	noodles
	もち米	glutinous rice
	もも肉	round(牛)；ham(豚)；leg (鶏)；dark meat(鳥)
ら	ライ麦	common rye
	ライ麦粉	rye flour
	冷凍肉	frozen meat
	冷肉	cold meat
	レバー(肝臓)	liver
わ	ワンタンの皮	wonton wrapper

	spring roll wrapper	春巻の皮
	starch	澱粉(でんぷん)
	steak	ステーキ(肉)
	sticks of bean jelly	春雨(はるさめ)
	stomach and intestines	牛の胃腸(シロ)
	strong flour	強力粉
T	tapioca	タピオカ
	T-bone (steak)	T-ボーン
	tenderloin	テンダーロイン, ヒレ肉
	the first crop of rice for the year	新米
	tongue	舌(タン)
	tree sparrow	雀
	turkey	七面鳥
U	unpolished (brown) rice	玄米
	upper wing	鶏の手羽もと
V	veal	子牛の肉
	venison	鹿(肉)
W	whales	くじら
	wheat	小麦
	wheat flour	小麦粉
	white meat	鶏のささみ
	wild boar	いのしし
	wild duck	鴨(かも)
	wonton wrapper	ワンタンの皮

PART 5

水産物・海産物などに関する重要語句 （和英）

あ あいなめ　　　　　　　greenling
青海苔(あおのり)　　　　　green string laver; seaweed flakes
あおやぎ　　　　　　　hen clam
あおりいか　　　　　　broad-mantle squid
赤貝　　　　　　　　　bloody clam
アカザ海老　　　　　　Japanese lobster
赤鯛(あかだい)　　　　　　red bream
赤むつ　　　　　　　　blackthroat seaperch
あさり　　　　　　　　*asari*; short-necked clam
あじ　　　　　　　　　yellowfin horse mackerel
穴子(あなご)　　　　　　　common Japanese conger eel
甘海老　　　　　　　　pink shrimp
甘鯛(あまだい)　　　　　　red horsehead
あみ　　　　　　　　　opossum shrimp
鮎(あゆ)　　　　　　　　*ayu*; sweetfish
新巻鮭　　　　　　　　lightly salted salmon
あわび　　　　　　　　abalone
あんこう　　　　　　　blackmouth goosefish; angler fish
アンチョビー　　　　　anchovy
いか　　　　　　　　　cuttlefish(甲いか); squid(甲なし)
胎貝(いがい)　　　　　　　native mussel
イクラ　　　　　　　　*ikura*; salmon roe
いさき　　　　　　　　threeline grunt
石垣鯛　　　　　　　　rock porgy
石鯛　　　　　　　　　striped beakperch
いしもち　　　　　　　white croaker
伊勢海老　　　　　　　Japanese spiny lobster; crawfish
いとう　　　　　　　　Japanese huchen

PART 5

水産物・海産物などに関する重要語句（英和）

A	abalone	あわび
	Alaskan king crab	たらば蟹
	alfonsino	金目鯛(きんめだい)
	anchovy	アンチョビー
	angler fish	あんこう
	apple snail	エスカルゴ
	arabesque greenling	ほっけ
	Atlantic cutlassfish	たちうお
	ayu	鮎(あゆ)
B	bigeya tuna	めばちまぐろ
	big-eyed flathead	めごち
	big-eye sardine	うるめいわし
	blackmouth goosefish	あんこう
	black porgy	黒鯛(くろだい)
	black rockfish	めばる
	blackthroat seaperch	赤むつ
	bloody clam	赤貝
	bluefin	黒まぐろ
	blue sprat	きびなご
	botan shrimp	ボタン海老
	broad-mantle squid	あおりいか
	brown sole	まがれい
	brutal moray	うつぼ
C	carp	鯉(こい)
	caviar	キャビア
	Ceylon moss	天草
	char	岩魚(いわな)
	chub mackerel	鯖(さば)
	chum salmon	鮭
	cockle	とり貝
	cod roe	たらこ

	いとより	goldenthread
	いなだ	very young yellowtail
	いぼ鯛	Japanese butterfish
	いわし(まいわし)	Japanese sardine
	岩魚(いわな)	char
	うぐい	Japanese dace
	うつぼ	brutal moray
	鰻(うなぎ)	eel
	うに	sea urchin roe
	うるめいわし	big-eye sardine
	うろこ	scale
	えい	Japanese stingray
	えいひれ	ray fillet
	エスカルゴ	apple snail; escargots
	海老	prawn; shrimp
	おこぜ	devil stinger
	オマール海老	lobster; homard〈仏〉
か	貝	shellfish
	海産物	seafood
	海草	seaweed
	貝柱	eyes of scallops
	かき	oyster
	かさご	marbled rockfish
	かじか	great sculpin
	数の子	herring roe
	かつお	skipjack tuna
	活魚	live fish
	蟹(かに)	crab
	蟹みそ	crab guts
	かます	Japanese barracuda
	からすみ	dried mullet roe
	かれい	flounder; flatfish
	川魚	river fish
	川海老	river shrimp
	かわはぎ	threadsail filefish
	かんぱち	great amberjack
	きす(白)	silver whiting
	きはだまぐろ	yellowfin tuna

	common Japanese conger eel	穴子(あなご)
	convict rock cod	はた
	cowrie	子安貝(こやすがい)
	cowry	子安貝(こやすがい)
	crab	蟹(かに)
	crab guts	蟹みそ
	crawfish	伊勢海老
	cuttlefish	甲いか
D	dace	はや
	devil stinger	おこぜ
	dried fish	干物(ひもの)
	dried mullet roe	からすみ
	dried sardines	めざし
	dried young sardine	白子(しらす)干し
E	edible frog	食用蛙
	eel	鰻(うなぎ)
	erctic lamprey	八目鰻
	escargots	エスカルゴ
	eyes of scallops	貝柱
F	fan shell	平貝
	first bonito	初がつお
	fishes	魚類
	fish full of fine bones	小骨の多い魚
	flatfish	かれい
	freshwater clam	しじみ
	fleshy prawn	大正海老
	flounder	かれい
	fresh fish	鮮魚
G	gaper	みる貝
	gizzard shad (fish)	こはだ
	goldenbanded fusilier	高砂(たかさご)
	goldenthread	いとより
	goldstriped amberjack	ひらまさ
	grass carp	草魚(そうぎょ)
	great amberjack	かんぱち
	great sculpin	かじか
	greenling	あいなめ
	green string laver	青海苔(あおのり)

きびなご	blue sprat
キャビア	caviar; caviare
きゅうり魚	toothed smelt
魚類	fishes
ぎんだら	sablefish
金目鯛（きんめだい）	alfonsino
鯨（くじら）	whale
くらげ	jellyfish
車海老	*kuruma* prawn; tiger prawn
黒鯛（くろだい）	black porgy
黒まぐろ	bluefin
毛蟹	horsehair crab
剣先いか	swordtip squid
鯉（こい）	carp
小海老	small shrimp
こはだ	gizzard shad (fish)
小骨の多い魚	fish full of fine bones
こまい	saffron cod
子安貝（こやすがい）	cowrie, cowry
昆布（こんぶ）	sea tangle; kelp
さ　桜海老	*sakura* shrimp
鮭	chum salmon
雑魚（ざこ）	small fish
さざえ	spiny top shell; turban shell
鯖（さば）	chub mackerel
鮫	shark
さより	Japanese halfbeak
さわら	spotted mackerel
秋刀魚（さんま）	Pacific saury
塩鮭	salted salmon
しじみ	*shijimi*; freshwater clam
ししゃも	*shishamo*; smelt
舌平目	sole
芝海老	shrimp
しめ鯖	mackerel marinated in vinegar
地元産魚介類	local seafood
しゃこ	squilla; mantis shrimp
上海蟹	Shanghainese mitten crab

H	hard clam	蛤(はまぐり)
	harvest fish	まながつお
	hen clam	あおやぎ, ばか貝
	herring	にしん
	herring roe	数の子
	hizikia	ひじき
	homard	オマール海老
	horsehair crab	毛蟹
I	ice fish	白魚(しらうお)
	ice goby	素魚(しろうお)
	ivory shell	ばい貝
J	Japanese barracuda	かます
	Japanese bluefish	むつ
	Japanese butterfish	いぼ鯛
	Japanese catfish	なまず
	Japanese dace	うぐい
	Japanese halfbeak	さより
	Japanese huchen	いとう
	Japanese lobster	アカザ海老
	Japanese sardine	いわし(まいわし)
	Japanese seaperch	すずき
	Japanese smelt	わかさぎ
	Japanese spiny lobster crawfish	伊勢海老
	Japanese stingray	えい
	Japanese *tsubugai* shellfish	つぶ貝
	jellyfish	くらげ
K	kelp	昆布(こぶ)
	kokanee	姫ます
	kuruma prawn	車海老
L	large catch	大漁
	largescale blackfish	めじな
	laver	海苔(海草)
	lightly salted salmon	新巻鮭
	live fish	活魚
	lobster	オマール海老
	local seafood	地元産魚介類
	longfinned tuna	びん長まぐろ

食用蛙	edible frog
白魚(しらうお)	ice fish
白子(しらこ)	milt
白子(しらす)	young sardine
白子干し	dried young sardine
素魚(しろうお)	ice goby
筋子(すじこ)	salmon roe
すずき	Japanese seaperch
すっぽん	soft-shelled turtle
スモークサーモン	smoked salmon
ずわい蟹	snow crab; queen crab
鮮魚	fresh fish
草魚(そうぎょ)	grass carp
た 鯛(たい)	sea bream
大正海老	fleshy prawn
平貝	pen shell ; fan shell
大漁	large catch
高砂(たかさご)	goldenbanded fusilier
たこ	octopus
たちうお	Atlantic cutlassfish
たにし	mud snail
たら	Pacific cod
たらこ	cod roe
たらば蟹	Alaskan king crab
ツナ	tuna
つぶ貝	Japanese *tsubugai* shellfish
天草	Ceylon moss
どじょう	oriental weatherfish
飛魚	opaquewing flyingfish
とらふぐ	ocellate puffer
とり貝	cockle
とろろ昆布	tangle flakes
な なまこ	sea cucumber
生魚(なまざかな)	raw fish
なまず	Japanese catfish
虹ます	rainbow trout
にしん	herring
煮干し	small dried fish

M	mackerel marinated in vinegar	しめ鯖
	mantis shrimp	しゃこ
	marbled rockfish	かさご
	mask crab	平家蟹
	masu trout	やまめ
	milt	白子(とこ)
	moule	ムール貝
	mud snail	たにし
N	native mussel	胎貝(いがい)
O	ocellate puffer	とらふぐ
	octopus	たこ
	olive flounder	ひらめ
	opaquewing flyingfish	飛魚
	opossum shrimp	あみ
	oriental weatherfish	どじょう
	oyster	かき
P	Pacific cod	たら
	Pacific saury	秋刀魚(さんま)
	pen shell	平貝
	pike eel	はも
	pink shrimp	甘海老
	prawn	海老
	puffer	ふぐ
Q	queen crab	ずわい蟹
R	rainbow trout	虹ます
	raw fish	生魚(なまざかな)
	ray fillet	えいひれ
	red bream	赤鯛(あかだい)
	red horsehead	甘鯛(あまだい)
	red salmon	紅鮭
	red sea bream	真鯛
	river fish	川魚
	river shrimp	川海老
	rock porgy	石垣鯛
S	sablefish	ぎんだら
	saffron cod	こまい
	sailfin sandfish	はたはた

	海苔	laver
は	ばい貝	ivory shell
	ばか貝	hen clam
	はぜ	yellowfin goby
	初がつお	first bonito
	はた	convict rock cod
	はたはた	sailfin sandfish
	蛤(はまぐり)	hard clam
	はまち	young yellowtail
	はも	pike eel
	はや	dace
	ひじき	hizikia
	姫ます	kokanee
	干物(ひもの)	dried fish
	ひらまさ	goldstriped amberjack
	ひらめ	olive flounder
	びん長まぐろ	longfinned tuna
	ふか	shark
	ふかひれ	shark's fin
	ふぐ	puffer
	ぶり	yellowtail
	平家蟹	mask crab
	紅鮭	red salmon
	帆立貝	scallop
	ほたるいか	*Toyama* squid
	ボタン海老	*botan* shrimp
	ほっき貝	surf clam
	ほっけ	arabesque greenling
	ぼら	striped mullet
ま	まかじき	striped marlin
	まがれい	brown sole
	巻き貝	snail
	まぐろ	tuna; tunny
	ます	trout
	真鯛	red sea bream
	まながつお	harvest fish
	まはた	sevenband grouper
	みる貝	gaper

sakura shrimp	桜海老
salmon roe	筋子(すじこ)，イクラ
salted salmon	塩鮭
scale	うろこ
scallop	帆立貝
sea bream	鯛(たい)
sea cucumber	なまこ
seafood	海産物
sea tangle	昆布(こんぶ)
sea urchin roe	うに
seaweed flakes	青海苔(あおのり)
seaweed	海草
sevenband grouper	まはた
Shanghainese mitten crab	上海蟹
shark	ふか，鮫
shark's fin	ふかひれ
shellfish	貝
short necked clam	あさり
shrimp	海老，芝海老
silver whiting	きす(白)
skipjack tuna	かつお
small dried fish	煮干し
small fish	雑魚(ざこ)
small shrimp	小海老
smelt	ししゃも
smoked salmon	スモークサーモン
snail	巻き貝
snow crab	ずわい蟹
soft-shelled turtle	すっぽん
sole	舌平目
speer squid	やりいか
spiny top shell	さざえ
spotted mackerel	さわら
squid	いか(甲なし)
squilla	しゃこ
striped beakperch	石鯛
striped marlin	まかじき
striped mullet	ぼら

	むつ	Japanese bluefish
	ムール貝	moule
	めかじき	swordfish
	めごち	big-eyed flathead
	めざし	dried sardines
	めじな	largescale blackfish
	めばちまぐろ	bigeya tuna
	めばる	black rockfish
や	八目鰻	erctic lamprey
	やまめ	*yamame*; *masu* trout
	やりいか	speer squid
わ	わかさぎ	Japanese smelt
	わかめ	*wakame* seaweed
	わたり蟹	swimming crab

	surf clam	ほっき貝
	sweetfish	鮎(あゆ)
	swimming crab	わたり蟹
	swordfish	めかじき
	swordtip squid	剣先いか
T	tangle flakes	とろろ昆布
	threadsail filefish	かわはぎ
	threeline grunt	いさき
	tiger prawn	車海老
	toothed smelt	きゅうり魚
	Toyama squid	ほたるいか
	trout	ます
	tuna	ツナ，まぐろ
	tunny	まぐろ
	turban shell	さざえ
V	very young yellowtail	いなだ
W	*wakame* seaweed	わかめ
	whale	鯨(くじら)
	white croaker	いしもち
Y	yellowfin goby	はぜ
	yellowfin horse mackerel	あじ
	yellowfin tuna	きはだまぐろ
	yellowtail	ぶり
	young sardine	白子(しらす)
	young yellowtail	はまち

PART 6

野菜・果物・山菜などに関する重要語句 （和英）

あ	青菜	greens
	青ねぎ	scallion
	赤いも	red taro
	赤かぶ	rad beet
	赤唐辛子	red chili pepper
	赤ピーマン	sweet pepper
	あけび	chocolate vine; five-leat akebia
	あさつき	chive
	あざみ	thistle
	アスパラガス	asparagus
	アセロラ	acerola
	アーティチョーク	artichoke
	アボカド	avocado
	アーモンド	almond
	アルファルファ	alfalfa
	あんず	apricot
	いちご	garden strawberry
	いちじく	fig
	一年草	annual herb
	芋（いも）	potato
	いよかん	*lyo* langor
	いんげん豆	kidney bean
	うずら豆	mottled kidney beans
	うど	spikenard
	梅	*ume*; Japanese plum
	瓜（うり）	gourd
	エシャロット	échalote
	枝豆	green soybeans
	えのきたけ	velvet-stemmed agaric
	エンダイブ	endive
	えんどう豆	green pea

PART 6

野菜・果物・山菜などに関する重要語句 (英和)

A acerola アセロラ
alfalfa アルファルファ
almond アーモンド
annual herb 一年草
apple りんご
apricot あんず
arrowhead くわい
artichoke アーティチョーク
asparagus アスパラガス
asparagus bean ささげ豆
avocado アボカド
B baby corn ヤングコーン
balsam pear 苦瓜(にがうり)
bamboo shoot たけのこ
banana バナナ
bean sprouts もやし
blackberry ブラックベリー
black soybean 黒豆
blueberry ブルーベリー
boneset コンフリー
bracken わらび
brightly colored vegetables 緑黄色野菜
broad bean そら豆, お多福豆
broccoli ブロッコリー
Brussels sprouts 芽キャベツ
Burma bean ビルマ豆
C cabbage キャベツ
candied fruit 砂糖づけ果物
carrot にんじん
cashew nut カシューナッツ
cauliflower カリフラワー

	オクラ	okra
	お多福豆	broad bean
	オリーブ	olive
	オレンジ	orange
か	かいわれ大根	white radish sprouts
	カカオ豆	cocoa bean
	柿	*kaki*; Japanese persimmon
	果樹	fruit tree
	カシューナッツ	cashew nut
	果肉	flesh
	果皮	peel
	かぶ	turnip
	カボス	*kabosu* citron
	かぼちゃ	pumpkin; squash
	からし菜	leaf mustard
	カリフラワー	cauliflower
	花梨(かりん)	Chinese quince
	柑橘類(かんきつるい)	citrus fruits
	乾燥果実	dried fruit
	乾燥野菜	dehydrated vegetable
	かんぴょう	dried gourd shavings
	きいちご(ラズベリー)	raspberry
	キーウィ	Chinese gooseberry; kiwi berry [fruit]
	菊芋(きくいも)	Jerusalem artichoke; girasole
	きくらげ	cloud ear mushroom
	きのこ	mushroom
	木の実	nuts
	木の芽	leaf buds
	キャベツ	cabbage
	胡瓜(きゅうり)	cucumber
	京菜	pot herb mustard
	きんかん	oval kumquat
	銀杏(ぎんなん)	ginkgo nut
	グアバ	guava
	茎(くき)	stalk
	グーズベリー	gooseberry
	果物	fruit

celeriac	セルリアク
celery	セロリ
chaco	隼人瓜 (はやと)
chayota	隼人瓜
cherry tomato	ミニトマト
chick pea	ひよこ豆
chicory	チコリ
chili	唐辛子
Chinese cabbage	白菜
Chinese chive	にら
Chinese citron	夏みかん
Chinese gooseberry	キーウィ
Chinese parsley	香菜
Chinese quince	花梨 (かりん)
Chinese vegetables	中国菜
chive	あさつき, チャイブ
chocolate vine	あけび
citrus fruits	柑橘類 (かんきつるい)
cloud ear mushroom	きくらげ
cocoa bean	カカオ豆
coconut	ヤシの実
coconut palm	ココナッツ
coltsfoot	ふき
coltsfoot bud	ふきのとう
common comfrey	コンフリー
common pea	さやえんどう
coriander	香菜
corn	とうもろこし
cowpea	ささげ豆
cranberry	クランベリー
cucumber	胡瓜 (きゅうり)
D date palm	なつめやしの実
dehydrated vegetable	乾燥野菜
devil's tongue	こんにゃく
dried fruit	乾燥果実
dried gourd shavings	かんぴょう
dried persimmon	干し柿
durian	ドリアン

	クランベリー	cranberry
	栗	Japanese chestnut
	グリーンピース	green pea
	グリーンリーフ	green leaf
	胡桃(くるみ)	Japanese walnut
	クレソン	watercress
	グレープフルーツ	grapefruit; pomelo
	黒豆	black soybeans
	くわい	arrowhead
	桑の実	mulberry
	香菜	Chinese parsley; coriander
	ココナッツ	coconut palm
	小玉ねぎ	pearl onion
	ごぼう	edible burdock root
	小松菜	leafy green vegetable
	根菜	root vegetable
	こんにゃく	devil's tongue
	コンフリー	common comfrey; boneset
さ	さくらんぼ	sweet cherry
	ざくろ	pomegranate
	ささげ豆	cowpea; asparagus bean
	さつま芋	sweet potato
	里芋	taro
	砂糖づけ果物	candied fruit
	さやいんげん	kidney bean
	さやえんどう	common pea; garden pea
	サラダ菜	salad
	サラダ用青葉	salad greens
	山菜	edible wild plants
	山椒	Japanese pepper
	椎茸	*shiitake* mushroom
	四角豆	winged bean
	しし唐(辛子)	*shishito*; small Japanese green pepper
	紫蘇(しそ)	perilla
	しめじ	*shimeji* mushroom
	じゃがいも	potato
	春菊	garland chrysanthemum

E	échalote	エシャロット
	edible burdock root	ごぼう
	edible chrysanthemum	食用菊
	edible flower	食用花
	edible wild plants	山菜
	eggplant	なす
	endive	エンダイブ
F	field horsetail	つくし
	fig	いちじく
	five-leat akebia	あけび
	flesh	果肉
	fruit	果物
	fruit tree	果樹
G	garden beet	ビーツ
	garden lettuce	レタス
	garden pea	さやえんどう
	garden strawberry	いちご
	garland chrysanthemum	春菊
	garlic	にんにく
	ginger	しょうが
	ginkgo nut	銀杏（ぎんなん）
	girasole	菊芋（きくいも）
	gooseberry	西洋すぐり，グーズベリー
	gourd	瓜（うり）
	grapefruit	グレープフルーツ
	grapes	ぶどう
	green leaf	グリーンリーフ
	green pea	えんどう豆，グリーンピース
	green pepper	ピーマン
	greens	菜葉（なっぱ），青菜
	green soybeans	枝豆
	guava	グアバ
H	*Hakuran*	白藍（はくらん）
	hazelnut	ヘーゼルナッツ
	hen of the wood	舞茸（まいたけ）
	hop	ホップ
J	Japanese chestnut	栗
	Japanese ginger	みょうが

じゅんさい	watertarget
しょうが	ginger
食用菊	edible chrysanthemum
食用花	edible flower
越瓜(しろうり)	oriental pickling melon
西瓜(すいか)	watermelon
ずいき	taro
スイートコーン	sweet corn
すだち	*sudachi* citron
ズッキーニ	zucchini; summer squash
すもも	Japanese plum
青果	vegetables and fruits
西洋かぼちゃ	squash
西洋すぐり	gooseberry
西洋梨	pear
西洋ねぎ	leek
芹(せり)	water dropwort
セルリアク	celeriac
セロリ	celery
ぜんまい	reyal fern
そら豆	broad bean
た 大根	*daikon*; white radish
大豆	soybean
高菜	leaf mustard
たけのこ	bamboo shoot
蓼(たで)	water pepper
玉ねぎ	onion
チコリ	chicory
チャイブ	chive
中国菜	Chinese vegetables
つくし	field horsetail
てんさい	sugar beet
唐辛子	chili
冬瓜(とうがん)	wax gourd
とうもろこし	corn
トマト	tomato
ドリアン	durian
トリュフ	truffle

	Japanese honewort	三つ葉
	Japanese loquat	びわ
	Japanese orange	みかん
	Japanese pear	梨
	Japanese pepper	山椒
	Japanese persimmon	柿
	Japanese plum	梅, すもも
	Japanese walnut	胡桃(くるみ)
	Japanese yam	大和芋
	Jerusalem artichoke	菊芋(きくいも)
	Jew's marrow	モロヘイヤ
K	*kabosu* citron	カボス
	kidney bean	いんげん豆, さやいんげん
	kiwi berry [fruit]	キーウィ
L	leaf buds	木の芽
	leaf mustard	からし菜, 高菜
	leafy green vegetable	小松菜
	leechee	ライチー
	leek	リーク, 西洋ねぎ, にら
	lemon	レモン
	lily bulb	百合根
	lime	ライム
	litchi	ライチー
	long green onion	長ねぎ
	long yam	長いも
	lotus	はす
	lotus root	蓮根(れんこん)
	lyo langor	いよかん
M	macadamia nuts	マカダミアナッツ
	mandarin (orange)	みかん
	mango	マンゴー
	mangosteen	マンゴスチン
	matsutake mushroom	松茸
	melon	メロン
	mint	はっか
	mottled kidney beans	うずら豆
	mountain yam	山芋
	mugwort	よもぎ

な	長いも	long yam
	長ねぎ	long green onion
	梨	Japanese pear
	なす	eggplant
	なた豆	sword bean
	菜葉(なっぱ)	greens
	夏みかん	Chinese citron
	なつめやしの実	date palm
	菜の花	rape blossoms
	なめこ	*nameko* mushroom
	苦瓜(にがうり)	balsam pear
	にら	Chinese chive; leek
	にんじん	carrot
	にんにく	garlic
	ねぎ	spring onion
	ネクタリン	nectarine
は	パイン(パイナップル)	pineapple
	白菜	Chinese cabbage
	白藍(はくらん)	*Hakuran*
	はす	lotus
	パセリ	parsley
	はっか	mint
	二十日大根	radish
	パッションフルーツ	passion fruit
	バナナ	banana
	パパイヤ	papaya
	隼人瓜(はやとうり)	chayota; chaco
	春玉ねぎ	scallion
	ピスタチオナッツ	pistachio
	ビーツ	garden beet
	ピーナッツ	peanut
	ひまわり	sunflower
	ピーマン	sweet pepper; green pepper
	ひよこ豆	chick pea
	平茸(ひらたけ)	oyster mushroom
	ビルマ豆	Burma bean
	びわ	Japanese loquat
	ふき	*fuki*; coltsfoot

	mulberry	桑の実
	muscat	マスカット
	mushroom	きのこ
	muskmelon	マスクメロン
N	*nameko* mushroom	なめこ
	nectarine	ネクタリン
	nuts	木の実
O	okra	オクラ
	olive	オリーブ
	onion	玉ねぎ
	orange	オレンジ
	oriental pickling melon	越瓜(しろうり)
	oval kumquat	きんかん
	oyster mushroom	平茸
P	papaya	パパイヤ
	parsley	パセリ
	passion fruit	パッションフルーツ
	peach	桃
	peanut	ピーナッツ，落花生
	pear	洋梨
	pearl onion	小玉ねぎ
	peel	果皮
	perilla	紫蘇(しそ)
	pineapple	パイン(パイナップル)
	pine nut	松の実
	pistachio	ピスタチオナッツ
	plum	プラム
	pomegranate	ざくろ
	pomelo	グレープフルーツ
	potato	じゃがいも，芋(いも)
	pot herb mustard	京菜
	prune	プルーン
	pumpkin	かぼちゃ
R	rad beet	赤かぶ
	radish	二十日大根
	raisin	レーズン，干しぶどう
	rakkyo	らっきょう
	rape blossoms	菜の花

	ふきのとう	coltsfoot bud
	ぶどう	grapes
	ブラックベリー	blackberry
	プラム	plum
	ブルーベリー	blueberry
	プルーン	prune
	ブロッコリー	broccoli
	ヘーゼルナッツ	hazelnut
	へちま	sponge gourd
	紅しょうが	red pickled ginger
	紅花	safflower
	ほうれん草	spinach
	干し柿	dried persimmon
	干しぶどう	raisin
	ホップ	hop
ま	舞茸(まいたけ)	hen of the wood
	マカダミアナッツ	macadamia nuts
	マスカット	muscat
	マスクメロン	muskmelon
	またたび	silver vine
	松茸	*matsutake* mushroom
	松の実	pine nut
	マンゴー	mango
	マンゴスチン	mangosteen
	みかん	mandarin (orange); Japanese orange
	三つ葉	Japanese honewort
	ミニトマト	cherry tomato
	みょうが	*mioga*; Japanese ginger
	紫キャベツ	red cabbage
	芽キャベツ	Brussels sprouts
	メロン	melon
	桃	peach
	もやし	bean sprouts
	モロヘイヤ	Jew's marrow
や	野菜	vegetable
	ヤシの実	coconut
	山芋	mountain yam

	raspberry	きいちご，ラズベリー
	red cabbage	紫キャベツ
	red chili pepper	赤唐辛子
	red currant	レッドカラント
	red pickled ginger	紅しょうが
	red taro	赤いも
	reyal fern	ぜんまい
	rhubarb	ルバーブ
	rocket salad	ロケットサラダ(菜)
	root vegetable	根菜
S	safflower	紅花
	salad	サラダ菜
	salad greens	サラダ用青葉
	scallion	春玉ねぎ，青ねぎ
	shiitake mushroom	椎茸
	shimeji mushroom	しめじ
	silver vine	またたび
	small Japanese green pepper	しし唐(辛子)
	soybean	大豆
	spikenard	うど
	spinach	ほうれん草
	sponge gourd	へちま
	spring onion	ねぎ
	squash	西洋かぼちゃ
	stalk	茎(くき)
	sudachi citron	すだち
	sugar beet	てんさい
	summer squash	ズッキーニ
	sunflower	ひまわり
	sweet cherry	さくらんぼ
	sweet corn	スイートコーン
	sweet pepper	赤ピーマン
	sweet pepper	ピーマン
	sweet potato	さつま芋
	sword bean	なた豆
T	taro	里芋，ずいき
	thistle	あざみ
	tomato	トマト

	大和芋	Japanese yam
	ヤングコーン	baby corn
	ゆず	*yuzu* citron
	百合根	lily bulb
	洋梨	pear
	よもぎ	mugwort
ら	ライチー	litchi; leechee
	ライム	lime
	ラズベリー(木いちご)	raspberry
	落花生	peanut
	らっきょう	*rakkyo*
	リーク	leek
	緑黄色野菜	brightly colored vegetables
	りんご	apple
	ルバーブ	rhubarb
	レーズン	raisin
	レタス	garden lettuce
	レッドカラント	red currant
	レモン	lemon
	蓮根(れんこん)	lotus root
	ロケットサラダ(菜)	rocket salad
わ	わけぎ	Welsh onion
	わらび	bracken

	truffle	トリュフ
	turnip	かぶ
V	vegetable	野菜
	vegetables and fruits	青果
	velvet-stemmed agaric	えのきたけ
W	watercress	クレソン
	water dropwort	芹(せり)
	watermelon	西瓜(すいか)
	water pepper	蓼(たで)
	watertarget	じゅんさい
	wax gourd	冬瓜(とうがん)
	Welsh onion	わけぎ
	white radish	大根
	white radish sprouts	かいわれ大根
	winged bean	四角豆
Y	*yuzu* citron	ゆず
Z	zucchini	ズッキーニ

スパイス＆ハーブ （Spices and Herbs）

アニス	anise
うこん	turmeric
エストラゴン	estragon
オールスパイス	allspice
オレガノ	oregano
からし	brown mustard
カルダモン	cardamon
クミン	cumin
クローブ	clove
ケイパー	caper
月桂樹	laurel ; sweet bay
こしょう	pepper
コリアンダー	coriander
コンフリー	common comfrey
サフラン	saffron crocus
山椒	Japanese pepper
シナモン	cinnamon
セイジ	sage
タイム	garden thyme
ターメリック	turmeric
タラゴン	tarragon
ディル	dill
唐辛子	red pepper ; chili pepper
ナツメグ	nutmeg
バジル（スウィート）	sweet basil
パセリ	parsley
はっか	peppermint ; Japanese mint
八角（はっかく）	star anise
バニラ	vanilla
パプリカ	paprika
フェンネル	fennel
ペパーミント	peppermint
マジョラム	marjoram
ミント	mint
レモングラス	lemon grass
レモンバーム	lemon balm
ローズマリー	rosemary
わさび	*wasabi* ; horseradish
キャラウェー	caraway
グリーンペパー	green pepper
チャービル	chervil

Spices and Herbs （スパイス＆ハーブ）

allspice	オールスパイス
anise	アニス
brown mustard	からし
caper	ケイパー
cardamon	カルダモン
chili pepper	唐辛子
cinnamon	シナモン
clove	クローブ
common comfrey	コンフリー
coriander	コリアンダー
cumin	クミン
dill	ディル
estragon	エストラゴン
fennel	フェンネル
garden thyme	タイム
Japanese mint	はっか
Japanese pepper	山椒
laurel	月桂樹
lemon balm	レモンバーム
lemon grass	レモングラス
marjoram	マジョラム
mint	ミント
nutmeg	ナツメグ
oregano	オレガノ
paprika	パプリカ
parsley	パセリ
pepper	こしょう
peppermint	はっか、ペパーミント
red pepper	唐辛子
rosemary	ローズマリー
sage	セイジ
saffron crocus	サフラン
star anise	八角（はっかく）
sweet basil	バジル（スウィート）
sweet bay	月桂樹
tarragon	タラゴン
turmeric	うこん、ターメリック
vanilla	バニラ
wasabi ; horseradish	わさび
caraway	キャラウェー
chervil	チャービル
green pepper	グリーンペパー

PART 7

調味料などに関する重要語句 （和英）

あ 赤砂糖　　　　　　　　　brown sugar
　　味塩(あじしお)　　　　　　seasoned salt; salt and MSG. mixture
　　味ぽん酢　　　　　　　　citron vinegar and soy sauce
　　アップルソース　　　　　apple sause
　　アニス　　　　　　　　　anise
　　油　　　　　　　　　　　oil
　　荒びき黒こしょう　　　　coarsely grounded black pepper
　　一味唐辛子　　　　　　　chili pepper flakes; cayenne pepper
　　薄口しょうゆ　　　　　　thin soy sauce
　　ウスターソース　　　　　worcester sauce
　　エッセンス　　　　　　　extracts
　　オイスターソース　　　　oyster sauce
　　オニオンソルト　　　　　onion salt
　　オリーブ油　　　　　　　olive oil
　　オールスパイス　　　　　allspice
　　オレガノ　　　　　　　　oregano
か 海鮮醤　　　　　　　　　hoisin sauce
　　化学調味料　　　　　　　monosodium glutamate (MSG.)
　　かき油　　　　　　　　　oyster sauce
　　角砂糖　　　　　　　　　cube sugar
　　かつお節　　　　　　　　dried bonito flakes
　　からし　　　　　　　　　mustard
　　辛味　　　　　　　　　　sharp taste; hot taste
　　ガラム・マサラ　　　　　garam masala
　　ガーリックソルト　　　　garlic salt
　　ガーリックパウダー　　　garlic powder
　　カルダモン　　　　　　　cardamon
　　カレー粉　　　　　　　　curry powder

PART 7

調味料などに関する重要語句 (英和)

A	allspice	オールスパイス
	anise	アニス
	apple sause	アップルソース
	artificial coloring	着色料
	artificial flavoring	着香料
	artificial sweetener	合成甘味料，人工甘味料
B	baking powder	ベーキングパウダー
	baking soda	ベーキングソーダ
	barbecue sause	焼肉のたれ
	bitter taste	苦味
	black pepper	黒こしょう
	black sesame seeds and salt	黒胡麻塩
	bouillon	ブイヨン
	brown sugar	赤砂糖
	butter	バター
C	cardamon	カルダモン
	catsup 〈米〉	ケチャップ
	cayenne pepper	一味唐辛子，七味唐辛子
	celery	セロリ
	chili pepper	唐辛子
	chili pepper flakes	一味唐辛子
	chili powder	チリパウダー
	chili sauce	チリソース
	Chinese hot sauce	辣油
	chocolate syrup	チョコレートシロップ
	cider vinegar	りんご酢
	cinnamon	シナモン
	citron vinegar	ぽん酢
	citron vinegar and soy sauce	味ぽん酢
	clove	クローブ，チョウジ

岩塩	rock salt
甘味	sweet taste
甘味料	sweetener
強力粉	hard-wheat flour
魚醤	*nam pla*; fish sauce
グラニュー糖	granulated [table] sugar
黒こしょう	black pepper
黒胡麻塩	black sesame seeds and salt
黒砂糖	raw [unrefined] sugar
クローブ	clove
削り節	dried bonito flakes
ケチャップ	ketchup; catsup〈米〉
月桂樹	laurel; sweet bay
減塩しょうゆ	very low salt soy sauce
濃口しょうゆ	thick soy sauce
香辛料	spice; condiment
合成甘味料	artificial sweetener
香味	flavor
氷砂糖	crystal [rock] sugar
香料	flavoring
五香粉	five spice powder
ココナッツオイル	coconut oil
ココナッツクリーム	coconut cream [milk]
こしょう	pepper
粉チーズ	Parmesan cheese
胡麻(ゴマ)	sesame seeds
胡麻塩	sesame seeds and salt
米酢	rice vinegar
さ 砂糖	sugar
サフラン	saffron crocus
サラダドレッシング	salad dressing
サラダ油	salad oil
ざらめ糖	granulated sugar
サワークリーム	sour cream
山椒	*sansho*; Japanese pepper
サンバル	sambal
サンフラワー油	sunflower seed oil
ジアスターゼ	diastase

	coarsely grounded black pepper	荒びき黒こしょう
	coconut cream [milk]	ココナッツクリーム
	coconut oil	ココナッツオイル
	common salvia	セージ
	condiment	香辛科；薬味
	crystal [rock] sugar	氷砂糖
	cube sugar	角砂糖
	curry powder	カレー粉
D	diastase	ジアスターゼ
	dill	ディル
	dip	たれ
	dressing	ドレッシング
	dried bonito flakes	かつお節，削り節
	dry mustard	ドライマスタード
E	extracts	エッセンス
F	fermented soybean paste	味噌
	five spice powder	五香粉
	flavor	香味；調味する
	flavoring	風味料，香料
G	garam masala	ガラム・マサラ
	garden thyme	タイム
	garlic powder	ガーリックパウダー
	garlic salt	ガーリックソルト
	gelatin	ゼラチン
	granulated sugar	ざらめ糖
	granulated [table] sugar	グラニュー糖
	grated white radish and chili	もみじおろし
H	hard-wheat flour	強力粉
	herb	ハーブ(香草)
	hoisin sauce	海鮮醬
	honey	はちみつ
	hops	ホップ
	horseradish	西洋わさび
	hot brown bean sauce	豆板醬
	hot taste	辛味
J	Japanese horseradish	わさび
	Japanese mustard	和がらし

塩	salt
塩味	salty taste
塩こしょう	salt and pepper mixture
しし唐辛子	small green pepper
紫蘇(しそ)	*shiso* leaves; perilla
七味唐辛子	seven-spice pepper; cayenne pepper
シナモン	cinnamon
ジャム	jam
上白糖	powdered sugar
しょうゆ	soy sauce
食塩	table salt
ショートニング	shortening
白こしょう	white pepper
シロップ	sirup〈米〉; syrup〈英〉
人工甘味料	artificial sweetener
酢	vinegar
すし酢	sweetened vinegar for *sushi*
ステーキソース	steak sauce
スパイス	spice
西洋わさび	horseradish
セージ	common salvia; sage
ゼラチン	gelatin
セロリ	celery
ソース	sauce
た タイム	garden thyme
タバスコ	Tabasco（sauce）
タルタルソース	tartar sauce
たれ	sauce; dip
着香料	artificial flavoring
着色料	artificial coloring
チョウジ	clove
調味する	season; flavor
調味料	seasoning
チョコレートシロップ	chocolate syrup
チリソース	chili sauce
チリパウダー	chili powder

	Japanese pepper	山椒
	Japanese *sake*	日本酒
K	ketchup	ケチャップ
L	lard	ラード
	laurel	月桂樹
	lemon extract	レモンエッセンス
M	maple sugar	メイプルシュガー
	margarine	マーガリン
	mayonnaise	マヨネーズ
	mint	ミント
	monosodium glutamate (MSG.)	化学調味料
	mustard	からし，マスタード
N	*nam pla*	魚醬
	nutmeg	ナツメグ
O	oil	油
	olive oil	オリーブ油
	onion salt	オニオンソルト
	oregano	オレガノ
	oyster sauce	かき油，オイスターソース
P	paprika	パプリカ
	Parmesan cheese	粉チーズ
	parsley	パセリ
	pepper	こしょう
	pepper mint	はっか
	perilla	紫蘇(しそ)
	powdered sugar	上白糖
R	raw [unrefined] sugar	黒砂糖
	red pepper	唐辛子
	relish	薬味
	rice vinegar	米酢
	rice wine	日本酒
	rock salt	岩塩
S	saffron crocus	サフラン
	sage	セージ
	salad dressing	サラダドレッシング
	salad oil	サラダ油
	salt	塩

	ディル	dill
	唐辛子	red pepper; chili pepper
	豆板醤	hot brown bean sauce
	トマトケチャップ	tomato ketchup
	トマトピューレー	tomato puree
	トマトペースト	tomato paste
	ドライイースト	yeast
	ドライマスタード	dry mustard
	ドレッシング	dressing
な	ナツメグ	nutmeg
	苦味	bitter taste
	日本酒	Japanese *sake*; rice wine
は	薄力粉	soft-wheat flour
	バジル	sweet basil
	パセリ	parsley
	バター	butter
	はちみつ	honey
	はっか	pepper mint
	八角	star anise
	バニラエッセンス	vanilla extract
	ハーブ（香草）	herb
	パプリカ	paprika
	ピーナッツバター	peanut butter
	ひまわり油	sunflower seed oil
	ブイヨン	bouillon
	風味料	flavoring
	ベーキングソーダ	baking soda
	ベーキングパウダー	baking powder
	ホップ	hops
	ホワイトソース	white sauce
	ぽん酢	citron vinegar
ま	マーガリン	margarine
	マスタード	mustard
	マーマレード	marmalade
	マヨネーズ	mayonnaise
	味噌	*miso*; fermented soybean paste
	味醂（みりん）	sweet cooking *sake*
	ミント	mint

salt and MSG. mixture	味塩(あじしお)
salt and pepper mixture	塩こしょう
salty taste	塩味
sambal	サンバル
sauce	ソース，たれ
season	調味する
seasoned salt	味塩(あじしお)
seasoning	調味料
sesame seeds	胡麻(ごま)
sesame seeds and salt	胡麻塩
seven-spice pepper	七味唐辛子
sharp taste	辛味
shiso leaves	紫蘇(しそ)
shortening	ショートニング
sirup 〈米〉	シロップ
small green pepper	しし唐辛子
soft-wheat flour	薄力粉
sour cream	サワークリーム
soy sauce	紫(むらさき)，しょうゆ
spice	スパイス，香辛料，薬味
star anise	八角
steak sauce	ステーキソース
sugar	砂糖
sunflower seed oil	ひまわり油，サンフラワー油
sweet basil	バジル
sweet bay	月桂樹
sweet cooking *sake*	味醂(みりん)
sweetened vinegar for *sushi*	すし酢
sweetener	甘味料
sweet taste	甘味
syrup 〈英〉	シロップ
T Tabasco (sauce)	タバスコ
table salt	食塩
tartar sauce	タルタルソース
thick soy sauce	濃口しょうゆ
thin soy sauce	薄口しょうゆ
tomato ketchup	トマトケチャップ
tomato paste	トマトペースト

	紫 (むらさき)	soy sauce
	メイプルシュガー	maple sugar
	もみじおろし	grated white radish and chili
や	焼肉のたれ	barbecue sause
	薬味	spice; relish; condiment
	ゆず	*yuzu* citron
ら	ラード	lard
	辣油	Chinese hot sauce
	りんご酢	cider vinegar
	レモンエッセンス	lemon extract
わ	ワインビネガー	wine vinegar
	和がらし	Japanese mustard
	わさび	*wasabi*; Japanese horseradish

ソース （Sauces）

アイオリ・ソース	Aioli sauce
アメリケーヌ・ソース	Americaine sauce
イタリアン・ドレッシング	Italian dressing
ヴィネグレット・ソース	Vinaigrette sauce
ヴルーテ・ソース	Veloutō sauce
オランデーズ・ソース	Hollandaise sauce
オーロラ・ソース	Aurora sauce
サウザンアイランド	thousand island
デミグラ・ソース	demiglace sauce
トマト・ソース	tomato sause
ブラウン・ソース	brown sause
フレンチ・ドレッシング	French dressing
ベアルネーズ・ソース	Béarnaise sause
ベシャメル・ソース	bechamel sause
ホワイト・ソース	white sauce
マスタード・ソース	mustard sauce

	tomato puree	トマトピューレー
V	vanilla extract	バニラエッセンス
	very low salt soy sauce	減塩しょうゆ
	vinegar	酢
W	white pepper	白こしょう
	white sauce	ホワイトソース
	worcester sauce	ウスターソース
Y	yeast	ドライイースト
	yuzu citron	ゆず

Sauces（ソース）

Aioli sauce	アイオリ・ソース
Americaine sauce	アメリケーヌ・ソース
Aurora sauce	オーロラ・ソース
Béarnaise sause	ベアルネーズ・ソース
bechamel sause	ベシャメル・ソース
brown sause	ブラウン・ソース
demiglace sauce	デミグラ・ソース
French dressing	フレンチ・ドレッシング
Hollandaise sauce	オランデーズ・ソース
Italian dressing	イタリアン・ドレッシング
mustard sauce	マスタード・ソース
thousand island	サウザンアイランド
tomato sause	トマト・ソース
Veloutō sauce	ヴルーテ・ソース
Vinaigrette sauce	ヴィネグレット・ソース
white sauce	ホワイト・ソース

食用油 (Cooking Oils)

オリーブ油	olive oil
オレンジ油	orange oil
肝油	liver oil
牛脂	beef tallow
魚油	fish oil
くるみ油	walnut oil
ココナッツ油	coconut oil
コプラ油	coconut oil
胡麻油	sesame oil
米ぬか油	rice bran oil
コーン油	corn oil
サラダ油	salad oil
脂肪	lard (豚) ; suet (牛・羊)
植物油	vegetable oil
大豆油	soybean oil
天ぷら油	*tempura* oil
なたね油	rape oil
パーム油	palm oil
バター	butter
ビター・アーモンド油	bitter almond oil
ひまわり油	sunflower seed oil
フルーツ・ピール油	fruit peel oil
紅花油	safflower oil
マーガリン	margarine
綿実油 (めんじつゆ)	cottonseed oil
ラード	lard
落花生油	peanut oil
レモン油	lemon oil

Cooking Oils （食用油）

beef tallow	牛脂
bitter almond oil	ビター・アーモンド油
butter	バター
coconut oil	ココナッツ油
coconut oil	コプラ油
corn oil	コーン油
cottonseed oil	綿実油 （めんじつゆ）
fish oil	魚油
fruit peel oil	フルーツ・ピール油
lard	脂肪 （豚）, ラード
lemon oil	レモン油
liver oil	肝油
margarine	マーガリン
olive oil	オリーブ油
orange oil	オレンジ油
palm oil	パーム油
peanut oil	落花生油
rape oil	なたね油
rice bran oil	米ぬか油
safflower oil	紅花油
salad oil	サラダ油
sesame oil	胡麻油
soybean oil	大豆油
suet	脂肪 （牛・羊）
sunflower seed oil	ひまわり油
tempura oil	天ぷら油
vegetable oil	植物油
walnut oil	くるみ油

PART 8

食器・器具・用具などに関する重要語句 (和英)

あ	浅めの片手鍋	pan
	圧力釜	pressure cooker
	圧力計	manometer
	穴あきお玉	skimmer
	油差し	oiler
	アーミーナイフ	army knife
	網目用カッター	tart-top cutter
	洗い桶	dishpan
	洗い物かけ	dish rack
	洗い用具	cleaning up
	アルコール・ランプ	alcohol lamp
	アルミホイル	aluminum foil
	泡立て器	whisk
	1クォート計量カップ	1 quart measuring cup
	浮きばかり(液体比重計)	hydrometer
	受け皿	saucer
	臼(うす)	mortar
	器(うつわ)	container
	裏ごし器	strainer
	柄付き深鍋	sauce pan
	遠心分離器	centrifuge
	桶	pail; bucket
	大さじ	tablespoon
	お玉	ladle
	落としぶた	drop-lid
	オーブン	oven
	オーブントースター	toaster oven
	オーブン用調理器具	kitchenware for the oven
	重石	weight for pressing down
	おろし金	grater
	温度計	thermometer

食器・器具・用具などに関する重要語句 (英和)

A	alcohol lamp	アルコール・ランプ
	aluminum foil	アルミホイル
	apple corer	芯抜き器
	apple parer	りんご皮むき器
	apron	前掛け
	army knife	アーミーナイフ
	automatic wash	自動洗浄器
B	bagging machine	袋詰め機
	baking shovel	釜べら
	bamboo rolling mat	巻き簀(す)
	barrel	樽(たる)
	basket	かご
	blender	ミキサー
	boning knife	骨すきナイフ
	bottle opener	栓抜き(せんぬき)
	bowl	ボール；椀(わん)；丼(どんぶり)
	bread knife	パン切り包丁
	bread plate	パン皿
	brush	ブラシ，たわし
	bucket	バケツ
C	cabinet	食器戸棚
	cake divider	等分器
	cake pan	ケーキ用鍋
	can opener	缶切り
	carving knife	肉用切り分け包丁
	cask	樽(たる)
	casserole	蒸し焼き鍋
	casserole pan	口広がりの両手鍋
	centrifuge	遠心分離器
	Chinese pan	中華鍋
	Chinese soup spoon	れんげ

	温度調節器	thermoregulator
か	回転台	turntable
	かき混ぜ器	rotary hand beater
	かご	basket
	果汁絞り器	juice squeezer
	ガス台	gas range; stove
	カスタード用カップ	custard cup
	ガスバーナー	gas burner
	型	mold, mould
	片手鍋	saucepan
	金網台	dipping wire
	釜(湯沸かし用)	kettle
	釜べら	baking shovel
	紙ナプキン	paper napkin
	皮削り器	peeler
	皮むき器	parer, peeler
	皮むき用ナイフ	paring knife
	缶(ケーキ用)	tin
	換気扇	ventilation [exhaust] fan
	缶切り	can opener
	乾燥機	desiccator
	木べら	wooden spatula
	急須	teapot
	霧吹き	spray
	串	skewer
	果物ナイフ	fruit knife
	口金	tube; piping tube
	口広がりの両手鍋	casserole pan
	クッキー用シート	cookie sheet
	グラス	glass
	くり抜き器	fruit ball spoon
	グリル(肉焼き器)	grill
	クレンザー	cleanser
	計量カップ	measuring cup
	計量スプーン	measuring spoon
	ケーキ用鍋	cake pan
	検温器	hygroscope
	合成洗剤	detergent

chopper	チョッパー
chopping board	〈英〉まな板
chopstick rest	箸置き
chopsticks	箸(はし)
clay pot	土鍋
cleaning up	洗い用具
cleanser	クレンザー，洗剤
coffee cup	コーヒーカップ
coffee pot	コーヒーポット
container	器(うつわ)；貯蔵庫；容器
cooker	レンジ
cookie sheet	クッキー用シート
cooking chopsticks	菜ばし
cooking fork	二股調理用フォーク
cooking grill	焼き綱
cook's cap	コック帽
cook's coat	白衣
cooler	冷房機
corkscrew	コルク(栓)抜き
cover	ふた
cradle	丸底の杓子
cupboard	戸棚，食器戸棚
custard cup	カスタード用カップ
cutter	裁断器
cutting board	まな板
D deep freeze	冷凍庫
desiccator	乾燥機
detergent	合成洗剤
dining table	食卓
dipper	平底の杓子(しゃくし)
dipping wire	金網台
dish	深皿，盛り皿
dish detergent	洗剤(台所用)
dish drainer	水切りかご
dishes	皿
dishpan	洗い桶
dish rack	洗い物かけ
dish towel	〈米〉皿ふき用ふきん

小刀(こがたな)	knife
小型の片手鍋	pan; skillet
小型包丁	little kinfe
小さじ	teaspoon
小皿	plate
コック帽	cook's cap
コップ	glass
コーヒーカップ	coffee cup
コーヒーポット	coffee pot
ゴミ箱	trash [garbage] can⟨米⟩; dustbin⟨英⟩
ゴミ袋	garbage bag
ゴムべら	rubber spatula; scraper
コルク(栓)抜き	corkscrew
裁断器	cutter
菜ばし	cooking chopsticks
杯(さかずき)	*sake* cup
魚包丁	kitchen knife for fish
作業台	kitchen table
皿	dishes
皿洗い機	dish washer
皿ふき用ふきん	dish towel⟨米⟩; tea towel⟨英⟩
ざる	draining basket; sieve
三角コーナー	sink strainer
湿度計	hygrometer
自動洗浄器	automatic wash
絞り袋	forcing bag
杓子(しゃくし)	dipper(平底); cradle(丸底)
蛇口	tap; faucet⟨米⟩
しゃもじ	spatula
じょうご	funnel
消毒器	sterilizer
しょうゆ差し	soy sauce cruet
食卓	dining table
食料貯蔵戸棚	larder
食器	tableware
食器戸棚	cupboard; cabinet

さ

	dish washer	皿洗い機
	disposable chopsticks	割箸
	doubleedged knife	両刃(りょうば)
	dough mixer	練り機
	drainer	水切り
	draining basket	ざる
	drop-lid	落としぶた
	dustbin	〈英〉ゴミ箱
	dustpan	ちりとり
E	earthenware mortar	すり鉢
	earthenware pot	土鍋
	egg cup	ゆで卵立て
	8 ounce measuring cup	8オンス計量カップ
	electric rice cooker	電気炊飯器
F	faucet	蛇口
	floorcloth	雑巾(ぞうきん)
	food processor	フード・プロセッサー
	forcing bag	絞り袋
	fork	フォーク
	freezer	冷凍庫
	freezing room	冷凍室
	fridge	冷蔵庫
	fruit ball spoon	くり抜き器
	fruit knife	果物ナイフ
	frying pan	フライパン
	frying pan with cover	ふた付きフライパン
	funnel	じょうご
G	garbage bag	ゴミ袋
	garbage pail	生ゴミ入れ
	gas burner	ガスバーナー
	gas range	ガス台
	glass	グラス, コップ
	grater	おろし金
	gravimeter	比重計
	grill	グリル(肉焼き器)
H	hand mill	ひきうす
	hatchet	鉈(なた)
	hole nozzle	丸形口金

	芯抜き器	apple corer
	炊飯器	rice cooker
	すきやき鍋	*sukiyaki* pan
	ストロー	straw
	スープ皿	soup plate
	スープ鍋	stock pot
	スープ用スプーン	soup spoon
	スプーン	spoon
	スポンジ	sponge
	スライサー	slicer
	すりこぎ	wooden pestle
	すり鉢	earthenware mortar
	製菓用オーブン	oven for pastry
	成形器	molding machine
	赤外線オーブン	infrared oven
	赤外線ランプ	infrared lamp
	膳(ぜん)	small dining table; tray
	洗剤(台所用)	dish detergent; cleanser
	洗濯機	washing machine
	栓抜き(せんぬき)	bottle opener
	雑巾(ぞうきん)	floorcloth
	掃除機	vacuum cleaner
	ソースパン	saucepan
た	大コップ(取っ手・足なし)	tumbler
	大コップ(取っ手付き)	tankard
	台所用はさみ	kitchen shears
	台所用品	kitchen utensils
	タイマー	timer
	大理石台	marble table [counter]
	卓上用塩・こしょう入れ	salt and pepper shaker
	棚(たな)	shelf
	卵焼き鍋	rectangular omelet pan
	樽(たる)	barrel; cask
	たわし	brush; steel wool
	茶こし	tea strainer
	茶さじ	teaspoon
	茶たく	saucer
	茶筒	tea caddy

	hot iron	焼きごて
	hydrometer	浮きばかり(液体比重計)
	hygrometer	湿度計
	hygroscope	検温器
I	infrared lamp	赤外線ランプ
	infrared oven	赤外線オーブン
J	Japanese broad-bladed kitchen knife for chopping	出刃包丁
	jug	水差し
	juice squeezer	果汁絞り器
K	kettle	やかん；釜(湯沸かし用)
	kitchen bleaches	漂白剤
	kitchen knife	包丁
	kitchen knife for fish	魚包丁
	kitchen shears	台所用はさみ
	kitchen table [counter]	調理台, 作業台
	kitchen towel	ふきん
	kitchen utensils	台所用品
	knife	ナイフ, 小刀(こがたな)
	knife sharpener	ナイフとぎ
	kitchenware for the oven	オーブン用調理器具
L	ladle	お玉, 柄杓(ひしゃく)
	larder	食料貯蔵戸棚
	lemon squeezer	レモン絞り器
	lid	ふた(箱)
	little kinfe	小型包丁
M	manometer	圧力計
	marble table [counter]	大理石台
	measure	計り(量)
	measuring cup	計量カップ
	measuring spoon	計量スプーン
	microwave oven	電子レンジ
	milkpan	ミルクパン
	mincer	挽き肉器
	mixer	ミキサー
	mixing bowl	混ぜ合わせ用ボール
	molding machine	成形器
	mold	型

茶碗	rice bowl
中華鍋	Chinese pan; wok
銚子 (ちょうし)	*sake* bottle
調理台	kitchen table [counter]
貯蔵庫	container
チョッパー	chopper
ちりとり	dustpan
使い捨てコップ	throwaway [disposable] cup
爪楊枝 (つまようじ)	toothpick
吊り戸棚	wall cupboard
ティシュー	tissues
ティースプーン	teaspoon
出刃包丁	Japanese broad-bladed kitchen knife for chopping
テーブルクロス	tablecloth
テーブルスプーン	tablespoon
電気炊飯器	electric rice cooker
電子レンジ	microwave oven
天ぷら鍋	*tempura* pan
砥石 (といし)	whetstone
糖度計	syrup hydrometer
等分器	cake divider
トースター	toaster
戸棚	cupboard
徳利 (とっくり)	*sake* bottle
土鍋	clay pot; earthenware pot
取り皿	plate
丼 (どんぶり)	bowl
な ナイフ	knife
ナイフとぎ	knife sharpener
流し	sink
鉈 (なた)	hatchet
ナプキン	table napkin
鍋	pan(浅い); pot(深い)
鍋つかみ	pot holder
鍋ぶた	pot lid
生ゴミ入れ	garbage pail
肉用切り分け包丁	carving knife

	mop	モップ
	mortar	臼(氵)
	mould	型
	mug	マグカップ
O	oiler	油差し
	1 quart measuring cup	1クォート計量カップ
	oven	オーブン
	oven for pastry	製菓用オーブン
P	pail	桶, バケツ
	pan	浅めの片手鍋, 平鍋, 小型の片手鍋
	paper napkin	紙ナプキン
	paper towel	ペーパータオル
	parer	皮むき器
	paring knife	皮むき用ナイフ
	peeler	皮削り器, 皮むき器
	percolator	ろ過装置付きコーヒー沸かし
	pie plate	パイ皿
	pie tin	パイ用ティン
	pincette	ピンセット
	piping tube	口金
	pitcher	水差し
	plastic bag	ポリ袋
	plastic wrap	ラップ
	plate	取り皿, 小皿
	platter	〈米〉肉・魚用盛り皿
	polishing powder	みがき粉
	pot	深めの両手鍋
	pot holder	鍋つかみ
	pot lid	鍋ぶた
	pressure cooker	圧力釜
Q	quern	ひきうす
R	range	レンジ
	rectangular omelet pan	卵焼き鍋
	refrigerator	冷蔵庫
	rice bowl	茶碗
	rice cooker	炊飯器
	roaster	ロースター

食器・器具・用具などに関する重要語句　**107**

	練り機	dough mixer
	残り物入れ	storing leftover
	のし棒	rolling pin
	のばし機	roller; rolling pin
は	パイ皿	pie plate
	パイ用ティン	pie tin
	計り	measure〈量〉; weight〈重さ〉
	秤	scale
	白衣	cook's coat
	バケツ	bucket, pail
	はさみ	scissors; sears
	箸（はし）	chopsticks
	箸置き	chopstick rest
	8オンス計量カップ	8 ounce measuring cup
	パン切り包丁	bread knife
	パン皿	bread plate
	飯台	wooden *sushi* bowl
	万能ナイフ	utility knife
	ひきうす	hand mill; quern
	挽き肉器	mincer
	柄杓（ひしゃく）	ladle
	比重計	gravimeter
	漂白剤	kitchen bleaches
	平鍋	pan
	ピンセット	pincette
	フォーク	fork
	深皿	dish
	深めの片手鍋	saucepan
	深めの両手鍋	pot
	ふきん	kitchen towel
	袋詰め機	bagging machine
	ふた	cover; lid〈箱〉
	ふた付きスープ壺	tureen
	ふた付きフライパン	frying pan with cover
	二股調理用フォーク	cooking fork; two tines
	フード・プロセッサー	food processor
	フライ返し	turner; spatula
	フライパン	frying pan; skillet〈米〉

	roller	粉砕機，のばし機
	rolling pin	麺棒，のし棒，のばし機
	rotary hand beater	かき混ぜ器
	round roasting pan with rack	ロースト用回転器
	rubber spatula	ゴムべら
S	*sake* bottle	銚子(ちょうし)，徳利(とっくり)
	sake cup	杯(さかずき)
	salt and pepper shaker	卓上用塩・こしょう入れ
	saucepan	片手鍋，ソースパン，深めの 片手鍋
	saucer	受け皿；茶たく
	scale	ものさし；秤
	scissors	はさみ
	scraper	ゴムべら
	sears	はさみ
	separator	分割器
	shelf	棚(たな)
	sieve	ふるい；ざる
	sifter	振りかけ容器(塩・こしょう)
	sink	流し
	sink strainer	三角コーナー
	skewer	串
	skillet	〈米〉フライパン；小型の片 手鍋
	skimmer	穴あきお玉
	slicer	スライサー
	small dining table	膳(ぜん)
	soup plate	スープ皿
	soup spoon	スープ用スプーン
	soy sauce cruet	しょうゆ差し
	spatula	しゃもじ，へら，フライ返し
	sponge	スポンジ
	spoon	スプーン
	spray	霧吹き
	star nozzle	星形口金
	steamer	蒸し器
	steel wool	たわし
	sterilizer	消毒器

	ブラシ	brush
	振りかけ容器(塩・こしょう)	sifter
	ふるい	sieve
	分割器	separator
	粉砕機	roller
	ペーパータオル	paper towel
	へら	spatula
	包装機	wrapping machine
	包丁	kitchen knife
	星形口金	wavy nozzle; star nozzle
	ポットカバー	tea cozy
	骨すきナイフ	boning knife
	ポリ袋	plastic bag
	ボール	bowl
	盆	tray
ま	前掛け	apron
	巻き簀(す)	bamboo rolling mat
	マグカップ	mug
	混ぜ合わせ用ボール	mixing bowl
	まな板	cutting board; chopping board 〈英〉
	丸形口金	hole nozzle
	みがき粉	polishing powder
	ミキサー	mixer; blender
	水切り	strainer; drainer
	水切りかご	dish drainer
	水差し	jug; pitcher
	ミルクパン	milkpan
	蒸し器	steamer
	蒸し焼き鍋	casserole
	麺棒	rolling pin
	木製調理用スプーン	wooden cooking spoon
	モップ	mop
	ものさし	scale
	盛り皿	dish; platter(肉・魚用)〈米〉
や	やかん	kettle
	焼きごて	hot iron
	焼き網	cooking grill

stewpot	両手付き大型シチュー鍋
stock pot	スープ鍋
storing leftover	残り物入れ
stove	ガス台
strainer	裏ごし器；水切り
straw	ストロー
sukiyaki pan	すきやき鍋
syrup hydrometer	糖度計
T tablecloth	テーブルクロス
table napkin	ナプキン
tablespoon	大さじ，テーブルスプーン
tableware	食器
tankard	大コップ(取っ手付き)
tap	蛇口
tart-top cutter	網目用カッター
tea caddy	茶筒
tea cozy	ポットカバー
teacup	湯呑み(ゆのみ)
teapot	急須
teaspoon	小さじ，茶さじ，ティースプーン
tea strainer	茶こし
tea towel	〈英〉皿ふき用ふきん
tempura pan	天ぷら鍋
thermometer	温度計
thermoregulator	温度調節器
throwaway [disposable] cup	使い捨てコップ
timer	タイマー
tin	缶(ケーキ用)
tissues	ティシュー
toaster	トースター
toaster oven	オーブントースター
toothpick	爪楊枝(つまよじ)
trash [garbage] can〈米〉	ゴミ箱
tray	盆；膳(ぜん)
tube	口金
tumbler	大コップ(取っ手・足なし)
tureen	ふた付きスープ壺

	野菜ラック	vegetable rack
	ゆで卵立て	egg cup
	湯呑み(ゆのみ)	teacup
	容器	container
ら	ラップ	plastic wrap
	両手付き大型シチュー鍋	stewpot
	両刃(りょうば)	doubleedged knife
	りんご皮むき器	apple parer
	冷蔵庫	fridge; refrigerator
	冷凍庫	freezer; deep freeze
	冷凍室	freezing room
	冷房機	cooler
	レモン絞り器	lemon squeezer
	れんげ	Chinese soup spoon
	レンジ	range, cooker
	ろ過装置付きコーヒー沸かし	percolator
	ロースター	roaster
	ロースト用回転器	round roasting pan with rack
わ	ワッフル焼き型	waffle iron
	割箸	disposable chopsticks
	椀(わん)	bowl

	turner	フライ返し
	turntable	回転台
	two tines	二股調理用フォーク
U	utility knife	万能ナイフ
V	vacuum cleaner	掃除機
	vegetable rack	野菜ラック
	ventilation [exhaust] fan	換気扇
W	waffle iron	ワッフル焼き型
	wall cupboard	吊り戸棚
	washing machine	洗濯機
	wavy nozzle	星形口金
	weight	計り(重さ)
	weight for pressing down	重石
	whetstone	砥石(とい)
	whisk	泡立て器
	wok	中華鍋
	wooden cooking spoon	木製調理用スプーン
	wooden pestle	すりこぎ
	wooden spatula	木べら
	wooden *sushi* bowl	飯台
	wrapping machine	包装機

PART 9

色彩などに関する重要語句 （和英）

あ 藍（あい）色　　　　　　　indigo
　　青　　　　　　　　　　blue
　　青緑　　　　　　　　　sea green
　　赤　　　　　　　　　　red
　　明るい（色）　　　　　bright
　　明るい黄色　　　　　　bright; light color
　　浅緑　　　　　　　　　light［pale］green
　　鮮やかな（色）　　　　vivid
　　鮮やかなピンク　　　　vivid pink
　　あずき色　　　　　　　russet
　　あっさりした色　　　　plain color
　　淡い（色）　　　　　　light
　　淡い中間色　　　　　　pastel color
　　暗褐色　　　　　　　　dark brown
　　暗色　　　　　　　　　dark color
　　暗緑色（あんりょくしょく）　　dark green
　　色　　　　　　　　　　color〈米〉, colour〈英〉
　　色合い　　　　　　　　shade
　　薄い（色）　　　　　　pale
　　薄茶色　　　　　　　　light brown
　　薄紫　　　　　　　　　lavender
　　えび茶色　　　　　　　maroon
　　エメラルドグリーン　　emerald green
　　えんじ色　　　　　　　dark red
　　オイスターホワイト　　oyster white
　　黄褐色　　　　　　　　yellowish brown
　　黄赤色　　　　　　　　apricot
　　黄土色　　　　　　　　ocher〈英〉
　　黄緑色　　　　　　　　yellowish green
　　オリーブ色　　　　　　olive
　　オレンジ色　　　　　　orange

色彩などに関する重要語句 (英和)

A	amber	琥珀(こはく)
	apricot	黄赤色
	artificial color	合成着色料
B	beige	ベージュ
	black	黒色
	blue	青
	brick red	れんが色
	bright	明るい(色)
	bright red	真っ赤
	bright yellow	明るい黄色
	brown	茶色
C	change of color	変色
	chestnut brown	栗色
	cobalt blue	コバルトブルー
	coloration	着色
	coloring	色彩, 着色
	color of the earth	土色
	color scheme	配色
	color tone	色調
	color vision	色覚
	color	色
	cream	クリーム色
	crimson	深紅
D	dark	暗い(色)
	dark blue	暗い青, 紺色
	dark brown	こげ茶, 暗褐色, 茶褐色
	dark color	暗色
	dark green	暗緑色(あんりょくしょく)
	dark red	えんじ色
	deep	深い(色)
	deep [dark] green	深緑

か	カーキ色	khaki
	唐紅_(からくれない)	scarlet
	黄色	yellow
	きつね色(小麦色)	light brown
	黄緑	yellow green
	金色	gold
	銀色	silver
	草色	green; yellowish green
	暗い(色)	dark
	暗い青	dark blue
	栗色	chestnut brown
	クリーム色	cream
	黒色	black
	群青	ultramarine
	けばけばしい赤	gaudy red
	原色	original color
	濃い(色)	strong
	濃い赤	strong red
	合成着色料	artificial color
	こげ茶	dark brown
	琥珀_(こはく)	amber
	コバルトブルー	cobalt blue
	紺青	prussian deep blue
	紺色	dark blue; navy blue
	混色	mixed colors
さ	サーモンピンク	salmon pink
	三原色	three primary colors
	三色	three colors
	色覚	color vision
	色感	impression of a color
	色彩	coloring
	色調	color tone
	朱色	vermilion
	白	white
	深紅	crimson
	赤褐色	reddish brown
	象牙_(ぞうげ)色	ivory
	空色	sky blue

	dull grey	にぶい灰色
E	earth tone	土色
	emerald green	エメラルドグリーン
F	flesh colored	肉色の
G	gaudy red	けばけばしい赤
	gold	金色
	gray 〈米〉	灰色
	green	緑色，草色
	grey 〈英〉	灰色
I	impression of a color	色感
	indigo	藍(あい)色
	ivory	象牙(ぞうげ)色
K	khaki	カーキ色
L	lavender	薄紫
	light	淡い(色)
	light brown	きつね色(小麦色)，薄茶色
	light [pale] green	浅緑
M	maroon	えび茶色
	milky white	乳白色
	mixed colors	混色
N	navy blue	濃紺，紺色
O	ocher	〈英〉黄土色
	olive	オリーブ色
	orange	オレンジ色
	original color	原色
	oyster white	オイスターホワイト
P	pale	薄い(色)
	pale blue	水色
	pastel color	淡い中間色
	pink	桃色
	plain color	あっさりした色
	polka dot pattern	水玉模様
	prussian deep blue	紺青
	purple	紫色
R	red	赤
	reddish brown	赤褐色
	rose	バラ色
	russet	あずき色

た	暖色	warm color
	茶色	brown
	茶褐色	dark brown
	着色	coloration, coloring
	土色	color of the earth; earth tone
	透明な(色)	transparent
な	肉色の	flesh colored
	にぶい灰色	dull grey
	乳白色	milky white
	濃紺	navy blue
は	灰色	gray〈米〉, grey〈英〉
	配色	color scheme
	バラ色	rose
	半透明の	semi-transparent
	緋(ひ)色	scarlet
	深い(色)	deep
	深緑	deep [dark] green
	ベージュ	beige
	変色	change of color
ま	真っ赤	bright red
	水色	pale blue
	水玉模様	polka dot pattern
	緑色	green
	紫色	purple
	桃色	pink
ら	れんが色	brick red
わ	ワインレッド	wine red

S	salmon pink	サーモンピンク
	scarlet	緋(ひ)色，唐紅(からくれない)
	sea green	青緑
	semi-transparent	半透明の
	shade	色合い
	silver	銀色
	sky blue	空色
	strong	濃い(色)
	strong red	濃い赤
T	three colors	三色
	three primary colors	三原色
	transparent	透明な(色)
U	ultramarine	群青
V	vermilion	朱色
	vivid	鮮やかな(色)
	vivid pink	鮮やかなピンク
W	warm color	暖色
	white	白
	wine red	ワインレッド
Y	yellow	黄色
	yellow green	黄緑
	yellowish brown	黄褐色
	yellowish green	黄緑色，草色

食品の形状などに関する重要語句 （和英）

あ	厚い	thick
	上	upper; top
	うしろ（背面）	back
	薄い	thin
	内側	inside
	鋭角	acute angle
	円形	circle; round shape
	円弧	arc
	円周	circumference
	円錐（えんすい）	cone
	円柱	cylinder; column
	凹凸（おうとつ）	uneven
	大きい	big; large
	大きさ	size
	奥行	depth
	重さ	weight
か	外形	external [outward] form
	角	angle
	型	format
	硬い（肉など）	tough
	形	shape; form（形状）
	球形	globular form
	曲線	curved line
	五角形	pentagon
	極少の	microscopic
	ごく小さい	tiny
	固形物	solid body
さ	ざらざらする	feel rough
	三角形	triangle
	四角錐	pyramid
	ジグザグ線	zig zag

食品の形状などに関する重要語句 （英和）

A	acute angle	鋭角
	angle	角
	apex	頂点(三角形など)
	arc	円弧
	area	面積
B	back	うしろ(背面)
	base	底辺
	big	大きい，太い
	bottom	底面
C	capacity	容積
	center	中心
	circle	円形
	circumference	円周
	cone	円錐(えんすい)
	column	円柱
	cube	立方体
	curved line	曲線
	cylinder	円柱
D	depth	奥行
	diagonal	対角線
	diameter	直径
	diamond	ひし形
	dot	点
E	edge	ふち
	ellipse	楕円形
	external [outward] form	外形
F	feel rough	ざらざらする
	filling material	中身
	form	形(状)
	format	型
	front	前

	四辺形	quadrilateral
	小	small size
	上面(部)	top
	垂直線	perpendicular line
	筋だらけの(野菜など)	stringy
	正方形	square
	線	line
	扇形	sector
	側面	side
	外側	outside
た	大	large size
	対角線	diagonal
	体積	volume
	楕円形	oval; ellipse
	高さ	height
	縦	length
	卵形	oval
	小さい	little; small
	中	medium size
	中ぐらいの大きさ	middle
	中心	center
	頂点(三角形など)	apex
	長方形	rectangle; oblong
	直線	straight line
	直角	right angle
	直角三角形の斜辺	hypotenuse
	直径	diameter
	底辺	base
	底面	bottom
	点	dot
	突起	projection
	鈍角	obtuse angle
な	長さ	length
	中身	filling material
	斜め	slanting; oblique
	並	regular size
	波線	wavy line
	なめらかな	smooth

G	globular form	球形
H	half	半分
	height	高さ
	hexagon	六角形
	hypotenuse	直角三角形の斜辺
I	inside	内側
L	large	大きい
	large size	大
	left	左
	length	縦, 長さ
	line	線
	little	小さい
M	medium size	中
	microscopic	極少の
	middle	中ぐらいの大きさ
O	oblique	斜め
	oblong	長方形
	obtuse angle	鈍角
	outside	外側
	oval	卵形, 楕円形
P	parallel lines	平行線
	pentagon	五角形
	perfect circle	まん丸
	perpendicular line	垂直線
	projection	突起
	pyramid	四角錐
Q	quadrilateral	四辺形
R	radius	半径
	rectangle	長方形
	regular size	並
	right	右
	right angle	直角
	round	丸める
	round shape	円形
S	sector	扇形
	semicircle	半円
	shape	形
	short	短い

は	幅	width
	半円	semicircle
	半径	radius
	半分	half
	ひし形	diamond
	左	left
	表面	surface
	ふち	edge
	太い	big; thick
	平行線	parallel lines
	辺	side
	星形	star
	細い	thin
ま	前	front
	丸める	round
	まん丸	perfect circle
	右	right
	短い	short
	面積	area; size
や	やわらかい	soft; tender
	容積	capacity
	横	width
ら	ら線	spiral
	立体	solid
	立方体	cube
	六角形	hexagon

	side	側面，辺
	size	大きさ，面積
	slanting	斜め
	small	小さい
	small size	小
	smooth	なめらかな
	soft	やわらかい
	solid	立体
	solid body	固形物
	spiral	ら線
	square	正方形
	star	星形
	straight line	直線
	stringy	筋だらけの(野菜など)
	surface	表面
T	tender	やわらかい
	thick	厚い，太い
	thin	薄い，細い
	tiny	ごく小さい
	top	上面(部)，上
	tough	硬い(肉など)
	triangle	三角形
U	uneven	凹凸(おうとつ)
	upper	上
V	volume	体積
W	wavy line	波線
	weight	重さ
	width	横，幅
Z	zig zag	ジグザグ線

PART 11

食の世界に関する重要語句（和英）

あ 和え物　　　　　　　　　foods dressed with sauce
　　青かび　　　　　　　　　blue mold
　　灰汁（あく）　　　　　　　harshness
　　悪臭　　　　　　　　　　bad [nasty] smell
　　揚げ油　　　　　　　　　oil for frying
　　揚げ物　　　　　　　　　deep-fried food
　　味　　　　　　　　　　　taste; flavor
　　味を覚える　　　　　　　acquire a taste for
　　味をしめる　　　　　　　get a taste of success
　　厚切りの食パン　　　　　thick sliced bread
　　あっさりした食べ物　　　light food
　　集める　　　　　　　　　bring together; collect
　　あと味　　　　　　　　　aftertaste
　　甘い食べ物　　　　　　　sweet food
　　甘口　　　　　　　　　　sweetish
　　甘味　　　　　　　　　　sweetness
　　あらかじめ　　　　　　　beforehand
　　あり合わせの　　　　　　available
　　アルコール　　　　　　　alcohol
　　アレルギー　　　　　　　allergy
　　泡　　　　　　　　　　　bubble; foam
　　生簀（いけす）　　　　　fish preserve
　　居酒屋　　　　　　　　　tavern; Japanese-style bar
　　衣食住　　　　　　　　　food, clothing and shelter
　　板長　　　　　　　　　　chef
　　板前　　　　　　　　　　cook
　　炒め物　　　　　　　　　fried food
　　市場　　　　　　　　　　market; shopping center
　　インスタント食品　　　　convenience food
　　ウエーター　　　　　　　waiter
　　ウエートレス　　　　　　waitress

食の世界に関する重要語句 （英和）

A	ability	腕前
	acidity	酸性
	acquire a taste for	味を覚える
	additive-free food	無添加食品
	additives	添加物
	after a meal	食後
	aftertaste	あと味
	alcohol	アルコール
	allergy	アレルギー
	alley	小路
	all of a size	粒ぞろい(大きさ)
	allowance(s)	手加減
	all sorts of delicacies	山海の珍味
	all the members	全員
	amply	たっぷり
	analyze	分解する
	animal fat	動物性脂肪，動物油脂
	animal fiber	動物性繊維
	animal food	動物の餌
	appetite	食欲
	appliances	設備
	appreciate	賞味する
	apron	前掛け
	arrangements	仕度
	article for sale	売り物
	article specially made to order	特注品
	artificial flavor	人工香料
	ashtray	灰皿
	assistance	手伝い
	assistant	助手
	association	付き合い

腕利き	man of ability
腕前	ability
腕まくり	roll up one's sleeves
うま味	taste; flavor
売り物	article for sale
熟れる	ripen
衛生	hygiene
栄養(素)	nutrition
栄養学	dietetics
栄養価の低い食品	junk food
栄養士	dietician
栄養失調	malnutrition
栄養食品	nourishing food
栄養不良	malnutrition
エキス	extract; essence
エキスパート	expert
駅弁	boxed lunch sold at a railroad station
エチケット	etiquette
エチルアルコール	ethyl alcohol
エッセンス	essence
宴会	dinner party; banquet(公式)
宴会場	banquet hall
エンゲル係数	Engel's coeffcient
塩分(ナトリウム)	sodium; salt content
園遊会	garden party
おいしい	nice; tasty; delicious
おかず	dishes to go with rice; side dish
おすすめ	special of the day
おせち料理	festive food for the New Year
御供(おそなえ)	offering
おひらき	break up; close
おまかせ	chef suggestions
か 買い入れ	buying
会合	meeting; gathering
外国の食べ物	foreign food
会食	have (take) a meal together
外食する	eat out; dine out

	assortment	詰め合わせ
	atrificial preservative	合成保存料
	available	あり合わせの
B	baby food	ベビーフード
	bad [nasty] smell	悪臭，臭気
	bad time	不景気
	baker	パン職人
	bamboo grass	笹
	banquet	酒宴(祝宴)，宴会
	banquet hall	宴会場
	barhopping	〈米〉はしご酒
	before a meal	食前
	beforehand	あらかじめ
	be hard to chew	歯ごたえがある
	be on a diet	減食する
	bit of contrivance	ひと工夫
	bleaching	漂白剤
	blood	血
	blue mold	青かび
	boiled food	ゆでた食べ物
	boiling	沸騰
	booth	屋台
	boxed lunch sold at a railroad station	駅弁
	brand new	新品の
	breakfast	朝食
	breakfast food	朝食用加工食品
	break up	おひらき
	brewing	醸造
	bring together	集める
	brochette	串焼き
	brokerage	仲買い
	bubble	泡
	business	商用，仕事
	business depression	不景気
	buying	買い入れ
C	caffeine	カフェイン
	cakes served with tea	茶菓子

カカオ油脂	cocoa fat
加工	processing
加工食品	process food
加工年月日	date of packaging
菓子(総称)	confectionery
華氏(°F)	Fahrenheit
過重	overweight
カッテージチーズ	cottage cheese
加糖練乳	condensed milk
かび	mold, mould
カフェイン	caffeine
嚙む(食物をかむ)	chew one's food
辛い	hot; spicy
カルシウム	calcium
カロチン	carotene
カロリー(熱量)	calorie
カロリーだけが高い食べ物	junk food
皮	skin; peel; rind
間食	snack
元祖	originator; founder
乾燥食品	dried food
簡単な食事	plain food
缶詰	canned food〈米〉; tinned food〈英〉
看板	signboard
乾パン	hardtack;〈米〉ship biscuit;〈英〉ship's biscuit
含有栄養素表示	nutrition facts
含有量	content
規格	standard
企画	plan; planning
汚い	dirty; grubby
喫茶店	tearoom; coffee shop
技能	technical skill; ability
客	customer; guest(招待客)
客席	seat
嗅覚	sense of smell
給食(学校)	school meals

calcium	カルシウム
calorie	カロリー(熱量)
calories from fat	油脂による熱量
cancellation	取り消し
canned food	〈米〉缶詰
carbohydrate	炭水化物
care	使用上の注意
carotene	カロチン
catering [delivery] service	出前
caution in use	使用上の注意
celebration	祝賀, 祝典
Celsius	摂氏(℃)
ceremony	祝祭
charcoal broiled	炭火焼き
charge	担当
charge for a room	席料
chef	コック長, 板長
chef's suggestions	おまかせ
chew one's food	(食物を)噛む
chlorophyll	葉緑素
choice	粒より
choose	より取り
citric acid	クエン酸
close	おひらき
coagulating agent	凝固剤
coarse food	粗食
cocoa fat	カカオ油脂
coffee shop	喫茶店
collect	集める
coloring matter	色素
commercial	商用
completion	修了
condensed milk	加糖練乳, 練乳
confectionery	菓子(総称)
congelation	凝固
congratulatory address	祝辞
congratulatory telegram	祝電
consumption	消費

行儀	manners
凝固	congelation
凝固剤	coagulating agent
器用な	skillful; clever
協力	cooperation
切り売り	sell by the piece [slice]
切り身	slice
食いしん坊	glutton
食道楽	epicurism
空席	vacant seat
空腹	hunger
クエン酸	citric acid
くさった食べ物	spoiled food; rotten food
くさりやすい食べ物	perishable food
串焼き	brochette
軽食堂	snack bar; lunchroom
健康	health
健康(管理・保持)食品	health food
健康によい食品	healthy food
原産国名	country of origin
原産地	place [country] of origin
減食	diet; dieting
減食する	be on a diet
原料(原材料名)	ingredients
減量	reduce the quantity
高価な食べ物	expensive food
豪華な	splendid
高級	high class
公休日	holiday
広告	public notice
高脂肪	high fat
小路	alley
合成保存料	atrificial preservative
酵素	enzyme
好評	favorable reception
好物	favorite food
酵母	yeast
顧客(得意客)	customer

content	含有量
contents	中味(内容)
convenience food	インスタント食品
cook	調理，料理；板前
cookery	料理法
cooking	料理
cook one's own food	自炊
cool down	冷める
cooperation	協力
cottage cheese	カッテージチーズ
country of origin	原産国名
criticize	品定めする
crops	作物
cultivation	栽培
custom	習わし
customer	顧客(得意客)，客
dainty	珍味(食品)
damp	湿気
date of import	輸入年月日
date of manufacture	製造年月日
date of packaging	加工年月日
deep-fried food	揚げ物
delicatessen	デリカテッセン，調製食品店
delicious	おいしい
delivery	納入
density	濃度
deteriorate	変質する
diastase	ジアスターゼ
diet	減食
dietetics	栄養学
dietician	栄養士
dieting	減食
digestion	消化
dine out	外食する
dining car	食堂車
dining room [hall]	食堂
dining table	食卓
dinner	夕食

D dainty

	固形食	solid food
	午餐(ごさん)	luncheon
	コック長	chef
	言葉遣い	wording
	粉	flour
	粉ミルク	milk powder; dry milk
	小人数	small number of people
	小袋(食品)の内容量	serving size
	古米	old rice
	ごみ	garbage
さ	最小提供単位(食品)	serving
	菜食	vegetable diet
	菜食主義	vegetarianism
	栽培	cultivation
	酒樽	*sake* cask
	肴(さかな)	side dish
	酒屋	*sake* [wine] shop
	作物	crops
	酒癖が悪い	turn nasty when drunk
	酒飲み友達	drinking companion
	笹	bamboo grass
	ささみ	white meat of chicken
	殺菌する	sterilize; pasteurize
	冷める	cool down; get cold
	さや	shell; pod
	山海の珍味	all sorts of delicacies
	酸化する	oxidize
	酸性	acidity
	産物	product
	ジアスターゼ	diastase
	仕入れる	lay [buy] in stock
	自営	self-employment
	塩辛い食べ物	salty food
	視覚	eyesight; (sense of) sight
	自活	self support
	色素	coloring matter
	嗜好(しこう)	taste
	仕事	work; job; business

	dinner party	宴会
	dirty	汚い
	disciple	弟子(従弟)
	dishes to go with rice	おかず
	disinfection	消毒
	display	陳列
	distribute boiled rice	炊き出し
	distributor	発売元
	doggie bag	持ち帰り用バッグ
	dried food	乾燥食品
	drink	飲む
	drinking companion	酒飲み友達
	dry milk	粉ミルク
	dust	ほこり
E	earlier visitor	先客
	eat out	外食する
	eat too much	食べ過ぎ
	egg powder	粉末卵
	employee	従業員
	emulsifier	乳化剤
	Engel's coeffcient	エンゲル係数
	enzyme	酵素
	epicurism	食道楽
	essence	エッセンス, エキス
	ethnic restaurant	民族料理店
	ethyl alcohol	エチルアルコール
	etiquette	エチケット
	evaporated milk	無糖練乳
	evening meal	夕食
	excellent *sake*	美酒
	excessive drinking and eating	暴飲暴食
	expense account	社用族
	expensive food	高価な食べ物
	expert	エキスパート
	extract	エキス
	eyesight	視覚
F	Fahrenheit	華氏(°F)
	fast food	ファーストフード

指示	instruct
試食	sample; taste
自炊	cook one's own food
自然食品	natural food
仕度	arrangements
下地	groundwork
下働き	subordinate work
地卵	locally produced eggs
湿気	damp
実習生	student apprentice
湿度	humidity
湿度測定	hygrometry
師弟	master and pupil
品薄	shortage [scarcity] of stock
品書き	menu
品切れ	out of stock
品定めする	criticize; judge
市販	goods on the market
脂肪	fat
脂肪がつく食べ物	fattening food
社用族	expense account
臭気	bad smell
従業員	employee; worker
修業	study; get one's education
集計	total
就職する	find a job
収納伝票	receipt
重箱	nest of boxes
十分な食べ物	sufficient food
修了	completion
酒宴(祝宴)	banquet
祝賀(祝典)	celebration
祝祭	ceremony
祝辞	congratulatory address
祝日	national [legal] holiday
祝電	congratulatory telegram
祝杯	toast
熟練	skill; experience

fat	脂肪
fattening food	脂肪がつく食べ物
favorable reception	好評
favorite food	好物
feel	手ざわり
fellowship	付き合い
fermented milk	発酵乳
festive food for the New Year	おせち料理
find a job	就職する
finger food	指でつまんで食べる食物
fish-paste products	ねり物
fish preserve	生簀(いけす)
flavor	味, うま味
flour	粉
foam	泡
food	食べ物, 食品(食料)
food additive	食品添加物
food chemistry	食品化学
food, clothing and shelter	衣食住
food expenses	食費
food hygiene	食品衛生
food poisoning	食中毒
foods dressed with sauce	和え物
food security	食糧安全保障
foreign food	外国の食べ物
foundation	創業
founder	元祖
freezing	冷凍
fresh flower	生花
fresh food	新鮮な食べ物
freshness	鮮度
fresh water	淡水
fried food	炒め物
frozen food	冷凍食品
fully	たっぷり
G garbage	ごみ
garden party	園遊会
gathering	会合

主催	sponsor
主食	principal food; staple food
主成分	principal ingredient
準備	preparation
消化	digestion
紹介	introduction
蒸気	steam
上質	high quality
使用上の注意	care; caution in use
少食である	have a small appetite
滋養食	nutritious food
常食	staple [daily] food
精進料理	vegetarian diet
焼成温度	temperature
醸造	brewing
招待	invitation
招待する	invite
上達	progress
消毒	disinfection
消費	consumption
上品な	refined
賞味期限	to be eaten by this date
正味重量	net weight
賞味する	appreciate
商用	business; commercial
食後	after a meal
食事時間	mealtime
食前	before a meal
食卓	dining table
食中毒	food poisoning
食通	gourmet
食堂	dining room [hall]
食堂車	dining car
職人	skilled worker
食費	food expenses
食品（食料）	food
食品衛生	food hygiene
食品化学	food chemistry

	get a taste of success	味をしめる
	get cold	冷める
	get drunk	酔う
	glutton	食いしん坊
	goods on the market	市販
	gourmand	大食家
	gourmet	食通
	gourmet food	美食家の食事
	grain	粒
	gravy	たれ(肉汁)
	grilled food	焼き物
	grocery [food] store	食糧品店
	ground fish meat	すり身(魚)
	groundwork	下地
	grubby	汚い
	guest	客，招待客
H	hangover	二日酔
	hardtack	乾パン
	harshness	灰汁(ゑ)
	have a small appetite	少食である
	have [take] a meal together	会食
	health food	健康(管理・保持)食品
	healthy food	健康によい食品
	heap up	山盛り
	heavy drinking	深酒
	help	手伝い
	high class	高級
	high fat	高脂肪
	high quality	上質
	holiday	公休日
	hot	辛い
	humidity	湿度
	hunger	空腹
	hygiene	衛生
	hygrometry	湿度測定
I	importer	輸入業者
	ingredients	原料(原材料名)
	inorganic matter	無機物

食品添加物	food additive
植物性脂肪	vegetable fat
植物油	vegetable oil
食物繊維	vegetable fiber
食欲	appetite
食糧	provisions
食糧安全保障	food security
食糧品店	grocery [food] store
助手	assistant
人工香料	artificial flavor
新鮮な食べ物	fresh food
新任の	newly appointed
新品の	new; brand new
辛抱	patience
スチーム	steam
炭火焼き	charcoal broiled
すり身(魚)	ground fish meat
寸志	small present
生花	fresh flower
製作	manufacture
生鮮食料品	perishable food
製造者	manufacturer
製造年月日	date of manufacture
製法	recipe
責任者	person in charge
席料	charge for a room
摂氏(℃)	Celsius
設備	appliances
絶品	superb piece of work
全員	all the members
先客	earlier visitor
洗浄	washing
鮮度	freshness
先約	previous engagement
創業	foundation; initiation
壮行会	send-off party
即席	instant
粗食	coarse food; poor meal

	instant	即席
	instruct	指示
	instrument	道具
	introduction	手ほどき；紹介
	invitation	招待
	invite	招待する
	iron	鉄
J	Japanese-style bar	居酒屋
	job	仕事
	judge	品定めをする
	junk food	カロリーだけが高い食べ物，栄養価の低い食品
K	kitchen	台所
L	lay [buy] in stock	仕入れる
	lay [set] the table	配膳
	light food	あっさりした食べ物
	locally produced eggs	地卵
	loss leader	目玉商品
	low fat	低脂肪
	lunch	昼食
	luncheon	午餐(ごさん)
	lunchroom	軽食堂
M	macrobiotic food	野菜中心の自然食
	main table	メーンテーブル
	malnutrition	栄養失調，栄養不良
	malt	麦芽
	manage	取り計らう
	maneuvering	手さばき
	manners	行儀
	man of ability	腕利き
	manufacturer	製造者
	market	市場
	master and pupil	師弟
	mealtime	食事時間
	meeting	会合
	menu	メニュー，品書き
	meringue	メレンゲ，卵白生地
	midnight snack	夜食

	そば屋	noodle restaurant
た	大食家	gourmand
	台所	kitchen
	炊き出し	distribute boiled rice
	脱脂粉乳	nonfat milk powder
	たっぷり	fully; amply
	店子 (たな)	tenant; renter
	食べ頃	ready to eat
	食べ過ぎ	eat too much; overeat
	食べ物	food
	たれ	sauce (かけ汁); gravy (肉汁)
	炭酸ソーダ	sodium carbonate
	淡水	fresh water
	断水	suspension of water supply
	炭水化物	carbohydrate
	担当	charge
	段取り	plan; program
	タンニン	tanin, tannin
	蛋白質	protein
	血	blood
	茶会	tea party
	茶菓子	cakes served with tea
	昼食	lunch
	注文	order
	朝食	breakfast
	朝食用加工食品	breakfast food
	調理 (料理)	cook
	調製食品店	delicatessen
	貯蔵する	store
	沈殿物	sediment
	珍品	rare article
	珍味 (食品)	dainty
	陳列	display
	付き合い	association; fellowship
	粒	grain
	粒ぞろい (大きさ)	all of a size
	粒より	choice; picked
	詰め合わせ	assortment

	milk fat	乳脂
	milk powder	粉ミルク
	milk sugar	乳糖
	mineral	ミネラル
	mold	かび
	mouthful	ひと口
N	national [legal] holiday	祝日
	natural essence	天然香料
	natural food	自然食品
	nest of boxes	重箱
	net weight	正味重量，内容量
	new	新品の
	newly appointed	新任の
	nice	おいしい
	no additives	無添加
	no agricultural chemicals	無農薬栽培
	noncalorie	ノンカロリー
	nonfat milk powder	脱脂粉乳
	noodle restaurant	そば屋
	nourishing food	栄養食品
	no-brand products	無印商品
	nutrition	栄養(素)
	nutrition facts	含有栄養素表示
	nutritious food	滋養食
O	obtain	取り寄せる
	offering	御供(おそなえ)
	oil for frying	揚げ油
	old rice	古米
	one's favorite pupil	愛弟子
	one's feeling after drinking	酔心地
	order	注文
	organic food	有機食物
	originator	元祖
	out of stock	品切れ
	overcooked food	料理しすぎた食べ物
	overeat	食べ過ぎ
	overweight	過重
	oxidize	酸化する

	低脂肪	low fat
	手加減	allowance(s)
	適量	proper quantity
	手さばき	maneuvering
	手ざわり	feel; touch
	弟子	pupil(門弟); disciple(従弟)
	手順	process
	鉄	iron
	手伝い	help; assistance
	手っ取り早い	quick; prompt
	手並	skill
	手ほどき	introduction
	出前	catering [delivery] service
	デリカテッセン	delicatessen
	添加物	additives
	天然香料	natural essence
	でんぷん	starch
	でんぷん質の食品	starchy food
	同期	same period
	同級	same class
	同郷	same district
	道具	tool; instrument
	同種	same kind
	動物性脂肪	animal fat
	動物性繊維	animal fiber
	動物の餌	animal food
	動物油脂	animal fat
	糖分	sugar; sugar content
	糖類	sugars
	特製	special
	特注品	article specially made to order
	取って置き	reserved
	取りあえず	for the time being
	取り消し	cancellation
	取り計らう	manage; arrange
	取り寄せる	get; obtain
な	内容量	net weight; volume
	仲居	waitress

P	packed [boxed] lunch	弁当
	paint	塗る
	pasteurize	殺菌する
	patience	辛抱
	peel	皮
	perishable food	生鮮食料品；くさりやすい食べ物
	person in charge	責任者
	place an order	発注する
	place [country] of origin	原産地
	plain food	簡単な食事
	plan	企画，段取り
	pod	さや
	poisonous	有毒な
	polish	みがく
	poor meal	粗食
	preparation	準備，用意
	preserve	保存する
	preserved food	保存食
	previous engagement	先約
	price	値段
	principal food	主食
	principal ingredient	主成分
	process	手順
	process food	加工食品
	processing	加工
	product	産物
	product name	品名
	progress	上達
	proper quantity	適量
	protein	蛋白質
	provisions	食糧
	pub crawling	〈英〉はしご酒
	public notice	広告
	pupil	弟子(門弟)
Q	quality	品質
	quick	手っ取り早い
R	rare article	珍品

仲買い	brokerage
中味(内容)	contents
習わし	custom; tradition
乳化剤	emulsifier
乳脂	milk fat
乳糖	milk sugar
ぬか	rice bran
塗る	paint
値段	price
ねり物	fish-paste products
濃厚(高栄養価)な食べ物	rich food
濃度	density
納入	delivery
飲み込む	swallow
飲む	drink
のれん	shop curtain
ノンカロリー	noncalorie
は　灰皿	ashtray
配膳	lay [set] the table
麦芽	malt
歯ごたえがある	be hard to chew
はしご酒	barhopping〈米〉; pub crawling 〈英〉
発酵乳	fermented milk
発注する	place an order
発売	sale
発売元	distributor
パーム油	palm oil
パン職人	baker
販売者	seller
美酒	excellent *sake*
比重	specific gravity
美食家の食事	gourmet food
ビタミン	vitamin
ひと口	mouthful
ひと工夫	bit of contrivance
漂白剤	bleaching
品質	quality

	ready to eat	食べ頃
	receipt	収納伝票
	recipe	製法，料理法
	reduce the quantity	減量
	refined	上品な
	reserved	取って置き
	restaurant	料亭
	rice bran	ぬか
	rich food	濃厚（高栄養価）な食べ物
	ripen	熟れる
	roll up one's sleeves	腕まくり
	rot	腐敗する
	rotten food	腐った食べ物
S	*sake* cask	酒樽
	sake [wine] shop	酒屋
	sale	発売
	salty food	塩辛い食べ物
	same class	同級
	same district	同郷
	same kind	同種
	same period	同期
	sample	試食
	saturated fat	飽和油脂
	sauce	たれ（かけ汁）
	school meals	給食（学校）
	seat	客席
	sediment	沈殿物
	self-employment	自営
	self support	自活
	sell by the piece [slice]	切り売り
	seller	販売者
	send-off party	壮行会
	sense of smell	嗅覚
	sense of taste	味覚
	separate	分割する
	serving	最小提供単位（食品）
	serving size	小袋（食品）の内容量
	shell	さや

	品種	variety
	品名	product name
	ファーストフード	fast food
	深酒	heavy drinking
	拭く	wipe
	不景気	bad time; business depression
	不揃い	uneven
	二日酔	hangover
	沸騰	boiling
	腐敗する	rot; spoil, go bad
	プロセスチーズ	processed cheese
	分解する	analyze
	分割する	separate
	粉末卵	egg powder
	β-カロチン	beta-carotene
	ベビーフード	baby food
	変質する	deteriorate
	偏食	unbalanced diet
	弁当	packed [boxed] lunch
	暴飲暴食	excessive drinking and eating
	忘年会	year-end party
	飽和油脂	saturated fat
	ほこり	dust
	保存試験	storage test
	保存食	preserved food
	保存する	preserve; store
	保存方法	storage information
	ほろ酔い	slight intoxication
ま	前掛け	apron
	愛弟子	one's favorite pupil
	味覚	sense of taste
	みがく	polish
	ミネラル	mineral
	民族料理店	ethnic restaurant
	無機物	inorganic matter
	無印商品	no-brand products
	無駄になった食べ物	waste food
	無着色の	uncolored, uncoloured

ship biscuit	乾パン
shop curtain	のれん
shortage [scarcity] of stock	品薄
side dish	肴(さかな)，おかず
sight	視角
signboard	看板
skill	手並，熟練
skilled worker	職人
skillful	器用な
skin	皮
slice	切り身
slight intoxication	ほろ酔い
small number of people	小人数
small present	寸志
snack	間食
snack bar	軽食堂
sodium	塩分(ナトリウム)
sodium carbonate	炭酸ソーダ
soft food	軟らかい食べ物
solid food	固形食
soluble	溶解する
sort out	より分ける
special	特製
special of the day	おすすめ
specific gravity	比重
spicy	辛い
splendid	豪華な
spoil	腐敗する
spoiled food	くさった食べ物
sponsor	主催
stall	屋台
standard	規格
staple [daily] food	常食，主食
starch	でんぷん
starchy food	でんぷん質の食品
steam	スチーム，蒸気，湯気
sterilize	殺菌する
storage information	保存方法

	無添加	no additives
	無添加食品	additive-free food
	無糖練乳	evaporated milk
	無農薬栽培	no agricultural chemicals
	無漂白	unbleached
	目玉商品	loss leader
	メニュー	menu
	メレンゲ	meringue
	メーンテーブル	main table
	持ち帰り	take out〈米〉; take away〈英〉
	持ち帰り用バッグ	doggie bag
や	焼き物	grilled food
	野菜中心の自然食	macrobiotic food
	夜食	midnight snack
	屋台	stall; booth
	山盛り	heap up
	軟らかい食べ物	soft food
	有機食物	organic food
	夕食	dinner; evening meal
	有毒な	poisonous
	湯気(蒸気)	steam
	油脂による熱量	calories from fat
	ゆでた食べ物	boiled food
	輸入年月日	date of import
	輸入業者	importer
	指でつまんで食べる食物	finger food
	酔心地	one's feeling after drinking
	酔う	get drunk
	用意	preparation
	溶解する	soluble
	用途	uses
	葉緑素	chlorophyll
	より取り	choose
	より分ける	sort out
ら	卵白生地	meringue
	料亭	restaurant
	料理	cooking
	料理しすぎた食べ物	overcooked food

	storage test	保存試験
	store	貯蔵する，保存する
	student apprentice	実習生
	study	修業
	subordinate work	下働き
	sufficient food	十分な食べ物
	sugar	糖分
	sugar content	糖分
	superb piece of work	絶品
	suspension of water supply	断水
	swallow	飲み込む
	sweet food	甘い食べ物
	sweetish	甘口
	sweetness	甘味
T	take away	〈英〉持ち帰り
	take out	〈米〉持ち帰り
	tanin	タンニン
	taste	嗜好(しこう)；試食；うま味，味
	tasty	おいしい
	tavern	居酒屋
	tea party	茶会
	tearoom	喫茶店
	technical skill	技能
	temperature	焼成温度
	tenant	店子(たな)
	thick sliced bread	厚切りの食パン
	tinned food	〈英〉缶詰
	toast	祝杯
	to be eaten by this date	賞味期限
	tool	道具
	total	集計
	touch	手ざわり
	tradition	習わし
	turn nasty when drunk	酒癖が悪い
U	unbalanced diet	偏食
	unbleached	無漂白
	uncolored	無着色の
	uneven	不揃い

料理法	cookery; recipe
冷凍	freezing
冷凍食品	frozen food
練乳	condensed milk

	uses	用途
V	variety	品種
	vegetable diet	菜食
	vegetable fat	植物性脂肪
	vegetable fiber	食物繊維
	vegetable oil	植物油
	vegetarian diet	精進料理
	vegetarianism	菜食主義
	vitamin	ビタミン
	volume	内容量
W	waiter	ウエーター
	waitress	ウエートレス，仲居
	washing	洗浄
	waste food	無駄になった食べ物
	wipe	拭く
	wording	言葉遣い
	work	仕事
	warker	従業員
Y	year-end party	忘年会
	yeast	酵母

PART 12

料理方法などに関する重要語句 （和英）

あ	和える	dress with
	あく抜きをする	remove the harshness
	あくを取る	skim the foam; remove scum
	揚げる	deep fry
	味つけは塩こしょう	salt and pepper to taste
	味見する	taste; sample
	味をつける	season; flavor
	味を調える	season
	温め直す	rewarm
	温める	warm; heat
	厚い	thick
	熱い	hot; warm
	熱いうちに供する	serve hot
	あっさり味をつける	season slightly
	あっさりした料理	light food
	穴をあける	make holes
	脂っこい	greasy; rich
	油をひく	grease; oil
	あぶり焼きした	broiled
	あぶる	broil(肉や魚); toast(パンなど)
	甘い	sweet
	甘くする	sweeten; sugar
	網焼きした	grilled
	洗う	wash
	あられに切る	cut in small cubes
	泡立てる	beat; whip; whisk
	安定させる	stabilize
	炒める	stir-fry; sauté
	いちょう切りにする	cut into quarter-rounds
	いっぱいにする	fill
	いる	roast; toast

料理方法などに関する重要語句 (英和)

A	add	加える，添加する
	admix	加える
	annex	添加する
	a pinch [dash] of salt	ひとつまみの塩
	appetizing food	食欲をそそる食べ物
	aromatize	香りをつける
	at high temperature	高温で
	at low temperature	低温で
	avoid scorching	焦がさないようにする
B	bake	焼く
	barbecued	直火焼きにした
	beat	泡立てる，かき混ぜる
	become solid	凝固する
	bitter	苦い
	blend	混ぜる
	boil	沸かす，炊く，煮る，ゆでる，煮沸(しゃふつ)する
	boil down	煮詰める
	boiling water	煮え湯，熱湯
	boil up	煮立てる
	bone	骨を抜く(魚・肉など)
	bread	パン粉をまぶす
	breadcrumb	パン粉をまぶす
	breaded	パン粉をつけた
	break	割る
	bring to a boil	沸騰させる
	broil	焼く，あぶる
	broiled	あぶり焼きした
	broil with salt	塩焼きにする
	brown	焦がす
	brush	塗る

入れる		put in
色が変わるまで		untill color changes
薄く切る		slice; cut into thin slices
うす塩		low salt
薄める		dilute
うま味		taste; flavor
裏返す		turn over
裏ごしする		strain
うろこを取る		scale
上火		upper flame
液化する		liquefy
押す		push; press
遅い		slow
おろす(大根など)		grate
温度		temperature
温度調節		temperature control
か	解凍する	thaw out; defrost
	改良する	improve; refine
	香りをつける	flavor; flavour; aromatize
	かき混ぜる	stir; mix; beat(卵・クリーム)
	嗅ぐ	smell; scent
	角むきにする	remove both ends and then peel thick
	加工する	process
	重ね置く	layer
	飾り線を入れる(ナイフで)	pink out
	飾る	decorate
	カス	scrap
	堅い(肉など)	tough
	型から取り出す	demold; demould
	片づける	clear away; clean up
	型取り	demolding; demoulding
	かつらむきにする	cut into thin sheet
	加熱する	overheat
	釜入れする	place in the oven
	釜出しする	draw from the oven
	空にする	empty
	軽いきつね色	light brown

	burn	燃やす(炎で)
C	chill	さます
	chilled	冷たくした
	chop	刻む
	clasp	握る
	clean a fish	わたを抜く(魚)
	clear away	片づける
	coat	まぶす
	combine	混ぜる
	compound	調合する
	cook	炊き, 料理する, 煮る
	cooking	煮炊き
	cooking instruction	作り方
	cooking time	調理時間
	cook uncovered	ふたをしないで料理する
	cool	冷やす, 冷ます
	cool down	冷却する
	cover	ふたをする
	creamed	クリーム状にした
	crisscross	十字目を入れる
	crush	砕(くだ)く(氷など)
	cube	さいの目に切る
	cut coarsely	ざく切りにする
	cut diagonally	斜め切りにする
	cut finely	みじん切りにする
	cut in halves [two]	二つに切る
	cut in rectangles	短冊切りにする
	cut in round slices	輪切りにする
	cut in small cubes	あられに切る
	cut into bar rectangles	拍子木切りにする
	cut into bite-size pieces	ひと口切りにする
	cut into half-moons	半月切りにする
	cut into quarter-rounds	いちょう切りにする
	cut into rolling wedges	乱切りにする
	cut into slices	小口切りにする
	cut into small pieces	細かく切る
	cut into thin sheet	かつらむきにする
	cut into thin slices	薄く切る

乾かす	dry; dry out
皮をむく	pare; peel; remove
刻む	chop; mince
きつね色に焼く	roast
凝固する	become solid
切り刻む	hash
切り分ける	cut out
霧を吹きかける	spray
切る	cut; slice(薄く)
きれいに盛った	dressed
切れ目を入れる(肉など)	score; make cuts
吟味する	examine closely
くし形に切る	cut into wedges
串に刺す	skewer
砕(くだ)く	crush(氷など); pound(つく)
ぐつぐつ煮る	simmer
クリーム状にした	creamed
加える	add; admix
燻製(くんせい)にした	smoked
計量する	measure; weigh
削る	shave
減塩	very low salt
検査	test; check
高温	high temperature
高温で	at high temperature
香料を加える	spice; season with spice
焦がさないようにする	avoid scorching
焦がす	scorch; brown
こくがある	have plenty of body
濃くする	darken
小口切りにする	cut into slices
焦げ目をつける	grill until surface get brown
焦げる	scorch
こす	filter; strain
こする	rub
こってりした味	rich [heavy] taste
粉をふる	flour
こねる	knead; dough

	cut into two or three pieces	2-3 こに切る
	cut into wedges	くし形に切る
	cut into 2-cm lengths	2センチの長さに切る
	cut out	切り分ける
	cut the back open	背開きにする(魚)
D	darken	濃くする
	dash	ひとつまみ
	decorate	飾る
	decrease	減らす
	deep fry	揚げる
	defrost	解凍する
	dehydrate	水分を取る(除く)
	demold	型から取り出す
	demolding	型取り
	devein	背わたを取る(海老)
	dice	さいの目に切る
	dilute	薄める
	dip	つける(浸す)
	dish up	盛りつける
	dissolve	溶かす
	dissolved cornstarch	水溶き片くり粉
	dough	こねる,練る
	drain	水を切る
	draw from the oven	釜出しする
	dress with	和える
	dry	干す,乾かす
	dust	まぶす
E	empty	空にする
	examine closely	吟味する
	exchange	取り替える
	extract	抽出する(絞り出す)
F	fill	いっぱいにする,詰める(中身)
	filter	こす,ろ過する
	finish	仕上げる
	fire	点火する
	flavor	香りをつける,味をつける;うま味

	5分おいておく	let stand 5 min.
	こぼす	spill; drop
	細かく切る	cut into small pieces
	混合した物	mixture
さ	さいの目に切る	dice; cube
	酒蒸しにする	steam steeped in *sake*
	裂く	tear
	ざく切りにする	cut coarsely
	酒をふりかける	sprinkle with *sake*
	ささがきにする	shave
	さっと混ぜる	toss
	さます	chill, cool
	さらす	soak; rinse
	酸味	sourness
	仕上げる	finish
	塩辛い	salty; salt
	塩出しする	make less salty
	塩焼きにする	broil with salt
	直火焼きにした	barbecued
	仕込む	prepare
	試食する	taste; sample
	下火	lower flame
	しなびる	wither
	しなやか	supple
	渋い味のする	puckery
	しぼむ	wither; wilt
	絞り出す（口金から）	pipe
	絞る（果汁など）	squeeze; press
	湿らす（浸す）	soak
	煮沸（しゃふつ）する	boil; scald
	十字目を入れる	crisscross
	熟成する	ripen; mature
	準備する	prepare
	食欲をそそる食べ物	appetizing food
	新鮮でない	stale
	新鮮な	fresh; new
	吸い上げる	suck up
	水分がほとんどなくなるまで	until almost no liquid is left

	flour	粉をふる
	flow	流す
	freeze	凍結させる
	fresh	新鮮な
G	garnish	付け合わせる，つまを添える
	get muddy	濁る
	glaze	つや出しをする
	grate	おろす(大根など)
	grease	油をひく
	greasy	脂っこい
	grilled	網焼きした
	grill until surface get brown	焦げ目をつける
	grind	すりつぶす，ひく
H	half-cooked	生煮えの
	hash	切り刻む
	have plenty of body	こくがある
	heat	温める
	high heat	強火
	high temperature	高温
	hot	熱い
I	improve	改良する
	increase	増やす
	in deep oil	たっぷりの油で
J	julienne	千切りにする
K	knead	こねる，練る
L	layer	重ね置く
	let stand 5 min.	５分おいておく
	level flatten	水平にする
	lick	なめる
	light food	あっさりした料理
	lower flame	下火
	low flame	とろ火
	low heat	弱火
	low salt	うす塩
	low temperature	低温
	lukewarm water	ぬるま湯
M	make cuts	切れ目を入れる
	make holes	穴をあける

	水分を取る(除く)	dehydrate; wipe off
	水平にする	level flatten
	酸っぱい	sour
	酢に漬けた	vinegared
	素早く	quickly
	すりつぶす	grind
	背開きにする(魚)	cut the back open
	背骨を取る	remove backbone
	背わたを取る(海老)	devein; remove black veins
	千切りにする	julienne
	注ぐ	pour
た	炊く	boil; cook
	たっぷりの油で	in deep oil
	種をとる	seed; remove seeds
	短冊切りにする	cut in rectangles
	中火	medium heat
	中火で	over medium heat
	中火にする	turn the heat to medium
	調合する	compound
	調理時間	cooking time
	調理方法	method of preparation
	抽出する(絞り出す)	extract
	突く(刃物で)	stab
	作り方	cooking instruction
	付け合わせる	garnish
	つける(浸す)	dip; soak
	包む	wrap; pack
	つぶす	mash
	つまを添える	garnish (with〜)
	冷たくした	chilled
	詰めものにした	stuffed
	詰める(中身)	stuff; fill
	つや出しをする	glaze
	強火	high heat
	強火で	over high heat
	強火にする	make the fire stronger
	低温	low temperature
	低温で	at low temperature

	make less salty	塩出しする
	make the fire stronger	強火にする
	mash	つぶす
	measure	計量する
	medium heat	中火
	melt	溶かす
	method of preparation	調理方法
	mince	刻む
	mince finely	みじん切りにする
	mix	混ぜる
	mixture	混合した物
	mix well by hand	手でよく混ぜる
	mix well together beforehand	前もってよく混ぜ合わせる
	moisten	ぬらす(水をかける)
O	oil	油をひく
	open	ふたを取る
	overcook	煮過ぎる
	overheat	加熱する
	over high heat	強火で
	over low heat	弱火で
	over medium heat	中火で
P	pack	包む
	parboil	ゆでる
	pare	皮をむく
	peel	皮をむく
	pinch	ひとつまみ
	pink out	飾り線を入れる(ナイフで)
	pipe	絞り出す(口金から)
	place in the oven	釜入れする
	plane off corners	面とりをする
	pour	注ぐ
	pour in just enough water to cover the meat	肉がかくれるまで水を入れる
	prepare	仕込む，準備する
	press	押す
	process	加工する
	puckery	渋い味のする
	pulverize	粉末にする

	手でよく混ぜる	mix well by hand
	手間取る	take time
	添加する	annex; add
	点火する	fire
	凍結させる	freeze
	溶かす	melt; dissolve
	取り替える	exchange
	取り出す	turn [take] out
	取り除く	remove
	とろ火	low flame
	とろみ	thickness
	とろみをつける	thicken
な	流す	flow
	斜め切りにする	cut diagonally
	生(なま)	raw
	生煮えの	half-cooked; underdone
	なめる	lick
	煮え湯	boiling water
	匂い	smell
	苦い	bitter
	握る	clasp; grasp
	肉がかくれるまで水を入れる	pour in just enough water to cover the meat
	煮込む	stew; boil well
	濁る	get muddy
	煮込んだ	stewed
	煮しめる	stew
	煮過ぎる	overcook
	2-3 こに切る	cut into two or three pieces
	2 センチの長さに切る	cut into 2-cm lengths
	煮炊き	cooking
	煮立てる	boil up
	煮詰める	boil down
	煮る	boil; cook; simmer
	二杯酢	vinegar with soy
	ぬらす(水をかける)	moisten
	塗る	brush
	ぬるい	tepid; lukewarm

push	押す
put in	入れる
put the lid on	ふたをする
quickly	素早く
raw	生(なま)
reduce heat	火を弱める
remove	取り除く
remove backbone	背骨を取る
remove black veins	背わたを取る(海老)
remove both ends and then peel thick	角むきにする
remove entrails	はらわたを取る
remove from heat	火から降ろす
remove scum	あくを取る
remove seeds	種を取る
remove the harshness	あく抜きをする
rewarm	温め直す
rich	脂っこい
rich [heavy] taste	こってりした味
rinse	さらす
ripen	熟成する
roast	きつね色に焼く，いる，焼く
roll (out)	のばす
roll up	巻く
rub	こする，もむ
salt and pepper to taste	味つけは塩こしょう
salt free	無塩
salty	塩辛い
sample	試食する，味見する
sauté	炒める
savor	風味
scald	煮沸する
scale	うろこを取る
scorch	焦げる，焦がす
score	切れ目を入れる(肉など)
scrap	カス
season	味を調える，味をつける
season slightly	あっさり味をつける

	ぬるま湯	tepid [lukewarm] water
	熱湯	boiling water
	練る	knead; dough
	のばす	roll; roll out
は	はらわたを取る	remove entrails
	半月切りにする	cut into half-moons
	パン粉をつけた	breaded
	パン粉をまぶす	bread; breadcrumb
	ひき肉にする	grind meat
	ひく (すりつぶす)	grind
	ひと口切りにする	cut into bite-size pieces
	ひとつまみ	pinch; dash
	ひとつまみの塩	a pinch [dash] of salt
	ひねる	twist
	冷やす	cool
	拍子木切りにする	cut into bar rectangles
	火を弱める	reduce heat
	火から降ろす	remove from heat
	風味	savor; flavor
	二つに切る	cut in halves [two]
	ふたをしないで料理する	cook uncovered
	ふたをする	cover; put the lid on
	ふたを取る	open; uncover; take the lid off
	沸騰させる	bring to a boil
	ふやかす	steep (in water)
	増やす	increase
	ふりかける	sprinkle; powder
	ふるう	sift(out); sieve
	粉末にする	pulverize
	減らす	decrease
	干す	dry
	細い	thin
	骨を抜く (魚・肉など)	bone
ま	前もってよく混ぜ合わせる	mix well together beforehand
	巻く	roll up
	まずい	unsavory; bad
	混ぜる	mix; blend; combine
	まぶす	coat; dust

seasos with spice	香料を加える
seed	種を取る
separate	分ける
serve hot	熱いうちに供する
shave	ささがきにする，削る
sieve	ふるう
sift (out)	ふるう
simmer	ぐつぐつ煮る，煮る
skewer	串に刺す
skim the foam	あくを取る
slice	薄く切る
slow	遅い
slowly	ゆっくりと
smell	匂い；嗅ぐ
smoked	燻製(くんせい)にした
soak	湿らす(浸す)，つける，さらす
soak in water	水につける
soften	やわらかくする
sour	酸っぱい
sourness	酸味
spice	香料を加える
spill	こぼす
spray	霧を吹きかける
sprinkle	ふりかける
sprinkle with *sake*	酒をふりかける
squeeze	絞る(果汁など)
squeeze out water	水気をしぼる
stab	突く(刃物で)
stabilize	安定させる
steam	蒸す
steam steeped in *sake*	酒蒸しにする
steep (in water)	ふやかす
stew	煮しめる，煮込む
stewed	煮込んだ
stir	かき混ぜる
stir-fry	炒める
strain	裏ごしする，こす，ろ過する

	みじん切りにする	cut finely; mince finely
	水気をしぼる	squeeze out water
	水溶き片くり粉	dissolved cornstarch
	水につける	soak in water
	水を切る	drain
	無塩	salt free
	蒸す	steam
	面とりをする	plane off corners
	もむ	rub
	燃やす (炎で)	burn; flame
	模様をつける	stamp emboss; decorate with a pattern
	盛りつける	dish up
や	焼く	bake; roast (肉); broil (魚肉)
	やわらかくする	soften
	ゆっくりと	slowly
	ゆでる	boil; parboil
	弱火	low heat
	弱火で	over low heat
ら	乱切りにする	cut into rolling wedges
	冷却する	cool down
	ろ過する	filter; strain
わ	沸かす	boil
	輪切りにする	cut in round slices
	分ける	separate; select
	わたを抜く (魚)	clean a fish
	割る	break

	stuff	詰める(中身)
	stuffed	詰めものにした
	suck up	吸い上げる
	supple	しなやか
	sweeten	甘くする
T	take the lid off	ふたを取る
	take time	手間取る
	taste	うま味；試食する，味見する
	tear	裂く
	temperature	温度
	temperature control	温度調節
	tepid water	ぬるま湯
	test	検査(する)
	thaw out	解凍する
	thicken	とろみをつける
	toast	焼く，あぶる，いる
	toss	さっと混ぜる
	tough	堅い(肉など)
	turn over	裏返す
	turn [take] out	取り出す
	turn the heat to medium	中火にする
	twist	ひねる
U	underdone	生煮えの
	until almost no liquid is left	水分がほとんどなくなるまで
	untill color changes	色が変わるまで
	upper flame	上火
V	very low salt	減塩
	vinegared	酢に漬けた
W	warm	温める，熱い
	wash	洗う
	whip	泡立てる
	whisk	泡立てる
	wither	しなびる，しぼむ
	wrap	包む

PART 13

状況別基本英会話

(1) 職場内の身近な会話

あ
1. 味が濃すぎませんか？
2. 頭に注意して！
3. あまりうまくないようですが。
4. 以上です。
5. 今すぐやってもらえないかな？
6. 今ちょっと手が離せないのですが。
7. いや、そうじゃない。
8. いや、予定より1時間遅れています。
9. エアコンを入れてくれる？
10. ええ、その通りです。
11. ええと。
12. 押し上げて。
13. 教えましょう。
14. 温度は何度ですか？

か
15. 火災の注意は大切です。
16. ガスくさくない？
17. ガスをつけて。
18. 彼の頼みを断れないよ。
19. 代わりに皿洗いしてくれない？
20. 機器のスイッチは入れたままにして下さい。
21. 機器のスイッチは切れている？
22. 機器のスイッチは入っている？
23. 機器のスイッチを入れて下さい。
24. 機器のスイッチを入れてはいけません。
25. 機器のスイッチを切って下さい。
26. 機器のスイッチを切ってはいけません。
27. 今日は風が強いですね。

Conversations and phrases

(1) At work

1. Isn't it too strong for you?
2. Watch your head!
3. I'm afraid this isn't good enough.
4. That's all.
5. Would you do it right away, please?
6. I'm a bit busy right now.
7. No, that's not right.
8. No, we're running about one hour behind schedule.
9. Will you turn on the air conditioner?
10. Yes, that's what I mean.
11. Let me see.
12. Push it up.
13. I'll show you.
14. What's the temperature?
15. It's essential to take precautions against fire.
16. Don't you smell gas?
17. Turn on the gas, please.
18. I can't turn down his request.
19. Will you do the dishes for me?
20. Keep the machine on.
21. Is the machine off?
22. Is the machine on?
23. Turn the machine on.
24. Don't turn the machine on.
25. Turn the machine off.
26. Don't turn the machine off.
27. It's windy today.

28. 今日はとても暑い[寒い]ですね。
29. 今日は冷えますね。
30. 今日は蒸し暑いですね。
31. 今日は予定どおり進んでいますか?
32. ここへ立って。
33. ここを見て。
34. この液体を保存するとき指定温度をチェックしてください。
35. この材料を保存する指定湿度はどれくらいですか?

36. この魚は涼しいところに置いておかないとだめになるよ。
37. このダイヤルで温度を調節します。
38. このバルブで圧力を調整します。
39. このパンかたくなっちゃった。
40. このボタンで照明を消します。
41. このボタンで電源を入れます。
42. このぼろは火災のもとになります。
43. このミルク酸っぱくなってるよ。
44. このようにして下さい。
45. これ返すよ。
46. これがナイフやフォークを入れておく引き出しです。
47. これは後ろ向きだ。
48. これは上下逆だ。
49. これは前後逆向きだ。
50. これを倉庫に保管してください。
51. これを保管棚に置いてください。
さ 52. さあ仕事に戻ろう。
53. さあ、自分でやってみて。
54. さあ始めよう。
55. 最後に……。
56. 最初に……。
57. 魚を裏返して。
58. 作業台の上に置いて。
59. 作業台の下に置いて。
60. 作業台のそばに置いて。
61. さて。
62. さて、ええと。
63. 事故の原因は何だったのですか?
64. 事故は不注意によるものでした。

28. It's very hot [cold] today.

29. It's chilly today.

30. It's very hot and humid today.

31. Are we running on schedule today?

32. Stand here.

33. Look here.

34. Check the temperature requirements for storing this liquid.

35. What are the humidity requirements for storing this material?

36. This fish will spoil if you don't keep it cool.

37. This dial controls the temperature.

38. This valve regulates the pressure.

39. This bread has gone stale.

40. This button turns off the light.

41. This button turns on the power.

42. These old rags are a fire hazard.

43. This milk has gone sour.

44. Do it like this.

45. I'll return it.

46. This is the drawer in which we keep our knives and forks.

47. This is backward.

48. This is upside down.

49. This is back to front.

50. Put this in the stockroom.

51. Put this on the storage rack.

52. Let's get back to work.

53. Now, try it yourself.

54. Let's get started.

55. Finally … .

56. First … .

57. Turn the fish.

58. Put it on the work bench.

59. Put it under the work bench.

60. Put it beside the work bench.

61. Well.

62. Well, let me see.

63. What was the cause of the accident?

64. The accident was caused by carelessness.

65. 静かに押して。
66. しっかり押して。
67. 実にすばらしい！

68. しばらくのあいだ自分で練習するように。
69. 自分の方に引っ張って。
70. (職場では)タバコは遠慮してください。

71. 慎重に！
72. すみませんが、わかりません。

73. 絶対です。
74. そう、そのとおり。
75. そうだといいですね。
76. そうに違いありません。
77. そうは思いません。
78. そこをもう一度説明してくださいませんか？
79. そのあと……。
80. そのとおりです。

81. それから……。
82. それはいいですね。

83. それは知りませんでした。
84. それは大変ですね。
85. それはどういう意味ですか？
86. それは無理です。
た 87. 大丈夫ですか？
88. 大丈夫ですよ。
89. 棚の上に置いて。
90. 多分そうでしょう。
91. 多分そうではないと思います。
92. 卵をひっくり返して。
93. 近くでよく見て。

65. Push it gently.
66. Push it firmly.
67. Incredible!
    That's great!
68. Practice it by yourself for a while.
69. Pull it toward you.
70. Don't smoke on the floor.
    Don't smoke here.
    No smoking in the workplace.
71. Be careful!
72. Sorry, I can't understand.
    I'm sorry I don't follow you.
73. I'm positive.
74. Yes, that's right.
75. I hope so.
76. It must be.
77. No, I don't think so.
78. Will you explain it again?
79. After that, ...
80. That's right.
    That's it.
    Quite so.
    Exactly.
    Absolutely.
81. Then, ...
82. That's a good idea.
    That'll be fine.
83. I didn't know that.
84. That's too bad.
85. What does it mean?
86. It's impossible.
87. Are you all right?
88. That'll be all right.
89. It goes on the shelf.
90. I suppose so.
91. No, I don't suppose so.
92. Turn the egg.
93. Watch closely.

94. 注意して！

95. ちょうど昼食の時間です。

96. ちょっと休もうじゃないか。

97. 次に……。

98. できるだけ早くするつもりです。

99. 手伝ってくれないか？

100. 手に注意して！

101. 電気を消した？

102. 同感です。

103. どうしたんですか？

104. 時計方向に回して。

な 105. 何か焦げ臭いぞ！

106. 何か問題があったら、わたしのところに来てください。

107. なるほど。

108. 煮過ぎないように。

109. のり（接着剤）をつけて。

110. のり（接着剤）をはがして。

は 111. はい。他に何か持ってきましょうか？

112. 廃棄処分にしてください。

113. 箱はどこに置きますか？

114. はっきりとはわかりません。

115. 火が通っていません。

116. 引き下げて。

117. 引き出しの中に入れて。

118. 左の奥にあります。

119. 1つずつやって見せてください。

120. 標準時間は 40 秒です。

121. 2つの端はそろえて。

ま 122. 右に回して。

123. ミルクがもうなくなってきたね。お店に行ってきてくれませんか？

124. 向こうの右側にあります。

125. 向こうへ押して。

126. もう一度おっしゃっていただけますか？

127. もう一度しっかりやってみて。

128. もう少し大きな声でおっしゃっていただけますか？

94. Watch out!
95. We are just in time for lunch.
96. Let's take a break.
97. Next, … .
98. I'll do it as soon as possible.
99. Can you give me a hand?
100. Watch your hands!
101. Did you turn off the light?
102. I agree.
103. What happened?
104. Turn it clockwise.
105. I smell something burning!
106. Come and see me if you have a problem.
107. Oh, I see.
108. Don't overcook.
109. Put glue on it.
110. Remove the glue.
111. Here you go. Can I get you anything else?
112. Scrap them.
113. Where should I put the box?
114. I'm not sure.
115. It's not cooked.
116. Pull it down.
117. Put it in the drawer.
118. It's in the back on the left.
119. Show me the steps.
120. The standerd time is forty seconds.
121. Align the two edges.
122. Turn it to the right.
123. We're running out of milk. Can you go to the store?

124. It's over there on your right.
125. Push it away from you.
126. Could you tell me again?
   I beg your pardon.
   Pardon?
127. You'll have to do it again.
128. Could you speak more loudly?

129. もちろん。
130. 元に戻すよ。
や 131. ゆっくりおっしゃってください。
132. よく見て！
ら 133. レバーを起こして。
134. レバーを倒して。
わ 135. わかってます。
136. わかりません。
137. わたしが行って聞いてくるよ。
138. わたしが行って取ってくる。
139. 私もそう思います。

(2) 店員の話す会話

あ 1. あいにく満員でございます。

2. 温めますか？

3. あらかじめ食券をお求めください。
4. 売り切れです。
5. お気をつけて。
6. お支払はどのようになさいますか？
7. お席はどこがよろしいですか？
8. お荷物をお預かりしましょうか？
9. お飲み物は何になさいますか？

10. お待たせして申し訳ありません。
か 11. かしこまりました。少々お待ちください。
12. かしこまりました。すぐお持ちいたします。
13. かしこまりました。はい、どうぞ。
14. かしこまりました。ほかに何かご注文はございませんか？
15. かしこまりました。レモンと砂糖をお入れしますか？
16. 片面焼きですか両面焼きですか？
17. 辛いカレーライスとあまり辛くないカレーライスとどちら
    がよろしいですか？
18. クリームと砂糖をお入れしますか？
19. ご注文はもうお決まりになりましたか？

129. Of course.
130. I'll put it back.
131. Please speak slowly.
132. Look out!
133. Raise the lever.
134. Lower the lever.
135. Yes, I know.
136. I don't know.
137. I'll go and ask him.
138. I'll go and get it.
139. Yes, I think so too.

⑵ By waiters and waitresses

1. I'm sorry all the tables are occupied now.
   I'm afraid we are full now.
2. Shall I warm it up for you?
   Do you want me to warm it up?
3. Please buy your meal tickets first.
4. We're out of that.
5. Take care.
6. How would you like to pay?
7. Where would you like to sit?
8. Would you like to check your things?
9. What would you like to drink?
   What will you have to drink?
10. I'm sorry to have kept you waiting.
11. Certainly. Just a moment, please.
12. Yes. I'll get you one right away.
13. Certainly. Here it is.
14. Certainly. Is there anything else you'd like to order?
15. All right. Would you like lemon and sugar in your tea?
16. Sunny side up or over easy?
17. Which kind of curry and rice do you like, spicy or mild?
    Would you like spicy or mild curry and rice?
18. With cream and sugar?
19. Have you decided what you'd like?

20. ご注文はよろしいですか？
21. ご注文を伺ってよろしいですか？

22. こちらのテーブルでよろしいでしょうか？
23. コーヒーになさいますか、紅茶になさいますか？
24. コーヒーはいかがですか？
25. コーヒーはお食事と一緒、それとも食後になさいますか？
26. コーヒーはどうしますか、砂糖かミルクを入れますか？
27. ごゆっくりどうぞ。
28. これはいっさいを含めてのお値段ですので、これ以外の余
    分なお支払いはございません。

さ 29. サラダはマヨネーズですか、それともサラダ用ドレッシン
    グですか？
30. 10分位です。
31. 少々お待ちください、すぐまいります。
32. すぐお持ちいたします。

33. ステーキの焼き加減はどのようにいたしましょう。
34. ステーキはどのようにいたしましょうか？
35. スープのお味はいかがですか？
36. すみませんがスパゲティはございません。
37. 前後酒はいかがですか？
38. 全部で23ドル56セントになります。
39. それでしたら、生ガキをご用意できますがいかがですか？
40. そんなにかかりません。

た 41. 卵はどのようにいたしますか？
42. ちょっと待っていただけますか？

43. デザートは何になさいますか？

44. どうぞこちらへ。
な 45. 何にいたしましょうか？
46. 何をお飲みになりますか？
47. 何を召し上がりますか？

48. 何人様ですか？

20. Are you ready to order?
21. May I take your order, please?
    Can I take your order?
22. Is this table all right?
23. Would you like coffee or tea?
24. Would you care for a cup of coffee?
25. Do you want coffee with the meal or after the meal?
26. How would you like your coffee, with sugar or cream?
27. Take your time.
28. This is an all inclusive price; there's nothing extra to pay.

29. Mayonnaise or salad dressing?

30. About 10 minutes.
31. Just a moment. I'll be right with you.
32. Coming right up.
    I'll have one for you in a moment.
33. How would you like your steak done?
34. How do you like your steak?
35. How do you like the soup?
36. I'm sorry we don't have spaghetti.
37. Would you care for an appetizer?
38. Twenty-three fifty-six in all.
39. Shall I get some fresh oysters for you?
40. Not long.
41. How would you like your eggs?
42. Could you wait a minute?
    Wait a minute, please.
43. What would you like for dessert?
    What kind of dessert would you like?
44. This way, please.
45. What do you like?
46. What would you like to drink?
47. What will you have?
    What would you like to have?
    What would you like to try?
48. How many people are you?
    How many of you are there?

49. 24 時間営業です。
50. 20 分位かかりますが、よろしいですか？
51. 飲み物は何がよろしいですか？
は 52. はいそれから？
53. はい。どのようなご用件でしょうか？
54. はい。何かお飲み物は？
55. 半熟ですか固ゆでですか？
56. ビフテキの焼き加減はどのようにいたしますか？

ま 57. またおいでください。

58. 待ちますか？
59. 満席です。
60. メインコースは何になさいますか？
61. メインは何になさいますか？
62. メニューをどうぞ。
63. もう少し待ってください。
や 64. 焼き具合はどういたしますか？
わ 65. ワインはお決めになりましたか？
66. 和風庭園の見える静かな部屋をとっておきました。

(3) 仲間同志の気楽な会話

あ 1. 朝まで騒ごう！
2. いいですね、行きましょう。
3. 家まで送るよ。
4. 息抜きに一杯やろう。
5. 一杯おごりましょう。
6. 一杯付き合いませんか？
7. うんありがとう、親切だね。
8. おごらせてください。
9. お酒くさーい。
10. おなかがすいて死にそうだ。
11. お腹へった。
か 12. 彼女は色気よりも食い気だ。

49. It's open around the clock.
50. It will take about twenty minutes. Will that be all right?
51. What kind of drink would you like?
52. And then?
53. Yes. What can I do for you?
54. Yes. Anything to drink?
55. Soft boiled or hard boild?
56. How would you like your steak?
    How do you want your steak?
57. I hope you'll come again.
    Please come again.
58. Would you like to wait?
59. There are no seats left.
60. What would you like for your main course?
61. And for your main dish?
62. Here's the menu.
63. Just a moment.
64. How would you like it cooked?
65. Have you decided on the wine, sir?
66. We've reserved a quiet room overlooking the Japanese garden.

(3) With friends and colleagues

1. Let's stay up!
2. Fine, let's go.
3. I'll drive you home.
4. Let's have a drink for a change.
5. I'll buy you a drink.
6. Won't you come with me for a drink?
7. Thanks. That's nice of you.
8. Let me pay.
9. You smell of liquor!
10. I could eat a horse.
11. I'm hungry.
12. She prefers eating to romance.
    She's fonder of food than of boys.

13. 軽い物が食べたい。
14. 彼はもう出来上がっている。
15. 乾杯！
16. 気の抜けたビールや炭酸飲料はごめんだね。
17. 君と話しができて楽しかったよ。

18. 君のが来ましたよ。
19. ケーキには目がないんですよ。
20. ここで食べます。
21. ごちそうさま、お腹がいっぱいです。
22. この酒は飲めるよ．
23. このへんで切り上げましょうか？
24. コーヒーでも飲みに行こう。
25. これはおいしくない。
26. これは何？
27. これは私のおごりです。

28. 今夜は外食にしよう。
29. 今夜パーティーに行きませんか？
30. 今夜僕と食事しない？
さ 31. さあ、着きましたよ！
32. 誘ってくれてどうも。
33. そこらの店で、ハンバーガーでも食べよう。
た 34. 食べるの早すぎるよ。
35. 誕生日に君を夕食に連れて行けたらなって思うんだけど、
土曜の夜は空いてる？
36. 朝食はまず1杯のオレンジジュースからにしたいね。
37. どういたしまして。
38. どう、コーヒーでも飲みませんか？
39. 同僚を紹介しましょう。
40. とてもおいしい！
な 41. 何か飲みたくてたまらない。
42. 飲みに行こう。

は 43. ひさしぶりだね。

44. ビールの一杯目はやっぱりうまいね！
45. 昼めしはホッドドッグですませておこう。

13. I'd like to eat something light.
14. He is already pretty drunk.
15. Cheers!
16. I don't like flat stale beer or gassy drinks.
17. Nice talking to you.
    It's been nice talking with you.
18. Here comes yours.
19. I'm crazy about cake.
20. I'll eat here.
21. I'm full.
22. This *sake* is good.
23. Shall we call it a day?
24. Let's go get some coffee.
25. I don't like this.
26. What's this?
27. This is my treat.
    This is on me.
28. Let's eat out tonight.
29. Would you like to go to a party tonight?
30. Why don't you have dinner with me tonight?
31. Here we are!
32. Thanks for asking me.
33. I'll grab a burger at a local fastfood restaurant.
34. You're eating too fast.
35. I'd really like to take you out to dinner for your birthday. Are you free Saturday night.
36. I'd like a glass of orange juice to start my breakfast with.
37. You're welcome.
38. How about coffee?
39. Let me introduce my colleagues.
40. Oh, delicious!
41. I'm dying for a drink.
42. Let's go out drinking.
    Let's go for a drink.
43. Long time no see.
    It's been a long time.
44. That first sip of beer sure tastes good, doesn't it!
45. I'll make do with a hot dog for lunch.

46. 太りますよ。
47. ぼくは酒に弱い。
48. ほろ酔い気分だ。

ま 49. また、近いうちに。
50. また、次の機会にでも。
51. また連絡ちょうだいね。
52. まだ宵の口だよ。
53. みんなで一杯やりましょう。
54. もう一軒行きませんか?

55. もう一皿[一杯]どう?

や 56. やっぱり、満員だ!
57. 夕食をおごるよ。
58. 酔っぱらっちゃった。

ら 59. ランチデートをしましょう。

わ 60. 私にごちそうさせてください。
61. 私に払わせてください。

62. 私にんじんが苦手なの。
63. 私は刺身が好き。
64. 私も。
65. 私も苦手だ。
66. 私も半分払います。
67. 割勘にしましょう。

⑷ 食事を計画する

あ 1. 朝から何も食べてないんだ、おなかがへって死にそうだ。
2. 明日会いましょう。

3. 明日一緒に昼食でもどうですか?
4. 明日コーヒーでも一緒にどう?
5. 明日 10 時に迎えに行くよ。
6. 明日の午後にお電話をさしあげます。
7. 明日夕食にお招きしたいのです。
8. 明日夕食でも食べに来ませんか?

46. You will put on weight.

47. I get drunk easily.

48. I'm tipsy.

49. See you again soon.

50. Maybe another time.

51. Keep in touch, OK.

52. The night is still young.

53. Let's have a drink.

54. Wouldn't you like to go to just one more place for a night-cap?

55. How about another plate [drink]?

56. Oh, I knew it. It's packed!

57. I'll buy you dinner.

58. I'm drunk.

59. Let's go out for lunch.

60. Let me treat you.

61. Let me pay.
    Let me take care of the bill.

62. I don't like carrots.

63. I like a raw fish.

64. Me, too. / me, either

65. Me, neither.

66. I'll pay half.

67. Let's split the cost.
    Let's split the bill.

(4) For planning to have a meal

1. I haven't eaten since this morning, and I'm dying of hunger.

2. See you tomorrow.
   I'll see you tomorrow.

3. How about having lunch with me tomorrow?

4. Let's meet for coffee tomorrow.

5. I'll pick you up at ten tomorrow.

6. I'll call you tomorrow afternoon.

7. I'd like to invite you to dinner tomorrow.

8. Won't you come and have dinner with us tomorrmw?

9. あっさりした和食が食べたいな。
10. あなたのおすすめのレストランを教えてくれませんか？
11. あのレストランはまずいよ。
12. いいすし屋を知っているので、そこへ行きませんか？
13. いいね、中華なんてどう？
14. いい焼鳥屋があるんです。
15. いいわよ、何時にする？
16. 行きましょうよ！
17. 一緒に昼食でもどうですか？
18. いつだとご都合がよろしいですか？

19. 一杯やりに行きませんか？
20. 今ちょっと無理なんです。
21. 今出られますか？
22. ええ、行きましょう。
23. おなかがすいてきた。
24. お昼ごはんに行きませんか？
25. お昼にしませんか、 テリーさん？
か 26. 会議のあと一緒に行きましょう。
27. 軽い食事がいいですね。
28. 今日はお弁当持ってきましたので。
29. 金曜日のご都合はいかがですか？

30. 9時にしませんか？
31. ご都合が悪くなければ、明晩夕食に招待したいのですが。

32. ご都合はいかがですか？

33. この地方の名物料理を出すレストランはどこでしょうか？
34. この辺で場所を替え、昼食をとりながら話しましょう。
35. この辺にバーガーキングはありますか？
36. この辺にファーストフードのレストランはありますか？
37. 今晩、一杯付き合ってくれませんか？
38. 今晩お暇ですか？
39. 今晩、みんなで一杯やりませんか？

40. 今晩、夕食をご一緒にしませんか？
41. 今夜は家で食べたくないな。

9. I want to eat some light Japanese food.
10. Can you suggest a good restaurant?
11. The food at that restaurant is awful.
12. I know a very good *sushi* restaurant. How about going there?
13. Great idea, Chinese food?
14. I know a good *yakitori* restaurant.
15. All right. When should we meet?
16. Oh, come on. Let's go!
17. Would you like to go out for lunch with me?
18. When is it convenient for you?
    When can you make it?
19. Would you like to go for a drink?
20. Sorry I can't right now.
21. Are you leaving now?
22. Sure, let's go.
23. I'm beginning to feel hungry.
24. Are you coming to lunch?
25. How about lunch, Terry?
26. We can go together after the meeting.
27. We'd like to have a light meal.
28. I brought my own lunch today.
29. Is Friday all right with you?
    Is Friday OK with you?
30. Shall we make it nine o'clock?
31. If it's not inconvenient for you, may I invite you to dinner
    tomorrow evening?
32. Will it be convenient for you?
    Is it all right with you?
33. Where can I have the local specialty?
34. Let's move to a restaurant now, and talk over lunch.
35. Is there a Burger King around here?
36. Do you know if there's a fastfood restaurant near here?
37. Won't you come with me for a drink this evening?
38. Are you free this evening?
39. Let's have a drink this evening.
    Would you like to go for a drink with us this evening?
40. Would you like to have dinner with me this evening?
41. I don't feel like eating at home tonight.

42. 今夜は外食しましょう。料理する気がしません。
43. 今夜はすし屋にお連れしましょう。
44. 今夜は外で食べましょう。
45. 今夜はどなたかと夕食の約束がおありですか？
46. 今夜夕食にお誘いしたいのですが。

さ 47. さあ、行きましょう。
48. 魚料理がいいですね。
49. 先に行って席を取っています。
50. 刺身もおいしいですよ。
51. じゃあ、先に行ってます。
52. じゃあ、下で待ってます。
53. 11時でどうですか？

54. 週末に上野公園でお花見を予定しています。

55. 週末に開く誕生パーティーにお招きしたいのですが。
56. 食事に出かけるのに、何時ごろならご都合がよろしいでしょうか？
57. 食事をする時間です。
58. すしを食べたことがありますか？
59. せっかく日本にいらしたのですから、日本食を食べてみませんか？
60. ぜひおつきあいしたいのですが、今日は少々疲れました。すみません。
61. そうだね、ええーと、1時でどう。
62. 外へ食事に行こう。
63. その日は時間がとれません。
64. その日は都合が悪いのです。
65. それはご親切に、ありがとうございます。
66. それはとてもおいしい食事です。
67. そろそろおなかが空いたでしょう。

た 68. ダイエット中なので、結構です。
69. 他にお約束がおありですか？
70. 近くに日本料理レストランはありますか？
71. 中華料理店へ行くのはどうですか？
72. 昼食に料亭の部屋を予約してあります。気に入っていただけるとよいのですが。
73. 昼食をお済ませになりましたか？

42. Let's go out to eat tonight. I don't feel like cooking.

43. Let me take you to a *sushi* restaurant tonight.

44. Let's eat out tonight.

45. Do you have a prior engagement for dinner tonight?

46. I'd like to take you out to dinner tonight.

47. Let's go.

48. I prefer seafood.

49. OK then, I'll save you a seat.

50. *Sashimi* is also good.

51. OK, I'll see you there.

52. I'll wait for you downstairs, then.

53. Is eleven OK?
    How about eleven o'clock?

54. We're going to have a *hanami* party this weekend at Ueno park.
    We're going to see the cherry blossoms this weekend at Ueno Park.

55. I'd like to invite you to my birthday party this weekend.

56. What time would be best for you to dine out?

57. It's time to eat.

58. Have you eaten *sushi* before?

59. Since you are in Japan, how about sampling some Japanese food?

60. I really wish I could go, but I'm a bit tired today. Sorry.

61. Let's make it at, say, one o'clock.

62. Let's go out for dinner.

63. I'll be busy that day.

64. That date doesn't really suit me.

65. That's very kind of you. Thank you.

66. That's really very good.

67. I suppose you must be hungry by now.

68. No thanks. I'm trying to lose weight.

69. Do you have another engagement?

70. Are there any Japanese restaurants around here?

71. Why not go to a Chinese restaurant?

72. I've booked a room at a *ryotei*, a traditional Japanese style restaurant, for lunch. I hope you like it.

73. Have you finished lunch?

74. 手ごろな値段のレストランを教えていただけませんか？
75. では、明日。
76. では7時にホテルにお迎えにあがります。
77. ではその時に。
78. 天ぷらやすき焼きを召し上がったことはありますか？
79. どうぞ奥さまもお連れください。
80. とくに食べてみたいものがありますか？
81. どこかいいレストランを教えていただけますか？
82. どこか値段も手軽でおいしい日本料理の食べられる店を知りませんか？
83. どこか安くておいしいレストランを知っていますか？
84. どこに行くんですか？
85. どんなものを召し上がりたいですか？
86. どんな料理がお好みですか？

な 87. 何かお好きなものがありますか？
88. 何が食べたい？
89. 何が食べたいですか？
90. 何か食べられないものはありますか？
91. 何時だと都合がいいですか？

92. 何時にお会いしましょうか？
93. 何時に私は来たらいいですか？
94. 何曜日がよろしいですか？

95. 肉は召し上がりますか？
96. 肉料理にしますか、それとも魚料理にしますか？
97. ～日にお会いしたいのですが。
98. 日本料理か中華料理の店を教えていただけますか？
99. 日本料理はお好きですか？

は 100. 腹ぺこです。
101. フランス料理のレストランへ行きませんか？
102. ベジタリアンに向くレストランはありますか？
103. 他の人とご一緒よろしいですか？
104. ぼくのなじみのレストランは高級だよ。
105. ホテルから店までは車で15分ほどです。

106. ホテルでひと休みしたら、あとで一緒に昼食でもいかがで

74. Could you tell me where I can find an inexpensive restaurant?

75. See you tomorrow.

76. Then I'll meet you at your hotel at 7.

77. See you then.

78. Did you ever have *tempura* or *sukiyaki*?

79. Please bring your wife with you.

80. Is there anything you are particularly interested in sampling?

81. Could you tell me the names of some good restaurants?

82. Do you know a reasonable place with good Japanese food?

83. Do you know any good, inexpensive restaurants?

84. Where are you going?

85. What kind of food would you like to have?

86. What kind of food would you prefer?

87. See anything you like?

88. What do you want to eat?

89. What would you like to eat?

90. Is there anything that you can't eat?

91. What time is convenient for you?
    What time will be convenient for you?
    What time do you have in mind?

92. What time shall we meet?

93. What time shall I come?

94. What's a good day?
    What's a good day for you?

95. Do you eat meat?

96. Do you prefer meat or seafood?

97. I would like to meet you ～.

98. Could you suggest a Japanese or Chinese restaurant?

99. Do you like Japanese food?

100. I'm hungry.

101. Why don't we go to a French restaurant?

102. Are there any restaurants for vegetarians?

103. Would you mind sharing a table?

104. My favorite restaurant is very exclusive.

105. It takes 15 minutes or so by car from your hotel to the restaurant.

106. Would you have lunch with me after you have a brief rest at

すか？
107. ホテルの中にシーフードのレストランはありますか？
108. 本格的メキシコ料理を食べたいです。

ま 109. まず刺身、続いて天ぷらというのはどうですか？
110. 万一場所がわからなくなったら、この番号に電話して私を
呼んでください。
111. 明晩7時にホテルのロビーにお迎えにあがります。

112. もう昼どきです、私はおなかが空きました。あなたもそう
じゃありません、何か食べに出ようじゃありませんか。
や 113. 夕食でもいかがですか？
114. 夕食でもご一緒にどうですか？
115. 夕食にお誘いしたいのですが。
116. 夕食にお招きしたいと思います、今晩と明晩どちらがご都
合がよいでしょうか？
117. 夕食にしゃぶしゃぶなどいかがでしょうか？
118. 夕食にすき焼きはいかがですか？

119. 夕食はどこに行きましたか？
120. 夕食は何にしましょうか？
121. 夕食をごちそうさせてください。
122. 有楽町にいい飲み屋があるんです。
123. 喜んで伺います。
124. 予約する必要がありますか？
ら 125. 来週の金曜日に忘年会を開きます。
わ 126. 私に接待させてください。
127. 私はいつでもかまいません、あなたにお任せします。

(5) 外食の予約・約束

あ 1. 明日何時に会いましょうか？
2. 明日の予約をしたいんですが。
か 3. 開店[閉店]は何時ですか？
4. カジュアルウエアでもいいですか？
5. 9時でどうですか？
6. 9時に2人分の席をお願いします。
7. 午後8時ということで店に予約を入れますが、さしつかえ

the hotel?

107. Is there any seafood restaurant in the hotel?

108. I'd like to have some real Mexican food.

109. How about ordering some *sashimi* followed by *tempura*?

110. In case you are lost, call me at this number.

111. I'll meet you at seven tomorrow evening in the lobby of your hotel.

112. Well, it's lunch time. I'm hungry and I imagine you are too. Let's go out for a bite.

113. Why don't you have dinner with me?

114. Would you like to go out for dinner with me?

115. I'd like to take you out to dinner.

116. I'd like to invite you for dinner. Which is more convenient for you, tonight or tomorrow evening?

117. How about trying *shabu-shabu* for dinner?

118. Would you like to try *sukiyaki* for dinner?
     How about having *sukiyaki* for dinner.

119. Where did you go for dinner?

120. What shall we have for supper?

121. Let me treat you to dinner.

122. I have a favorite bar in Yurakucho.

123. Thank you. I'd love to come.

124. Do we need a reservation?

125. We're going to have a year end party, what we call a *bonenkai*, next Friday.

126. Please be my guest.

127. I don't care when. It's up to you.

(5) For making a reservation

1. What time shall we meet tomorrow?

2. I'd like to make a reservation for tomorrow.

3. What time do you open [close]?

4. Is casual wear OK?

5. Is nine OK?

6. Two people at nine, please.

7. I'm booking a table at a restaurant for 8 p.m. tonight. Is that

ありませんか？

8. 御予算はいくらぐらいですか？

9. 今週の金曜日の予約をしたいんですが。

10. 今夜6時に2人お願いします。

さ 11. 残念ながら行かれそうもありません。

12. すてきね、電話して席を予約しておいてくださる？

13. 正装しなければなりませんか？

14. そろそろ行きましょうか？

た 15. 地図を描きましたので、タクシーの運転手に見せてください。店まで連れて行ってくれますから。

16. ディナーは何時からですか？

17. どの席でもかまいません。

な 18. 何時から開店ですか？

19. 何時だと都合がいいですか？

20. 何時まで開いていますか？

21. ネクタイ着用の必要はありますか？

22. ネクタイは必要ですか？

は 23. 8時頃に迎えに行くよ。

24. 8時ではいかがですか？

25. 8時に5人分の席をお願いします。

ま 26. 前払いですか？

27. まだ空席がありますか？

28. 窓際の席に座れますか？

29. 窓際の席をお願いします。

30. 明朝8時にお迎えにあがります。

31. 申し訳ありませんが、約20分遅れます。

や 32. 約束を取り消し[延期]したい。

33. 予約が必要ですか？

34. 予約をしたいのですが。

35. 喜んでまいります。

ら 36. レストランの住所と電話番号を書いておきました。このメ

all right?

8. How much would you like to spend?
   What price range do you have in mind?
9. I'd like to make a reservation for this Friday.
10. Table for 2 at 6 this evening, please.
11. I'm sorry to say that I won't be able to come.
12. Wonderful. Will you call up to reserve a table?
13. Do I have to be formally dressed?
    Do we have to dress up?
14. Shall we go now?
15. Here's the map to show your taxi driver for directions. He'll take you to the restaurant.
16. What time do you start serving dinner?
17. Any table is OK.
18. What time do you open?
19. What time is convenient for you?
20. How late are you open?
    What time is it open until?
21. Is a tie necessary?
    Do I have to wear a tie?
22. Should I wear a tie?
23. I'll pick you up around eight o'clock.
24. How about eight o'clock?
25. Five people at eight, please.
    I'd like a table for five people at eight o'clock.
26. Should I pay in advance?
27. Any seats left?
28. Can we sit by the window?
29. We'd like to have a table near the window.
30. I'll come and meet you tomorrow morning.
31. Excuse me, we will be 20 minutes late.
32. I have to cancel [postpone] my appointment.
33. Do we need a reservation?
34. Reservation, please.
    Can I make a reservation, please?
    I'd like to make a reservation, please.
35. I'd be delighted to.
36. I've written down the address and telephone number of the

モです。
37. 6時にしていただけますか？
38. 6時に迎えに行くよ。
39. 6時半に2人分の席をお願いします。

⑹ レストランに入る

あ 1. 相席してもよろしいですか？

2. あなたをファーストネームで呼んでもいいですか？
3. いつになったら席が空きますか？
4. 一品料理のメニューを見せてください。
5. 英語のメニューをもらいましょうか？
6. おすすめ品は何ですか？
7. お手洗いは廊下の突き当たりです。ご案内しましょう。

8. お店の自慢料理は何ですか？
か 9. カウンター席にしてください。
10. カウンターは空いていますか？
11. 軽い食事がしたいです。
12. 軽い食事ができますか？
13. 気に入りましたか？
14. 今日のおすすめは何ですか？

15. 今日のおすすめ料理は？
16. 今日のランチは何ですか？
17. 今日は何がおいしいですか？

18. 今日は何か特別料理はありますか？
19. 禁煙席をお願いできますか？

20. Kさんはそちらの席へ、Hさんはその隣りにおかけくださ
    いますか？
21. 景色の見える席。
22. ここのおすすめ料理は何ですか？
23. ここの自慢料理は何ですか？
24. ここには定食もありますよ。

restaurant for you. Here you are.
37. Can you make it six?
38. I'll pick you up at six.
39. We'd like a table for two at six thirty.

(6) At restaurants

1. Do you mind if I join you?
   Do you mind if I share the table with you?
2. May I call you by your first name?
3. When can we get a table?
4. May I see the a la carte menu?
5. Shall we ask for an English menu?
6. What do you recommend?
7. The restroom is at the end of the corridor. Let me show you the way.
8. What's the specialty of the house?
9. I'd like to sit at the counter.
10. Is there room at the counter?
11. Any snacks?
12. We'd like to have a light meal.
13. You like it?
14. What are the daily specials?
    What's today's specialty?
15. Will you recommend something today?
16. What is included in the lunch today?
17. What's good today?
    What do you recommend today?
18. Do you have any special dishes today?
19. Nonsmoking, please.
    Nonsmoking area, please.
20. Mr. K, please take a seat over there. Mr.H, will you sit next to Mr.K?
21. A table with a view.
22. What is the specialty of the house?
23. What's your specialty?
24. There is also a set menu.

25. ここはセルフサービスですか？
26. ここは北海道料理の店なので、北海道のよい地酒もそろってます。
27. こちらの床の間のそばにお座りください。
28. この座席よろしいですか？

29. この店はうなぎのかば焼きで有名です。
30. この店は海鮮料理が専門です。
31. この店は何時まで開いていますか？
32. このレストランははやっています。
33. これが本日のスペシャルメニューだと書いてあります。
34. これは会社持ちです。
35. 今晩は何をお召し上がりになりますか？
36. 今晩は。1人用のテーブルをお願いします。

さ 37. 最近は養殖うなぎを使っている店がほとんどですが、この店はちがいます。
38. 魚料理を食べたいのですが、何がおすすめですか？
39. さてと、何を食べましょうか？
40. 3人で、後からもう1人来ます。
41. 3人ですが空いていますか？
42. 3人分の席が欲しいんですが。
43. 時間はどれくらいかかりますか？
44. すき焼きとしゃぶしゃぶではどちらがいいですか？
45. スパゲティにします。
46. すみません。
47. 席はありますか？

48. 全部で4人です。
49. そうですね、ここはすき焼きがおいしいんです。
50. そうですね、ここは天ぷらで有名なんですよ。
51. そのテーブルで結構です。

た 52. たばこを吸ってかまいませんか？
53. 食べられないものがあれば、遠慮なく言ってください。

54. 食べるものは何にする？
55. 卵料理にはどんなものがありますか？
56. ちょっと面倒臭いな。
57. 連れを探してもいいですか？

25. Is this self service here?
26. This restaurant specializes in the regional cooking of Hokkaido. So, they have a large selection of good local *sake*.
27. Please have a seat by the alcove here.
28. Is this seat OK?
    Can I keep this here?
29. This restaurant is famous for barbecued eel, *kabayaki*.
30. This restaurant specializes in seafood.
31. How late are you open?
32. This restaurant is doing good business.
33. It says that this is their special menu for today.
34. This is a business expense.
35. What would you like to order tonight?
36. Good evening. A table for one, please.
37. Most *unagi* (eel) restaurants use cultured eels these days. However, this restaurant is one of the rare exceptions.
38. I'd like a seafood dish. What would you recommend?
39. Well, what shall we eat?
40. Three now and there's one more coming.
41. We are three. Can we have a table?
42. I'd like a table for three.
43. How long will it take?
44. Which would you prefer, *sukiyaki* or *shabu-shabu*?
45. I think I'll have the spaghetti.
46. Excuse me, waiter [Miss].
47. Any seats?
    Is there any place to sit down?
48. Four in all.
49. Well, one of their specialties is *sukiyaki*.
50. Well, they're famous for their *tempura*.
51. Yes, it's fine.
52. May I smoke?
53. Please don't hesitate to let me know if there's anything you can't eat.
54. What are you going to have to eat?
55. What kind of egg dishes do you have?
56. I can't be bothered.
57. Can I look for my party?

58. 定食はありますか？
59. 鉄板焼きがおいしいですよ。
60. では、待ちましょう。
61. テーブルを拭いてくださいませんか？
62. 通りに面した席
63. どのくらいかかりますか？
64. どのくらい待ちますか？

65. どの席でもかまいません。
66. どれもおいしそうですね、おすすめは何ですか？
67. どんな料理がありますか？
な 68. 何がお好きですか？
69. 何がおすすめですか？

70. 何か今日のおすすめのものはありませんか？
71. 何かつまみはありますか？
72. 何をとっていいかわからないな。おすすめは何ですか？

73. 何を召し上がりたいですか？すき焼き、寿司、天ぷら、それともほかにご希望がありますか？
74. 何を召し上がりますか？
75. 何名様ですか？
76. ２階でよろしいでしょうか？
77. 肉はお好きですか？
78. ２名で予約してあるんですが。
は 79. はい、少々お待ち下さい。
80. 早くできるものは何ですか？
81. ふぐ刺しは絶対おすすめですよ。

82. ２人分の席がありますか？
83. ボーイ長（マスター）を呼んでいただけますか？
84. 他に行きませんか？
85. 僕は天ぷらにしよう。
ま 86. 前払いですか？
87. まだ決まってません。
88. 待たせていただいてよろしいですか？
89. 待ち時間はどれくらいですか？

58. Do you have any set menu?

59. *Teppanyaki* is quite good.

60. OK, we will wait.

61. Would you clean this table?

62. A seat facing the street.

63. How long will you be?

64. About how long should we wait?
    How long must we wait?

65. Any table is OK.

66. It all looks good. Any suggestions?

67. What do you have?

68. What would you like?

69. What do you recommend?
    What would you recommend?

70. What do you recommend for today?

71. Do you have something to eat?

72. I don't really know what to order. What would you recommend?

73. Which would you like to eat? *Sukiyaki*, *sushi*, *tempura*, or would you rather have something different?

74. What would you like to have?

75. How many of you are there?

76. We have some room upstairs, if that's OK.

77. Do you like meat?

78. We booked a table for two.

79. Certainly. Just a minute, please.

80. What can you serve quickly?

81. I strongly recommend you try *fugusashi*, a globefish *sashimi* dish.

82. Do you have a table for two?

83. Would you send the manager?

84. Let's go somewhere else.

85. I'll have the *tempura*.

86. Should I pay in advance?

87. I haven't decided yet.

88. May we wait for a table?

89. How long is the wait?
    About how long will we have to wait?

90. 窓際の席に移りたいのですが。

91. 窓際の席に座れますか？
92. 店の自慢料理は何ですか？
93. みんなおいしそう。
94. メニューを見せてください。

95. メニューを見ながら、どれが何かご説明しましょう。
96. もう一度メニューを見せてください。
97. もうランチはやっていますか？
や 98. 野菜はどんな種類がありますか？
99. 4人ですけど、席は空いていますか？
100. 予約してあります。
101. 予約してある中村です。
ら 102. ランチセットはありますか？
わ 103. ワインリストを見せてください。
104. 和食になさいますか、西洋料理になさいますか？
105. 私の経費でおとします。

(7) 店内での注文

あ 1. ああ、お腹すいたなあ！
2. アップルパイをお願いします。
3. ありがとうございます、でも結構です。
4. あれと同じものをください。
5. いいえ、決めかねています。
6. いいですね、僕もそうしますよ。
7. 急いでくださいませんか？
8. 今注文したいのですが？
9. ウェルダンにしてください。
10. うん、もう一杯コーヒーが欲しいな。
11. ええ、お願いします。トマトスープとステーキをお願いします。
12. えーと、ホットケーキにしてみようかな。君は？
13. 塩分は控えめにしてください。

90. I'd like to move to the window table, please.
    I'd like to change to the seat by the window.
91. Can we sit by the window?
92. What's your specialty?
93. Everything looks good.
94. May I have a menu, please?
    Let me have a menu, please.
    Can I see the menu, please.
    I'd like the menu, please.
95. Let's see the menu and I'll explain to you what's what.
96. I'd like to see the menu again, please.
97. Are you serving lunch now?
98. What kinds of vegetables do you have?
99. Do you have a table for four?
100. I have a reservation.
101. I have a reservation, Nakamura.
102. Do you have a set lunch menu?
103. Wine list, please.
104. Are you in the mood for Japanese or Western food?
105. This is part of my expense account.

(7) For ordering

1. Oh, I'm starving.
2. I'd like apple pie.
3. Thank you, but no.
4. The same, please.
5. No, I just can't make up my mind.
6. That's a good idea. I think I'll join you.
7. Will you rush my order, please?
8. May I order, please?
9. Well done, please.
10. Yes. I'd like another cup of coffee.
11. Yes, please. I'd like some tomato soup and a steak.

12. Well, I think I'll try the pancakes. How about you?
13. Don't use too much salt.

14. おいしそうね、私も同じものを注文しよう。
15. お先にどうぞ召し上がってください。
16. おすすめの前菜はありますか?
17. オーダーを変えたいのですが?
18. 同じ物をお願いします。

か 19. カキが好物なのですが、カキはありますか?
20. 餃子はありますか?
21. 今日のおすすめは何ですか?
22. 今日の定食をお願いします。
23. ここの自慢料理は何ですか?
24. ここはセルフサービスですか?
25. このステーキは焼きすぎです。
26. この店のおすすめ品は何ですか?

27. この店の名物料理は何ですか?

28. この料理にサラダは付いていますか?
29. コーヒーだけ注文してもいいですか?

30. コーヒーは食後にお願いします。

31. これとこれをお願いします。
32. これは注文していません。
33. これはどんな料理ですか?
34. これは量が多すぎます。
35. これは私が注文したものと違います。

36. これをお願いします。

37. これをください。
さ 38. さっぱりしたデザートはありますか?
39. 砂糖を入れないでください。
40. サラダ用ドレッシングをお願いします。
41. サーロイン・ステーキをミディアムにして下さい。
42. 塩を使わないで料理してください。

14. That sounds good. I'm going to order the same thing.
15. Go ahead.
16. Do you have any special appetizers?
17. May I change my order?
18. Same, please.
    I'll have the same.
    The same for me, please.
    I'd like to order the same.
19. I like oysters very much. Do you have any oysters today?
20. Do you have fried dumplings?
21. What's today's specialty?
22. Today's special, please.
23. What's your specialty?
24. Is this self-service here?
25. This steak is over done.
26. What do you recommend?
    Would you recommend something?
27. What's your specialty?
    What's the specialty of this restaurant?
28. Do you serve salad with this?
29. Is it OK to order only a cup of coffee?
    May I have just a cup of coffee here?
30. I'd like my coffee after the meal, please.
    Coffee later, please.
31. I'll have this and this.
32. I didn't order this.
33. What kind of dish is this?
34. This portion is too large.
35. This isn't mine.
    This isn't what I ordered.
36. I'll have this, please.
    I'd like this, please.
37. Can I have this one, please.
38. Do you have any light desserts?
39. Without sugar, please.
40. Salad dressing, please.
41. I'll have a sirloin steak, medium rare.
42. Please don't use any salt when you cook it.

43. じゃあ、それにしましょう。

44. 食後にお茶を。
45. 食後にコーヒーをお願いします。
46. 酸っぱいものが食べたい気分です。
47. ステーキがまだ来ないのですが。
48. ステーキはどう？
49. ステーキはどの程度に焼きましょうか？

50. ステーキを生に近く焼いてください。
51. ステーキをほどよく焼いてください。
52. ステーキをよく焼いてください。
53. スプーンをもらいましょうか？
54. すみません、注文したいのです？
55. ぜひそれをお願いします。
56. 前菜を半分ずつ分けてもいいですか？
57. そうだね、トマトのスープにサラダをください。
58. そちらの単品をいくつかとってみませんか？

59. それがいいですね、あとガーデンサラダをください。
60. それからポテトも追加してください。
61. それにします。
62. それはいくらですか？
63. それはどんな味ですか？
64. それを３つ。
65. それをもう２個ください。

た 66. 卵はどういうのが好きですか？
67. 玉ねぎは入れないでください。
68. 注文したものがまだ来ないんてすが。
69. 注文してよろしいですか？

70. 注文をお願いします。
71. 付け合わせは何ですか？
72. 定食はありますか？
73. できるだけ辛くしてください。
74. デザートには何がありますか？

I'd like it cooked without salt.

43. OK. Why don't we try it ?
   Let's try it.

44. Tea after the meal, please.

45. I'll have a coffee after dinner, please.

46. I'm in the mood for something sour.

47. My steak hasn't come yet.

48. How about a steak ?

49. How would you like your steak ?
   How do you like your steak ?

50. Rare, please.

51. Medium, please.

52. Well done, please.

53. Shall I get you a spoon ?

54. Excuse me, may I order now ?

55. Please do.

56. Shall we split an appetizer ?

57. Well, I'd like tomato soup and a salad.

58. Shall we order some of those dishes from the a la carte menu ?

59. That sounds fine. I'd also like a garden salad, please.

60. And then, please add French fries.

61. I'll try it.

62. How much is it ?

63. What does that taste like ?
   How does it taste ?

64. Make that three.

65. Two more, please.

66. How would you like your eggs ?

67. Hold the onions, please.

68. Is my order ready yet ?

69. May I order, please ?
   I'm ready to order.

70. Will you take my order, please ?

71. What's the garnish ?

72. Do you have any set menu ?

73. Please make it as spicy as you can.

74. What do you have for dessert ?

75. デザートはけっこうです。
76. では、試してみましょう。
77. テーブルを拭いてくださいますか?
78. どうやって注文するのですか?
79. トーストは焼きすぎないようにしてください。それからコーヒーをください。
80. どのようにして食べるのですか?

81. とりあえず、それだけください。
82. どれが早くできますか?

83. ドレッシングはイタリアンをお願いします。
84. 豚かつはこってりしすぎるから、やめとこうかな。
な 85. なすの天ぷらをください。
86. 何か甘い物が食べたいです。
87. 何かお菓子はありませんか?
88. 何かおすすめ品はありますか?
89. 何か冷たい飲み物がほしいです。
90. 何か他の料理がいいですか?

91. 生ビールは置いていますか?
92. 生ビールをお願いします。

93. 肉が生焼けです。
94. 肉が焼けすぎです。
95. 肉はミディアムに焼いてください。
96. 肉はよく焼いてください。
97. 日本は今、鮎の季節なんです、ためしてみませんか?
は 98. はい、スパゲティを2つお願いします。
99. はじめる前に前菜はいかがですか?
100. パスタはどんな味つけですか?
101. 早くできるものは何ですか?

102. ピクルスは入れないでください。
103. ピザを注文したいのですが。
104. ひとりでは量が多すぎますか?
105. ビフテキをください。
106. ベーコン、レタス、トマトサンドイッチを下さい。

75. No space for dessert, thank you.
76. OK. I'll try it.
77. Would you clean this table?
78. How do I order?
79. I don't want my toast too dark. And a cup of coffee, please.

80. How do you eat this?
    Would you show me how to eat this?
81. That's all for now.
82. What's fast?
    What can you serve quickly?
83. Italian dressing, please.
84. A pork cutlet is very heavy so I think I'll skip it.
85. Give me an order *tempura* of eggplant.
86. I would like something sweet.
87. Do you have any sweets?
88. What do you recommend?
89. I want something cold to drink.
90. Could I get you something else?
    Anything else I can get you?
91. Do you have draft beer?
92. A draft, please.
    Could I have a draft beer, please?
93. This is too rare.
94. This is overdone.
95. Medium, please.
96. Well done, please.
97. It's the season now for *ayu*. Why don't you try it?
98. Yes, two spaghettis, please.
99. Shall we have some hors d'oeuvres before we start?
100. What is the pasta like?
101. What's fast?
    What can you serve quickly?
102. Hold the pickles, please.
103. I want to order a pizza.
104. Is it too much for one person?
105. I'd like to have a beefsteak, please.
106. Please give me a B.L.T.

107. べつにマカロニサラダをください。
108. ほかに何か召し上がりませんか？
109. ポタージュスープとグリーンサラダ、それとサーロインステーキをお願いします。
110. ポテトはいかがですか？

ま 111. マスタードをつけてください。
112. まだ決まっていません。

113. ミディアムにお願いします。それから野菜の盛り合わせサラダが欲しいのです。
114. ミディアムに焼いてください。

115. ミディアムレアでお願いします。
116. メインディッシュにはまぐりをくださいませんか。
117. 目玉焼きにしてください。
118. 麺類を食べたいのですが。
119. もう一度メニューを見せてください。
120. もう一本ビールをください。

121. もらいましょう。

や 122. 焼いた舌平目をいただいてみます。
123. ゆで卵にしてください。
124. よく焼いてください。

ら 125. ラムチョップはよく焼いたのにしてください。
126. 量を半分にしてもらえますか？
127. レアでお願いします。
128. レタスとトマトも入れてください。
129. ローストビーフをください。

わ 130. 私も同じ物をお願いします。
131. 私もそれにしよう。

⑻ 飲み物の注文

あ 1. 赤ワインを1本お願いします。
2. 赤ワインをグラスで2つお願いします。
3. 暑いよ。のどが渇いて死にそうだ。休んで何か飲もう。

107. I'll have a side order of macaroni salad.
108. Won't you have something else?
109. I'll have potage soup, green salad, and a sirloin steak, please.

110. Would you like French fries?
111. Put some mustard on it.
112. I'm not ready.
    I haven't decided on anything yet.
113. Medium, please. And I'd like mixed green salad.

114. Medium, please.
    Would you make my meat medium?
115. Medium rare, please.
116. Could I have the clams as a main course?
117. Sunny side up, please.
118. I'd like to have noodles.
119. May I see the menu again?
120. Another beer, please.
    May I have another bottle of beer?
121. I'll take it.
122. I think I'll try the broiled sole.
123. I'll have boiled eggs, please.
124. Well done, please.
    Could you cook my meat well done, please?
125. I'll have the lamb chops, well done, please.
126. Could you cut it in half?
127. Rare, please.
128. Please add some lettuce and tomato.
129. Please give me some roast beef.
130. Same, please.
131. I'll have that too.

(8) For ordering drinks

1. Could I have a bottle of red wine, please?
2. Two glasses of red wine, please.
3. It's so hot and I'm dying of thirst. Let's stop and get a drink.

4. あなたももう1杯いかがですか？
5. 甘くておいしいです。
6. いいえ、結構です。

7. いいですね、冷やでいただきます。
8. いただきます、スコッチはありますか？
9. 一杯飲めよ。
10. 今はいいです。
11. いや、ブラックで何も入れません。
12. ウイスキーはどうしますか？
13. ウイスキーをロックで。
14. ええ、お願いします。
15. ええ、ではビールをお願いします。
16. おいしいです。
17. おかわり (飲み物) をください。
18. お酒は燗をつけますか、それとも冷やがいいですか？
19. お砂糖をお願いします。
20. おすすめのカクテルは何ですか？
21. オレンジジュースは絞りたてですか？
22. オンザロックをお願いします。

か 23. かしこまりました、お飲み物は何にしますか？
24. 辛口の白ワインを選んでください。
25. 乾杯！
26. グラスワインを注文していいですか？
27. クリームだけお願いします。

28. 氷を入れてください。
29. このお酒は辛口、そちらはもっと甘口です。
30. この料理には辛口の日本酒が合いますよ。
31. コーヒーいかがですか？
32. コーヒーか紅茶をもっといかが？
33. コーヒーだけでもいいですか？
34. コーヒーでも飲みましょう。
35. コーヒーにはクリームと砂糖をお入れしますか？
36. コーヒーには何も入れません。
37. コーヒーはどのように飲まれますか？
38. コーヒーはブラックにしてください。

4. Would you also like another drink?
5. It's nice and sweet.
6. No, thanks.
   No, thank you.
7. Why not? I'll try it cold.
8. Thanks. Do you have Scotch?
9. Have a drink.
10. Actually, I'm OK. Thanks.
11. No, I have coffee black.
12. How would you like your whiskey?
13. Whiskey on the rocks, please.
14. Yes, please.
15. Yes, I'd like a beer, please.
16. It's good.
17. Could I get a refill?
18. Would you like to drink your *sake* warm or would you prefer it cold?
19. With sugar, please.
20. What's your special cocktail?
21. Is the orange juice freshly squeezed?
22. On the rocks, please.
23. Certainly. And what would you like to drink?
24. Please recommend a dry white wine.
25. Cheers!
26. May I order wine by the glass?
27. Only cream, please.
28. With some ice, please.
29. This *sake* is dry, while that one is sweeter.
30. Dry *sake* will go well with this dish.
31. Would you like some coffee?
32. Would anyone care for more coffee or tea?
33. Is it OK to order only a cup of coffee?
34. Let's have a coffee.
35. Will you have cream and sugar in your coffee?
36. I like my coffee black.
37. How would you like your coffee?
38. I like my coffee black.
    Black, please.

39. コーヒーを一杯いかがですか？
40. コーヒーをください。
41. コーラにレモンを入れてください。
さ 42. 最後に一杯いかがですか？
43. 砂糖とミルクをお願いします。
44. 砂糖を2つお願いします。
45. じゃあ、ちょっとだけいただきます。
46. ジュースかお茶をおとりしましょうか？
47. 焼酎というのは、穀類やイモで作った強い蒸留酒です。
48. 食後にコーヒー［紅茶］をお願いします。
49. 白ワインをいただければありがたいです。
50. 白ワインをグラスで2つお願いします。
51. ジントニックをお願いします。
52. ジントニックをもらおうかな。
53. スコッチのソーダ割りにしてください。
54. スコッチの水割りをいただきます。
55. そのままでいいです。
た 56. 炭酸水をください。
57. できればビールをいただきたいのですが。
58. とりあえずビールをお願いします。
59. どんな飲み物がありますか？
60. どんなフルーツジュースがありますか？
な 61. 何かお飲みになりますか？

62. 何か飲み物はいかがですか？
63. 何をお飲みになります？　日本酒をやってみますか？

64. 生ビールをいただけますか？
65. 日本の酒を召し上がったことがありますか？
66. 喉が乾いたなあ。
67. 飲み物のメニューを見せてください。
68. 飲み物は何がありますか？
69. 飲んだばかりなので。
は 70. ハウスワインはありますか？
71. はじめに飲み物をお願いします。
72. ハーブティーをください。
73. ビール、ウイスキー、ワイン、日本酒があります。何がよ
　　ろしいですか？

39. Will you have a cup of coffee?
40. Give me some coffee, please.
41. Coke with a slice of lemon, please.
42. How about one for the road?
43. With sugar and cream, please.
44. Two sugars, please.
45. OK. Just a little.
46. Shall I get you some juice or green tea?
47. *Shochu* is a strong spirit distilled from grain or potatoes.
48. I'll have coffee [tea] after dinner.
49. A glass of white wine would be fine, thank you.
50. Two glasses of white wine, please.
51. I'd love a gin tonic.
52. I think I'll have a gin tonic.
53. Could I have a scotch and soda?
54. Scotch and water would be fine.
55. No thanks. That's fine.
56. A carbonated water, please.
57. I think I'll have a beer, if you have any.
58. For the time being, beer, please.
59. What do you have to drink?
60. What kind of fruit juices do you have?
61. Would you like something to drink?
    Could I get you something?
62. Would you like something to drink?
63. What would you like to drink? Would you like to try some *sake*?
64. A draft, please.
65. Have you ever tasted Japanese *sake* before?
66. I'm thirsty.
67. Please show me the wine list.
68. What kind of drinks do you have?
69. I just had one.
70. Do you have a house wine?
71. We'd like to order drinks first.
72. I'll have some herb tea.
73. Which would you prefer, beer, whiskey, wine, or *sake*?

74. ビールにします。
75. ビールはどう？
76. ビールは何がありますか？
77. ビールをお願いします。
78. ビールをもう一杯いかがですか？
79. ブラックでお願いします。
80. 僕のコーヒーは甘くしてくれないかな？
81. ホワイトさん、お酒は飲むんですか？

ま 82. 水割りをください。
83. 水をもう一杯欲しいのですが。
84. ミルクだけお願いします。
85. ミルクとお砂糖を入れてください。
86. ミルクと砂糖は？
87. もう一杯いかがですか？
88. もう一杯、同じものを。
89. もう一杯ビールをください。
90. もう少し日本酒をお飲みになりませんか？
91. もうひとつグラスをください。

や 92. 酔いざましに水を1杯ください。
ら 93. 両方お願いします。
94. レモンだけにしてください。
95. レモンティーをください。

わ 96. ワインリストを見せてください。
97. 私が入れましょうか。
98. 私はソーダー水だけで結構です。

(9) 食事中の会話

あ 1. ああ、お願いします。
2. 揚げたての熱いうちに召し上がって下さい。
3. 明日市内観光にいらっしゃいませんか？おともしますよ。

4. アメリカでも最近日本食が人気だそうですね。
5. ありがとう。それはいいですね。
6. いえ、結構です。
7. 今デザートを召し上がりますか？
8. ええ、とても辛いですよ。

74. I'd like to have a glass of beer.
75. How about some beer?
76. What kind of beer do you have?
77. Beer, please.
78. Would you like another beer?
79. Black, please.
80. Could you make my coffee sweet?
81. Mr. White, do you drink?
82. Scotch and water, please.
83. Another glass of water, please.
84. Just milk, please.
85. With cream and sugar, please.
86. Do you want cream and sugar?
87. How about a refill?
88. The same one, please.
89. Could you bring me another beer?
90. Would you like to drink some more *sake*?
91. One more glass, please.
92. Give me a glass of water, so I can sober up.
93. Both, please.
94. Just lemon, please.
95. Give me tea with lemon, please.
96. Wine list, please.
97. Let me make it.
98. Just a club soda for me, please.

(9) At table

1. Oh, yes, please.
2. It must be eaten hot from the pan.
3. Would you like to go sightseeing around the city tomorrow?
   I'll accompany you.
4. They say Japanese food is becoming popular in the U.S.
5. Thank you. That would be nice.
6. No, thank you.
7. Would you like some dessert now?
8. Yes, it's very hot.

9. えーと、サラダはこちらの女性に。
10. おいしい！
11. おいしいですか？

か 12. このインドカレーは私には辛すぎる。
13. このキングサーモンのフライはとてもおいしいですね。
14. この頃は天気が変わりやすいですね。
15. この魚は淡白でいい味だ。
16. このソース、しょっぱすぎると思わない？
17. このトマトは天然の甘味があるね。
18. これが前菜ですか？
19. これは注文していません。
20. これは何ですか？
21. これは何のスープですか？

さ 22. さあ、ビールをもう一杯どうぞ。
23. 再会を祝して！
24. 最高においしい！
25. 魚の練り製品の一種です。
26. さて、今度はカラオケでもどうですか？
27. 砂糖を取ってくれませんか？
28. 砂糖をもうひとさじ入れて下さい。
29. 山椒の粉をうなぎにふって召し上がってみてください。
30. 塩をとっていただけますか？

31. 塩を回していただけますか？

32. 自己紹介させていただきます。
33. 仕事以外に、どこか観光などなさいましたか？

34. しょうゆにいろいろな調味料を合わせたつゆにつけて食べます。
35. しょうゆにつけて食べてください。
36. しょうゆをつけて召し上がってください。
37. すき焼きには、特別な飼料を与え丹精して育てた和牛が最

9. Well, the salad is for the lady here.
10. Delicious !
11. Is it good ?
    How does it taste ?
    How is it ?
    Does it taste good ?
12. This Indian curry is just too spicy for me.
13. This fried king salmon is excellent.
14. The weather is changeable these days.
15. This fish has a very delicate taste.
16. This sauce is too salty, don't you thihk ?
17. This tomato is naturally sweet.
18. Is this the first course ?
19. I didn't order this.
20. What's this ?
21. What's the base of this soup ?
22. Have another glass of beer.
23. To our second meeting !
24. It's very delicious.
25. It's a kind of fish paste cake.
26. How about going to a karaoke house now ?
27. Will you pass me the sugar ?
28. Please put one more spoonful of sugar in it.
29. Sprinkle the powdered *sansho* over the eel and eat it.
30. Could you pass me the salt, please ?
    Will you pass me the salt ?
    Salt, please.
31. Would you please pass the salt ?
    Would you mind passing the salt ?
    Please pass me the salt.
32. Let me introduce myself.
33. Have you had a chance to look around Japan apart from your business ?
34. Eat with a special sauce, which is made with soy sauce and other seasonings.
35. Eat it with soy sauce.
36. Please try it with soy sauce.
37. Cattle fed on special fodder with extra care are said to

高とされています。

38. すごくおいしいよ！

39. 少しだけにしておいたほうがいいですよ。
40. すし飯には、酢、砂糖、塩で味がついてます。
41. ステーキがまだ来ないのですが。
42. ステーキは私です。
43. すみませんが、まだかかりますか？
44. すみません、マスタードを取っていただけますか？
45. その手の味は苦手です。
46. それはどんなものですか？

た 47. 大好物です。

48. 大根おろしは薬味としてつゆに入れてください。

49. 滞在中にとくに行ってみたいところはありますか？
50. 大変おいしいです。
51. 食べ方を教えてくださいませんか？
52. 注文したものと違うんですけど。
53. ちょっと油っこいですね。
54. ちょっと失礼します。（中座する時）
55. デザートはいかがですか？
56. デザートをお持ちしてよろしいですか？
57. とても辛いですよ。

な 58. 何かいいにおいがしますね。
59. 何からできているのですか？
60. 日本のビールを飲んでみてください。

は 61. はい、オニオンスープをカップでお願いします。
62. 灰皿を換えてください。
63. パンのおかわりをください。
64. パンを回してください。
65. フォークを落としました、別のをくださいませんか？
66. 本当においしいですね。

ま 67. まだ作ってないならキャンセルしてください。
68. もう一杯水をいただけますか？

69. もう一本ビールをたのみましょうか？
70. もうひとつグラスをください。

produce the best quality Japanese beef for *sukiyaki*.

38. Oh, delicious!

It's delicious.

39. You'd better take a little.

40. *Sushi* rice is seasoned with vinegar, sugar and salt.

41. My steak hasn't come yet.

42. Waiter, the steak is for me.

43. Excuse me, but is my order ready?

44. Excuse me, please pass me the mustard.

45. I don't like such a taste.

46. What's that?

47. This is my favorite dish.

48. Mix some grated Japanese radish with the sauce as a condiment.

49. Are there any places you'd particularly like to go during your stay?

50. It's very delicious.

51. How do you eat this?

52. This is not what I ordered.

53. It's a little too greasy.

54. Please excuse me.

55. Would you like some dessert?

56. Are you ready for your dessert now?

57. It's very hot.

58. I smell something good.

59. What is it made from?

60. Try Japanese beer.

61. Yes. I'd like a cup of onion soup.

62. Please change the ashtray.

63. Could I have more bread, please.

64. Would you pass me the bread, please.

65. I dropped my fork. Can you give me another?

66. It's really tasty.

67. If you haven't started to make it, I'd like to cancel this order.

68. Another glass of water, please.

I'd like to have another glass of water, please.

69. Shall we order another bottle of beer?

70. One more glass, please.

71. もっとコーンをいただいていいですか？

や 72. 指でつまんで食べてかまいません。

⑽ 食後の会話

あ 1. 明日また私どものオフィスでお会いしましょう。
2. 後で電話して。
3. ありがとう、夕食おいしかったです。
4. ありがとう、チップです。
5. いずれまた機会がありましたら。
6. いろいろありがとうございました。
7. おいしかったです。シェフによろしく。
8. お話しできて楽しかったよ。
か 9. 君がいつも健康でそして幸せでいられますように。
10. ご親切に感謝します。
11. ごちそうさま。

12. このあとお酒でもいかがですか？　近くによいバーがある
んです。
13. この料理を持ち帰れますか？
14. 今度いつ会えますか？
さ 15. さて、コーヒーでも飲みながら、詳細を協議しましょうか。
16. 食事が終わったので、ちょっと仕事の話でもしますか？
17. 食事は済みましたか？
18. それから、お手洗いはどちらですか？
19. それを包装していただけますか？
20. そろそろ行きましょうか？
た 21. タクシーを呼びましょう。
22. デザートにはどんなものがありますか？

23. とてもいいお料理でした。
24. とてもおいしかったです。堪能しました。
25. とても結構な夕食でした。

な 26. 残ったものを詰めてもらえますか？

71. Can I have some more corn?
    Please pass the corn.
72. You can eat it with your fingers.

(10) After meals

1. See you again tomorrow at our office.
2. Give me a call later.
3. Thank you for the wonderful dinner.
4. Thank you. This is for you.
5. I hope we'll have another chance.
6. Thank you for everything.
7. My compliments to the chef.
8. Nice talking to you.
9. May you always be healthy and happy.
10. I appreciate your kindness.
11. I've had enough.
    I'm full.
12. Would you care for a drink? There's a good bar near here.

13. Can I take out this dish?
14. When can I see you again?
15. Well, let's discuss the matter in detail over coffee.
16. Since we've all finished, shall we talk about business a bit?
17. Are you through?
18. And which way is the bath room?
19. Would you wrap it up, please?
20. Shall we go now?
21. I'll get a taxi for you.
22. What kind of dessert do you have?
    What's for dessert?
23. We really enjoyed our dinner.
24. Well, that was an excellent meal. I enjoyed it very much.
25. That was an excellent dinner.
    That was a wonderful dinner.
    I thoroughly enjoyed that dinner.
26. Will you wrap it up?

27. 残った料理を袋に入れていただけますか？
28. 飲み物はもう結構です。
は 29. ビールは僕のおごりだよ。
ま 30. まだ少し時間がありますね。
31. 持ち帰りの注文はできますか？
32. 持ち帰ります。

(11) 支払い時の会話

あ 1. ありがとう、チップです。
2. いくらですか？
3. 今ここで払わなければなりませんか？
4. おいくらになりますか？
5. お勘定お願いします。

6. お勘定が間違ってます。
か 7. 会計でお支払いください。

8. 会計はどこでしょうか？

9. カードでお願いします。
10. カードは使えるのですか？

11. 今日は割り勘にしましょう。
12. 計算が間違ってませんか？
13. ここに請求してください。
14. ここは私のおごりです。
15. ごちそうさせてください。
16. このカードで払ってもいいでしょうか？

17. このクレジットカードで払えますか？
18. これにはサービス料（チップ）も含まれていますか？
19. これは何の料金ですか？
20. 今晩は夕食代私が払うわ。

27. Could you put these in a doggy bag?
28. Nothing more to drink, thanks.
29. The beer is on me.
30. We still have time.
31. Can I order a take out here?
32. I'll take them out.

⑾ For paying a bill

1. Thank you. This is for you.
2. How much is it?
3. Pay now?
4. How much do I owe you?
5. May I have the check, please?
   Could we have the bill, please?
   I'll take the check now.
   Would you bring me the check?
   Check, please.
6. There's a mistake in the bill.
7. Please pay the cashier.
   Please pay at the cashier's desk.
8. Where is the cashier?
   Would you tell me where the cashier is?
9. I'd like to pay with my credit card.
10. Is a credit card OK?
    Can I pay by credit card?
11. Today, let's split the cost.
12. Isn't this bill wrong?
13. This is my billing address.
14. This is my treat.
15. Please be my guest.
16. Is this card OK?
    Can I pay with this card?
17. Do you accept this credit card?
18. Does the bill include a service charge (the tip)?
19. What's this charge?
20. I'll pay for dinner tonight.

21. 今夜は夕食代僕が出すよ。
さ 22. サービス料は入っていますか？

23. 支払いはどこでするのですか？
24. 支払いは別々にしてください。
25. 税込みでいくらになりますか？
26. 全部でいくらになりますか？

27. 全部で～円［ドル］です。
28. そうしましょう。
た 29. テーブルで支払うのですか？
30. トラベラーズチェックでいいですか？
31. トラベラーズチェックは使用できますか？
な 32. 日本円で払ってもかまいませんか？

は 33. 半々にしましょう。
ら 34. 領収書をください。
わ 35. 私のおごりです。
36. 私の分はいくらですか？

37. 割り勘にしましょう。

⑿ ファースト・フード店での会話（客）

あ 1. アップルパイにするわ。
2. いいねえ、僕もそうしようっと。
3. いえ、けっこうです。
4. うん、コーヒー飲みたいね。
5. ええ、まずはトマトジュースを。
か 6. ケン、他に人が座れるように少しつめてくれませんか？

7. ここで食べます。

8. ここに座ってもいいですか？
9. この席は空いてますか？
10. この席は使っていますか？
11. コーヒーがいいわ。

228 PART 13

21. Dinner is on me tonight.
22. Does it include the service charge?
    Is the service charge included?
23. Where should I pay the check?
24. Separate checks, please.
25. How much does it come to, with tax?
26. What's the total?
    How much does that come to altogether?
27. That's ~ yen [dollars] altogether.
28. All right.
29. Should I pay the check at the table?
30. Do you take traveler's checks?
31. Do you accept traveler's checks?
32. Is Japanese money OK?
    Can I pay in Japanese money?
33. Let's split the bill.
34. Can I have a receipt?
35. It's my treat.
36. How much is mine?
    How much is my share?
37. Let's split the cost.

⑫ At fastfood restaurants

1. I think I'll have a piece of apple pie.
2. That sounds good. I think I'll have the same.
3. No, thank you.
4. Yes, I could have a cup of coffee.
5. Yes, first I'll have tomato juice.
6. Ken, could you please move over a little so someone else can sit down?
7. I'll eat here.
   For here.
8. May I sit here?
9. Is this seat taken?
10. Is this seat taken?
11. Coffee would be fine.

12. コーヒーだけでもいいですか？
13. コーヒーにするんでしょう？
14. コーラが飲みたいな。
15. コーラをお願い。

さ 16. スクランブルエッグとトーストにするよ、君は？

17. ステーキサンドにしてみます。
18. スモールをお願いします。
19. すわって待ってて、買ってくるから。
20. それからポテトも追加してください。

た 21. 卵 2 つにコーヒーを持ってきてください。
22. チーズバーガーとオレンジジュースをください。
23. チーズバーガーとフレンチフライを注文してくれるとありがたいわ。
24. チーズバーガー 2 つとコーラ 2 つお願いします。
25. チョコレート・シェイクがいいわ。
26. では、待ちましょう。
27. どうする？

な 28. 何がいい？
29. 何にする？
30. 何を注文しましょうか？
31. 飲み物は？
32. 飲み物はどうする？
33. 飲み物は何かいらない？

は 34. ハンバーガー 1 つ、チキンサンドイッチ 1 つ、ポテトの小 2 つ、それとコーラ 2 つお願いします。
35. ハンバーガー 1 つとコーラの小さいサイズをください。
36. ピクルスは入れないでください。
37. フレンチトーストがよさそうだな。君は何を注文するつもりだい？
38. フレンチフライの大を 2 つください。
39. 他には何にする？
40. ホッドドッグを 1 つください。
41. ポテトチップスとコーヒーを、いやいや、ハンバーガーとコーヒーをください。
42. ポテトはフライドポテトにしてください。

ま 43. 持ち帰りたいのですが。

12. Can I get a seat for just coffee?
13. You're having coffee, aren't you?
14. I feel like having a coke.
15. A coke, please.
16. I'm going to order scrambled eggs and toast. What about you?
17. I'll try a steak sandwich.
18. Small, please.
19. OK. Sit down and I'll get it.
20. And then, please add French fries.
21. Please bring me two eggs and coffee.
22. A cheeseburger and an orange juice, please.
23. An order of a cheeseburger and French fries would be great.

24. I'd like two cheeseburgers and two cokes.
25. I'd like a chocolate shake.
26. OK, we'll wait.
27. What do you want to do?

28. What do you want?
29. What are you going to have?
30. What shall I order for you?
31. How about something to drink?
32. Do you want something to drink?
33. Can I get you anything to drink?
34. One hamburger, one chicken sandwich, two small French fries, and two cokes, please.
35. One hamburger and a small size coke, please.
36. Hold the pickles, please.
37. French toast sounds good. What are you going to order?

38. I'd like two large orders of French fries, please.
39. What else are you going to have?
40. I'd like one hot dog, please.
41. I'd like potato chips and a cup of coffee. On second thought, make that a hamburger and a cup of coffee, please.
42. I'd like French fries.
43. I'd like to take it out.

44. 持ち帰ります。
ら 45. レタスとトマトのハンバーガーがいいわ。
わ 46. 私も。

(13) ファースト・フード店での会話（店員）

あ 1. いらっしゃいませ。
か 2. 決まりましたか？
3. こちらで召し上がりますか、お持ち帰りですか？
4. コーラは大、中、それとも小でしょうか？
5. こんばんわ、何にいたしましょうか？
さ 6. すみません、売り切れました。
な 7. 何か飲み物は？
8. 何になさいますか？
9. 何をつけますか、ケチャップですか、からしですか？　（ホットドッグなどを注文した場合）
は 10. ポテトはいかがですか？
ま 11. もう少し待ってください。
12. 持ち帰りますか、ここで食べますか？
ら 13. ルートビアーはラージですか、スモールですか？

(14) パーティーでの会話

あ 1. ありがとう、すてきなパーティーだったわ！
2. ありがとう、でも本当にもうこれ以上は食べられそうにないわ。
3. いいえ、結構です。

4. いいえ、結構です、十分いただきました。
5. いいえ、本当にもう、ありがとう。
6. いえ、結構です、とてもおいしいけれど、もう十分いただきましたから。
7. 一杯どうですか？
8. いらっしゃい、来ていただいてうれしいよ。
9. いらっしゃい、またお目にかかれてうれしいです。
10. いろいろとお世話になりました。

44. I'll take it out.
45. I'd like a hamburger with lettuce and tomato.
46. Me too.

(13) By employees at fastfood restaurants

1. May I help you?
2. Have you decided?
3. Is that for here or to go?
4. Would you like your coke large, medium or small?
5. Good evening. What will you have?
6. Sorry. We've sold out.
7. Would you like anything to drink?
8. What would you like?
9. What do you want on it, ketchup or mustard?

10. Would you like French fries?
11. Just a moment.
12. Will you take it out or eat here?
13. Would you like your root beer large or small?

(14) At party

1. Thanks very much. It was a great party!
2. Thank you, but I really can't eat any more.

3. No, that's OK.
   No, thank you.
4. No, thanks. I've had enough.
5. No, thanks all the same.
6. No, thank you. It's delicious, but I've had enough.

7. Can I get you a drink?
8. Hi, I'm happy you could make it.
9. Hello. It's a pleasure to see you again.
10. Thank you for everything.

11. うちにもいらしてください。
12. ええ、とくに予定はありません。
13. ええ、フレッシュフルーツ・カクテルをね。
14. ええ、本当にこれ以上はもう食べられないから。
15. ええ、まずシュリンプ・カクテルをもらいます。
16. ええ、もうたくさん、減量中っていうことになっていますから。
17. え、もう？　もっとコーヒーはいかが？
18. お会いするのを楽しみにお待ちしています。
19. お会いするのを楽しみにしていました。
20. お会いできて楽しかったです。

21. おいしいです。
22. お出でくださってありがとうございございました。

23. お気をつけてお帰りください。
24. お口に合わなければ、残してください。
25. 遅れてすみません。
26. お越しくださりありがとうございました。
27. お酒はいかがですか？
28. お酒は各自持参のパーティーです。
29. お酒は召し上がるでしょう？
30. お茶を1杯いただけませんか？

31. お茶をもう少しいかがですか？
32. おつきあいいただき、こちらこそありがとうございました。
　　料理を気に入っていただいたようで嬉しいです。
33. お待たせいたしました。
34. お待ちしておりました。
35. お招きくださってありがとう。
36. お召し上がりください。
37. お目にかかれてうれしいです。
38. お目にかかれてうれしく思います。
か 39. 彼女はパーティーに出席しないの？
40. 彼女はパーティーに出席しますか？
41. 彼は大学時代からの古い友人なんですよ。

11. Please come and see us.
12. Well, I haven't made any plans.
13. Yes. I'll have the fresh fruit cocktail.
14. No, thank you. I just can't eat any more.
15. Yes. I'll have the shrimp cocktail to start.
16. No, thanks. I'm supposed to be on a diet.

17. What? Already? Won't you have more coffee?
18. I'll be looking forward to meeting you.
19. Well, I've been looking forward to seeing you.
20. It was nice meeting you.
    I enjoyed meeting you.
21. This is delicious.
22. I'm glad you could come.
    I enjoyed having you.
    We enjoyed your company.
    Thank you for coming.
23. Take care on the way home.
24. If you don't like it, just leave it.
25. I'm sorry I'm late.
26. I'm glad you could come.
27. Would you care for a drink?
28. It's a bring your own bottle party.
29. You'll have a drink, won't you?
30. One tea, please.
    May I have a cup of tea, please?
31. Won't you have some more tea?
32. Thank you for your company. I'm glad you seemed to like the meal.
33. Thank you for waiting.
34. I have been expecting you.
35. Thank you for inviting me.
36. Help yourself.
37. It's a pleasure to meet you.
38. I'm glad to meet you.
39. Won't she attend the party?
40. Will she attend the party?
41. He's my old friend. We've known each other since we were

42. 来ていただいてうれしいです。
43. 来てくれてありがとう。
44. 気をつけてお帰りください。
45. クッキーでもどうぞ。
46. クッキーやお菓子をどうぞ。
47. ケーキをもうひとついかがですか？
48. ケーキをもっといかがですか？
49. こうして会って飲めるなんてとても嬉しいよ。
50. 紅茶とコーヒーのどちらをお飲みになりたいですか？
51. ご招待ありがとうございます。
52. こちらこそ楽しかったよ。
53. コーヒーと紅茶はどちらがいいですか？
54. コーヒーのおかわりはいかがですか？
55. コーヒーはどうしますか、砂糖かミルクを入れますか？
56. これ以上食べられないほどいただきました。
57. これはどうも。このパーティーに出るのを本当に楽しみにしていました。
58. 今晩は、ホワイトさん、ご招待いただきましてありがとうございます。
59. 今晩は、ようこそいらっしゃいました。
60. 今夜パーティーに来られますか？
61. 魚をお召し上がりですね。提案をしてもよろしいですか？
62. サラダはもう食べないの？
63. じゃあ、行かなくちゃ。
64. 自由にお菓子を召し上がってください。
65. じゅうぶん召し上がりましたか？

66. 出席できてよかったですよ。
67. すばらしいお食事をありがとうございました。
68. すばらしいディナーでした。
69. すばらしい日本料理をありがとうございました。
70. すばらしいパーティーをありがとうございました。
71. すばらしい夕食をありがとうございました。

72. すみませんが、そろそろ失礼します。
73. せっかくですが伺えません。
74. そう言っていただくとうれしいです。

university students.

42. I'm glad you could home.
43. Thank you for coming.
44. Take care on the way home.
45. Please help yourself to the cookies.
46. Help yourself to cookies and sweets.
47. How about another piece of cake?
48. Would you like some more cakes?
49. I'm so glad we could get together for a drink.
50. Which would you like to drink, tea or coffee?
51. Thank you for inviting us.
52. It was our pleasure.
53. Which would you prefer, tea or coffee?
54. Would you like some more coffee?
55. How would you like your coffee, with sugar or cream?
56. I've had more than enough.
57. Thank you. I've been looking forward to your party.

58. Good evening, Mr.White. Thank you for inviting us.

59. Good evening. I'm so happy you could come.
60. Can you come to the party tonight?
61. Well, you are having fish. May I make a suggestion?
62. Can't you eat the rest of the salad?
63. Well, I have to go.
64. Please help yourself to the cake.
65. Did you get enough to eat?
    Did you have enough?
66. It's nice to be here.
67. Thank you for a wonderful meal.
68. That was a great dinner.
69. Thank you very much for the superb Japanese dinner.
70. Thank you for the lovely party.
    Thank you for a wonderful party.
71. Thank you for the very enjoyable dinner.
72. Sorry but we're going to have to be leaving.
73. I'm afraid I won't be able to come.
74. I'm glad to hear that.

75. そう、こんなに早く行かなくちゃならないなんて残念だな。
76. そう、残念だなあ。
77. そう！　残念、もっといられたらいいのに。
78. そうしたいのですが、明日の朝早いものですから。
79. そうしたいんですが、もう遅いですから。
80. そうね、あなたが何か食べるなら私も食べることにするわ。
81. そうね、じゃあパイをひと切れいただきます。
82. そうね、でも先にオレンジジュースをもらいます。
83. その時間にお伺いします。
84. その日は他に用事はありません。
85. その日は約束はありません。
86. ソフトドリンクをご自由に召し上がってください。
87. それはいいですね、何時にディナーを食べましょうか？
88. それはどうも、あいにく肉はいただかないのです。
89. そろそろ行かないと。
90. そろそろおいとましないと。
91. そろそろおいとましなければなりません。
92. そろそろ失礼しなければなりません。

た 93. たいへん楽しかったです。

94. 楽しく過ごしました。招待してくださってありがとう。
95. できればシャンペンをグラスでほしいね。
96. デサートに何かいただこうよ。
97. デサートは食べられるでしょう？
98. デサートはどう？
99. デサートも食べないの？
100. テーブルのものを何でも勝手に取って食べてください。
101. どういたしまして、こちらこそ。
102. どういたしまして、また近いうちにいらしてください。
103. どうぞおかけください。
104. どうぞお召し上がりください。
105. どうぞお楽になさってください。
106. どうぞ召しあがれ。

107. どうもありがとう、とても楽しかったです。
108. とっても楽しい晩でした、ありがとう。

75. Well, I'm sorry you have to leave so early.
76. Well, it's too bad that you have to go.
77. Oh! I'm sorry. I wish you could stay.
78. I'd love to, but I have to get up early tomorrow.
79. I wish I could, but it's already late.
80. Well, I'll join you if you're having something.
81. Well, maybe I'll have just a small piece of pie.
82. Yes, but I think I'll have orange juice first.
83. I'll be there then.
84. I have no other business that day.
85. I have no appointments that day.
86. Help yourself to the soft drinks.
87. That's a great idea. What time shall we have dinner there?
88. Thanks, but I don't eat meat. Sorry.
89. I really should be on my way.
90. I'd better be going.
91. I think it's about time we got going.
92. I'm afraid I have to leave now.
93. I had a wonderful time.
    I enjoyed myself very much.
    I had the time of my life.
94. I had a wonderful time.Thanks for inviting me.
95. I'd like a glass of champagne, if possible.
96. Why don't we have something for dessert?
97. You're going to have dessert, aren't you?
98. Would you like some dessert?
99. Aren't you going to have dessert?
100. Help yourself to anything on the table.
101. You're quite welcome. It was my pleasure.
102. Don't mention it. I hope you can come again soon.
103. Please take a seat.
104. Please help yourself.
105. Please make yourself at home.
106. Help yourself.
     Go ahead.
     Please have some.
107. Thank you very much. We really had a good time.
108. Thank you for a very enjoyable evening.

109. とてもすてきなパーティーですね。
110. とてもすばらしい夕べでした。
111. とても楽しいパーティーでした。
112. とても楽しく過ごさせていただきました。
な 113. 中へどうぞ、またお会いできて良かった。
114. 何かお飲み物はいかがですか？
115. 何かもっと軽いものがよろしいでしょうか？
116. 何から何までありがとうございました。
117. 何をお飲みになりますか？
118. 何をお持ちしましょうか？
119. 何時だと都合がよろしいですか？
120. 肉をもっといかがですか？
121. 日本へようこそ、ケリーさん、ではみなさん、乾杯！
は 122. はい、おなかがいっぱいです。
123. パーティーにお招きいただいてありがとう。
124. パーティーの会費は5000円位がいいのじゃないですか？
125. 本当にもうお帰りにならなければならないのですか？
126. 本当はいけないんだけど、アイスクリームをちょっとだけ
    いただきます。
ま 127. まだいいでしょう！　せめてもう一杯。
128. まだ来たばかりじゃないですか、もう少しいいでしょう？
129. 皆様のご協力とご尽力を感謝いたします。
130. 名刺をいただけますか？
131. もうお帰りとは本当に残念です。
132. もうお帰りになるのですか？
133. もう失礼しなければなりません。

134. もう少しゆっくりしていってください。
135. もう、たくさん。減量中なのよ。
136. もう本当に失礼しないと。
137. もう？　もう少しいいじゃありませんか。
138. もちろん！7時にお宅にお邪魔するつもりです。
139. もっとサンドイッチをどうぞ。
140. もっとスープはいかが？
や 141. ゆっくりとお食事をお楽しみください。
142. よい週末を。

109. It's really a nice party.
110. Thank you for a very enjoyable evening.
111. I had a very good time at the party.
112. I had a very good time.
113. Come in. It's nice to see you again.
114. Would you care for something to drink?
115. Would you prefer to have something lighter?
116. Thank you for everything.
117. What would you like to drink?
118. What can I get you?
119. What time will be convenient?
120. Care for some more meat?
121. Now, welcome to Japan, Mr Kery. Everybody, cheers!
122. Yes, I'm full, thanks.
123. Thank you for inviting me to the party.
124. Isn't about 5000 yen each reasonable for the party?
125. Do you really have to go?
126. I really shouldn't, but I'll have a little ice cream.

127. Oh, not yet! At least have one for the road.
128. But you just got here. Can't you stay a little longer?
129. Thanks for your cooperation and efforts.
130. Could I have your business card?
131. Oh, it's a shame that you have to leave.
132. Do you really have to go?
133. I'm afraid I must be going.
    I'm afraid I have to leave now.
    I'm afraid I must be on my way.
    I'm afraid it's time to say goodbye.
134. Can't you stay a little longer?
135. No, thank you. I'm trying to cut down.
136. I really must be going now.
137. So soon? Why don't you stay a little longer?
138. Sure! I'll come to your house at seven.
139. Please have another sandwich.
140. Would you like some more soup?
141. Enjoy your meal!
142. Have a nice weekend.

143. ようこそ。
144. よくいらっしゃいました。
145. 喜んでいただいてなによりです。
146. 喜んでいただけてよかったです。
147. 喜んで伺います。

ら 148. 来週の金曜日にパーティーを開きます。
149. 来週の土曜日にささやかなパーティーを開きます。いらっしゃっていただけますか?
150. 両社の今後の友好と繁栄に乾杯しましょう。

151. 料理はいかがですか?
わ 152. ワインをもう少しいかがですか?
153. わかった、じゃあその時にね。
154. 私どもの大月社長が、今夜の歓迎夕食会であなたにお目にかかるのを楽しみにしております。
155. 私にコーヒーを一杯持って来てくれませんか?
156. 私の作ったクッキーです。召し上がってください。
157. 私のパーティーに来てください。

158. 私のパーティーに来ませんか?
159. 私の友人を紹介します。

⒂ 食品売り場での会話

あ 1. 甘いのはどっちだと思いますか?
2. いいえ、どちらかと言えば甘酸っぱいですよ。
3. 牛のひき肉を 500 g ください。
4. おいしいメロンを選んでくださいませんか?
か 5. カキはいまが旬ですよ、この品は漁港からの直送品です。

6. 今日はこの魚安いですよ。ひとついかがですか、奥さん?

7. この果物は少し酸っぱいです。
8. このパパイヤはどのくらい日持ちしますか?
9. このメロンは 4 、 5 日後が食べ頃です。
10. これは入荷したばかりの熱帯産のパパイヤです。
11. コンビーフを 5 ポンドください。

143. You're very welcome here.
144. It's nice to see you.
145. I'm glad you liked it.
146. I'm glad you enjoyed it.
147. I would love to come.
148. We're having a party next Friday.
149. We are giving a small party next Saturday. Would you be able to come?
150. Let's drink a toast to the future friendship and prosperity of our two companies.
151. How do you like it?
152. How about some more wine?
153. OK. I'll see you then.
154. Our president, Mr.Otsuki, is looking forward to seeing you at your welcome dinner tonight.
155. Would you bring me a cup of coffee?
156. Here are some cookies I made. Help yourself.
157. Please come to my party.
   I'd like you to come to my party.
158. Would you like to come to my party?
159. Let me introduce my friend.

⒂ At groceries

1. Which do you think is sweeter?
2. No, these are rather sour-sweet.
3. Give me 500 grams of ground beef please.
4. Would you select a good melon for me?
5. Oysters are now in season. These were sent directly from the fishing port.
6. The fish is quite reasonable today. How about trying this one, ma'am?
7. This fruit has a bit of an acid taste.
8. How long will this papaya last?
9. This melon will be ready to eat in a few days.
10. This is a fresh, tropical papaya.
11. (I want) Five pounds of corned beef, please.

さ 12. 試食してもいいですか？
  13. じゃあ、３びきいただきます。
  14. その淡い緑のものはなんですか？
  15. その魚高そうね、おいくらですか？
  16. そのほかに、にんじんをください。
  17. それ酸っぱいんでしょう？
  18. それをいただきます。
は 19. パンが焼き上がるのは何時ですか？
  20. ブラウンブレッドを２つください。

補遺・基本英会話

  1. あいにく、今日はありません。
  2. このブロック牛肉の半分をスライスしてください。
  3. 最近贅肉がついてきた。
  4. じゃ、魚は何がありますか？
  5. サケとスズキがあります。
  6. では、スズキを２匹、うろこと腹わたを取ってもらえますか？
  7. 頭と尻尾もとりますか？
  8. いえ、そのままにしておいてください。
  9. １０分したらガスの火を細くしてちょうだい。
 10. こんど開店した中華料理屋に行ってみようよ。
 11. どこか二次会にいかない？
 12. 私は見よう見まねで料理を覚えました。
 13. 火を（強く／弱く）してください。
 14. 火を止めてください。

12. Can I taste it?
13. Well, I'll take three.
14. What's the light green one?
15. That fish looks expensive. How much is it?
16. Give me a side order of carrots.
17. Those are sour, right?
18. I'll take it.
19. What time will the bread be baked?
20. Give me two loaves of brown bread, please.

補遺・基本英会話

1. Not today, I'm afraid.
2. I'd like half of this piece of beef cut in thin sliecs, please.
3. I'm getting flabby these days.
4. In that case, what kinds of fish do you have?
5. [We have] salmon and perch.
6. Could you give me two perch cleaned and scaled, please?
7. Shall I cut off the head and tail?
8. No, just leave them on.
9. Please turn down the gas in ten minutes.
10. Try that new Chinese restaurant.
11. Are we going on somewhere afterward?
12. I learned to cook [cooking] by watching other people.
13. Please turn (up/down) the flame.
14. please turn off the burner.

PART 14

食・ミニ情報（Tips for food, cooking, etc.）

1．蛋白質（Proteins）

　人体のほぼ3分の2は水で、残りの3分の1の約半分が、蛋白質との化合物です。蛋白質は、皮膚、毛髪、筋肉、骨髄など、各組織の最も重要な部分を形成している物質です。蛋白質は子供の成長に非常に重要な役割を果たしています。各組織の維持再生に不可欠で重要な物質なため、大人になっても、常に補給しなければなりません。

　また、蛋白質は、重要な働きをする体内物質の主成分です。血液中に見られる赤色素と蛋白質との化合物であるヘモグロビンは、酸素を肺から身体各部に運搬する働きをし、病原菌やウイルスと戦う抗体も、蛋白質からつくられます。「酸または酵素により加水分解を受けて、アミノ酸のみを生ずるものを単純蛋白質、他の有機物質類をも生成するものを複合蛋白質という。（広辞苑）」

2．炭水化物（Carbohydrates）

　炭水化物は、炭素・水素・酸素の三元素から成ります。糖類、澱粉などの形をとり、穀類、野菜、果物など、植物性食品に含まれています。摂取されると、燃焼されてエネルギー

となり、余ったものは脂肪となって、体内に蓄積されるので、運動量の少ない人にとっては、炭水化物のとりすぎ、なかでも砂糖のとりすぎは特に注意が必要です。

3．ミネラル（Minerals）

ミネラルとは微量元素のことで、正常な人体の約3％を占め、骨とか歯といった硬質な組織に大量に見られます。また他の組織でも、ミネラルは非常に重要な役割を果たしています。カルシウム・リン・マグネシウム・カリウム・ナトリウム・鉄・亜鉛・コバルト・マンガンの類で、普通は無機塩類の形で摂取されます。カルシウムとリンは、強い骨と歯を作り、それらを丈夫に保つミネラルです。カルシウムにはまた、出血したとき血を止める凝結作用のほか、神経と筋肉の働きを正常に保つ作用もあります。カルシウムが最も多い食品は、ミルクですが、ほうれん草のような青菜にも含まれています。

鉄は蛋白質と結合してヘモグロビンを作ります。ヘモグロビンは、身体各部に酸素を運搬する血液中の赤い色素です。

4．ビタミン（Vitamins）

人体内にあるビタミンの量は、どんなときでも、7グラムに満たないと考えられていますが、健康を保つうえで重要な役割を果たしています。各種ビタミンは、体内でほとんど生合成できませんので、植物や細菌が合成したものを直接または間接に摂取する方法しかありません。水溶性ビタミン類は、水に溶けるため、すぐに使い果たされ、体外に排泄され

る率も高いという性質があります。そのために、毎日欠かさず摂取する必要があります。また、水溶性ビタミン類は調理中に失われやすいので、水の使用量を減らして調理したり、調理時間を短くすれば、損失を少なくすることが出来ます。

5．脂肪（Fat）

　脂肪は、正常な人体の約15％を占め、寒いときに熱の消耗を防ぐなど、健康を保つうえで重要な役割を果たしています。栄養素としての最も大きな役目は、人に重要なエネルギーを供給することです。1グラム当たり、蛋白質は4カロリーですが、脂肪は9カロリーと、ぐんと熱量が高く、食べられた脂肪は、まず燃やされてエネルギーとなり、余ったものは体内に蓄積され、必要なときにエネルギー源として利用されます。脂肪は、労働量の多い人には、有用なエネルギー源となりますが、軽い労働や運動量の少ない人には、むしろやっかいなお荷物となります。

6．カロリー（Calories）

　カロリーは、食物中に含まれるエネルギー量をはかる厳密な単位です。純粋1キログラムを摂氏1度だけ高めるのに必要な熱量（エネルギー量）を1カロリーとしています。栄養学では普通には1キロカロリー（1,000カロリー）のことをカロリーと言います。接取された食物は、ほぼ酸素と化合して燃焼し、エネルギーとなります。成人男性の1日当たりのエネルギー所要量は平均2,550キロカロリーですが、1時間当たり、じっと座っているだけでも100カロリー、歩くと

300 カロリー以上を消費すると言われています。体を激しく使い、ごく少量の食物しかとらないことは、体力を急激に消耗します。過食状態では、燃やされない未消費の燃料が残り、肥満の原因となります。

7．動物性脂肪（Animal fat）

　動物性脂肪は、とりすぎると血液の流れを妨げ、心臓病の原因となるので、摂取全カロリー量の3分の1以下に押さえるべきだ、と考えられています。肉、乳製品、卵などの動物性脂肪を、摂取全カロリー量の6分の1以下に押さえるべきだとする意見もあります。また、血管内のコレステロールを過剰にするという問題もあります。コレステロールは、脳や神経組織に多く見られるとともに、肝臓で作られ、飽和脂肪（動物性脂肪）を血液内に運ぶ働きもする重要な物質ですが、動物性脂肪をとりすぎると体内での生産が過剰になり、動脈の壁に付着し、血液の流れを妨げます。その結果、心機能不全が起こりやすくなります。

8．コレステロール（Cholesterol）

人の脳・神経組織・臓器・血液中などに含まれる脂質成分。血管壁の組織にたまると動脈硬化の原因になります。コレステロールを全身に運ぶ役割を持つリポ蛋白には血管壁の組織の余分なコレステロールを抜き出して肝臓に戻す善玉(HDL)とコレステロールを肝臓で受け、血管を通って全身の組織へ運ぶ悪玉（LDL）があります。

9. コレステロールの比較的多い食品
(Foods with cholesterol)

いか・わかさぎ・車海老・鶏卵(卵黄)・鶏肉(もも)・かずのこ・うなぎ・たこ・豚肉(ロース)・鶏肉(レバー)・たらこ・しらす干し・ししゃも・すじこなど。

　これらの食品でも、良い成分をたくさん含んでいるものが多いので、バランスよく食べれば問題はありません。

10. DHA 〈ドコサヘキサエン酸〉
(Docosahexaenoic acid)

　さんま、まぐろなど特に青背の魚には多く含まれ、魚の脂肪分を構成する不飽和脂肪酸の一種。また、コレステロール値を下げる効果のある EPA(エイコサペンタエン酸)が含まれている。DHA には脳の機能を活性化する要素があるといわれ、記憶力の向上、老人性痴呆症の改善、動脈硬化の防止や血栓を予防する物質として知られています。

11. 食生活4つの基本的グループ
(Four fundamental groups)

　栄養のバランスの取り方には、単純な方法があります。毎日、4つの基本的グループに属する食品を、いろいろ取り合わせて食べるという方法です。4つの基本的グループとは1.乳製品グループ、2.肉グループ、3.パン・穀類グループ、4.野菜・果物グループです。一日30〜35品目をバランス良く適量摂取するのが理想的だと言われています。

12. 卵 (Eggs)

卵の用途は非常に広く、栄養価が高いうえに、消化もしやすい食品です。卵をゆでるときは、ナベの中の水が冷たいうちから入れ、それから火にかけ、水が沸騰するところまで加熱します。半熟にするときは、沸騰し始めたらすぐに、ナベを火から降ろし、そのまま、卵を熱湯の中に4分ほど放置します。固ゆでにするときは、沸騰し始めたところで、火を弱め、そのまま弱火で15分ほどゆでます。ゆでた卵は、すぐに冷水に浸すと殻をむくのが簡単になります。

13. 梅干 (Pickled *ume*)

人は、体内の物質代謝サイクルがうまくいかないと、摂取した栄養物の不完全燃焼が起こり、血液中に乳酸がたまってきます。乳酸は疲労の原因となり、筋肉中のタンパク質と結びつくと乳酸蛋白となり、これが筋肉を硬化させ、肩凝りや首の凝り、腰のだるさを引き起こします。さらに細胞の老化、動脈硬化、高血圧、肝臓病や腎臓病、神経痛などの原因にもなります。

代謝サイクルを円滑にする決め手がクエン酸です。梅干の酸っぱさの主成分はクエン酸です。梅干にはカルシウム・リン・鉄などのミネラルも含まれています。肉食中心で体質が酸性になりやすい現代の食生活では、ミネラルの多い食品を取り、血液を弱アルカリ性に保つ必要があります。梅干は百薬の長とも言われています。

14. 米（Rice）

　よい米は粒がそろっていて透明感があります。蛋白を含み、脂肪がほどほどあって、糖質を中心に澱粉があるもので、質の良い米にはさらにカルシウム、マグネシウム、カリウムの３つのミネラルがより多く含まれます。お米が脂肪の多い肉や、甘い煮物などよりもダイエットにいいことは確かなことです。

15. ご飯を炊く（Boiling rice）

　米は手早くかき回しながら数回洗えば十分です。研ぎ過ぎると粒がかけたり、表面が削られて、米粒中の蛋白質、ミネラル、アミノ酸などの成分が流出しやすくなります。米の澱粉は、水分と熱で分子の構造が変わって糊化します。糊化に必要な水量は、新米なら水を控えめに、古米なら多めにします。

　米が水を十分に吸収しないうちに加熱すると、糊化がうまくいかなく、澱粉を糖分に変える酵素の働きも不十分になり、ご飯の甘みにも影響します。またミネラルウォーターを少し加えると良く炊けます。１時間つければ、糊化には十分で、つけすぎると米の表面がふやけてご飯につやがなくなります。

16. 牛乳（Milk）

　牛乳は天然の食品の中で最も栄養価の高い食品で、タンパク質、脂肪、乳糖、カルシウム、リン、ビタミン類のほとん

どを含み、特にタンパク質の 80 ％がカゼインという物質で、
必須アミノ酸 8 種をすべて含んでいます。

　哺乳動物の赤ちゃんが乳で成長する姿を見ても、理想的な
栄養素をもっていると言えます。

17. 酢（Vinegar）

　品質のよい米や穀物が使われている酢は、アミノ酸やミネ
ラル類が豊富に含まれています。健康にも料理にもプラス効
果が大きく、殺菌作用があり、コレステロール値を下げ、ア
レルギーをおさえ、血液をさらさらにする有益な成分をもっ
ています。

18. 味噌（*Miso*）

味噌は味も栄養的にも日本の食卓に欠かせません。最近では
健康面での優れた効用が科学的に解明され、味噌の持つ健康
食品としての機能性が幅広く注目されています。その効用と
しては、コレステロールの制御、動脈硬化やガンの予防、胃
潰瘍・老化の防止や美肌効果など多岐に及んでいます。

19. 食物繊維を含む主な食品
　　（Foods with dietary fiber）

こんぶ・いんげん豆・オートミール・切り干し大根・バナ
ナ・寒天(乾燥)・ごぼう・納豆・おから・えのきだけ・干し
推茸・うずら豆・小豆・とうもろこし・キーウィ・しめじ・
きなこ・そば・干し柿・ひじき(乾燥)など。

20. ノンカロリーの主な食品 (Noncalorie foods)

こんにゃく・昆布・椎茸・えのきだけ・舞茸・しらたき・干し海苔・とろろ昆布・ひじき・松茸・しめじ・ひらたけ・青海苔・わかめ・いわ海苔・もずく・はつたけ・なめこなど。

21. カルシウムを含む主な食品
(Foods with calcium)

わかさぎ・小松菜・ひじき(乾燥)・木綿豆腐・切り干し大根・丸干しいわし・牛乳・高野豆腐・干しわかめ・桜海老・プロセスチーズ・ししゃも・干し海苔・はぜなど。

22. 鉄を含む主な食品 (Foods with iron)

豚肉(レバー)・虹ます・まぐろ(赤身)・煮干し・きなこ・ひじき(乾燥)・わかさぎ・大豆・切り干し大根・パセリ・ほうれん草・あさり・高野豆腐・いんげん豆・干し海苔・はまぐり(つくだ煮)・しじみなど。

23. ビタミンAを含む主な食品
(Foods with vitamin A)

鶏肉(レバー)・小松菜・にんじん・かぶ(葉)・パセリ・うなぎ・にら・鶏卵(卵黄)・バター・春菊・ほうれん草・マーガリン・プロセスチーズ・干しわかめ・牛の肝臓など。

24. ビタミン B₁ を含む主な食品
(Foods with vitamin B₁)

強化米・豚肉(ロース)・ロースハム・ベーコン・豚肉(ヒレ)・豚肉(バラ)・豚肉（モモ)・日本そば・大麦・胡麻・玄米・落花生など。

25. ビタミン B₂ を含む主な食品
(Foods with vitamin B₂)

豚肉(レバー)・かれい・ししゃも・丸干しいわし・干し推茸・鯖・魚肉ハム・アーモンド・鶏卵・プロセスチーズ・強化米・納豆・うずら卵・どじょうなど。

26. ビタミン C を含む主な食品
(Foods with vitamin C)

柿・いちご・小松菜・メロン・さつま芋・蓮根・ブロッコリー・夏みかん・ほうれん草・グレープフルーツ・ネーブルオレンジ・はっさく・カリフラワー・かぶ(葉)・グアバ・パパイヤ・ピーマンなど。

27. ビタミン D を含む主な食品
(Foods with vitamin D)

鮭・まぐろ(脂身)・鯖・さわら・めざし・めかじき・虹ます・さんま・さつま揚げ・しめじ・かれい・うなぎ・かつお・ぶり・生推茸・まいわしなど。

28. ビタミン E を含む主な食品
(Foods with vitamin E)

うなぎ・まぐろ・ほうれん草・鮭・たらこ・かぼちゃ・いか・にら・アボガド・高野豆腐・アーモンド・ぶり・さつま芋・マーガリン・鶏卵(卵黄)など。

29. ことわざ・名句あれこれ (Proverbs)

1. 新しい酒を古い皮袋に入れるな
   (釣り合わないことをするな)
   Do not put new wine into old bottles.

2. あのぶどうはすっぱい
   (あんな物欲しくない。手に入らぬときの負け惜しみ)
   The grapes are sour.

3. 網にかかるものは何でも魚だ
   All's fish that comes to the net.

4. 石塀の向こうのりんごはいちばんおいしい
   (人の物はよく見える)
   The apples on the other side of the wall are the sweetest.

5. いちばんいい魚は底の方を泳ぐ
   (最善のものは入手が困難だ)
   The best fish swims near the bottom.

6. 蟹をたてに歩かせることはできない
   (不可能なことはするな)
   You cannot make a crab walk straight.

7. 今日の卵ひとつは明日の鶏1羽にまさる

Better an egg today than a hen tomorrow.

8. 禁じられた果実はいちばんおいしい

（不義の快楽は最も楽しい）

Forbidden fruit is sweetest.

9. 空腹はいちばんのソース

（すき腹にまずいものなし）

Hunger is the best sauce.

10. 腐った魚と呼び売りするな

（自分のことを卑下するな）

Don't cry stinking fish.

11. 腐ったりんごは仲間を腐らせる

（悪友と交わるな）

The rotten apple injures its neighbour.

12. コックは大勢過ぎるとスープが台なしになる

（船頭多くして船山に登る）

Too many cooks spoil the broth.

13. 酒に誠あり

In wine there is truth.

14. 食物は生命の糧

Bread is the staff of life.

15. 卵を残らずひとつ篭に入れるな

（全財産を一事業に投資するな。危険は分散せよ）

Don't put all your eggs in one basket.

16. 卵を割らずにオムレツは作れない

（目的を達するには何か犠牲を払わねばならない）

You cannot make an omelet without breaking
eggs.

17. 読書と精神の関係は食物と肉体の関係と同じである

Reading is to the mind what food is to the body.

18. のど元過ぎれば熱さ忘れる

A crisis once past is too soon forgotten.

19. 腹が減っては戦ができぬ

An army marches on its stomach.

20. 半分のパンでもないよりはまし

Half a loaf is better than none.

21. 人の心をつかむには胃袋をねらえ

（うまいものを食べさせれば、夫はいつも妻を愛する）

The way to a man's heart is through his stomach.

22. 火のないところに煙は立たぬ

Where there's smoke, there's fire.

23. 袋に入った豚は買うな

（品物は見ないで買うな）

Never buy a pig in a poke.

24. 暴食は剣よりも多く人を殺す

（戦死する人より食い過ぎて死ぬ人の方が多い）

Gluttony kills more than the sword.

25. 水はいちばんの飲み物

Adam's ale is the best brew.

26. 実を食べようとする者はクルミを割らなくてはならぬ

（まず努力せよ）

He that would eat the kernel must crack the nut.

27. 楽あれば苦あり

Take the good with the bad.

28. 1日1個のリンゴで医者知らず

An apple a day keeps the doctor away.

29. 弱肉強食

the law of the jungle

30. 商業ビル内に関する重要語句
（At commercial bldg.）

案内所	information desk
1 階	first floor〈米〉; ground floor〈英〉
入り口	entrance
エスカレーター	escalator
エレベーター	elevator〈米〉; lift〈英〉
屋上	roof (top)
お手洗い	restroom
階段	stairs
化粧室	powder room
最上階	top floor
3 階	third floor〈米〉; second floor〈英〉
12 階	the 12th floor〈米〉; eleventh floor〈英〉
女子用手洗い	ladies' room, WOMEN〈米〉; LADIES〈英〉
男子用手洗い	men's room, MEN〈米〉; GENTLE-MEN〈英〉
地下（地下室）	basement
地下 1 階	the first basement
地下 2 階	the second basement
地下貯蔵庫	cellar
中 2 階	mezzanine
陳列台	market stall
手洗所	lavatory; wash room
出口	exit
テーブル	table
展望台	observatory
2 階	second floor〈米〉; first floor〈英〉
非常口、避難口	emergency exit
廊下	corridor

31. レストラン・酒場の標識・掲示
   (Signs at restaurants and bars)

営業時間　9時－5時

BUSINESS HOURS; 9 A.M.－5 P.M.

営業中

OPEN

衛生及び安全のため店内への犬の連れ込み禁止

FOR HEALTH AND SAFETY REASONS, DOGS CAN
NO LONGER BE PERMITTED INTO THE STORE

お席にご案内するまでお待ち下さい

PLEASE WAIT TO BE SEATED

お持ち帰り用の料理あります

FOOD TO GO(米), TAKE AWAY(英)

靴を履き、シャツを着用してください

SHOES, SHIRTS REQUIRED

靴を履いていなかったり、シャツを着ていない人には、飲食
物は出しません

NO SHOES, NO SHIRTS, NO SERVICE

コーヒーのお代わりは無料です

COFFEE REFILLS ON US; ENDLESS REFILLS;
ANOTHER CUP OF COFFEE ON US

小切手・つけお断り

NO CHECKS OR CHARGE

サービスタイム(6:00－7:00)

HAPPY HOUR (6:00－7:00)

15日まで臨時休業

CLOSED TEMPORARILY TILL THE 15TH

準備中
　IN PREPARATION; CLOSED FOR CLEANING
定休日
　HOLIDAY
定休日（毎週月曜日）
　CLOSED（ON MON.）
どうぞ自由にお座り下さい
　PLEASE SEAT YOURSELF
24時間営業
　OPEN 24 HOURS
　AROUND THE CLOCK SERVICE
日曜祭日も営業
　OPEN SUNDAYS AND HOLIDAYS
ネクタイ着用でない方はご遠慮いただきます
　GENTLEMEN WITHOUT NECKTIES WILL NOT
　BE SEATED
年中無休
　OPEN EVERY DAY OF THE YEAR
閉店時間
　CLOSING TIME
本日休業
　CLOSED TODAY
よそで買った食べ物を持ち込まないでください
　FOOD BOUGHT ELSEWHERE CANNOT BE
　BROUGHT IN
冷房中
　AIR-CONDITIONING ON
冷房完備

AIR-CONDITIONED
冷房装置
AIR-CONDITIONING

32. お祝いの表現 (Congratulations)

ご成功おめでとうございます。

Congratulations on your success.

ご卒業おめでとうございます。

Congratulations on your graduation.

ご就職おめでとうございます。

Congratulations on your new job.

銀婚式おめでとうございます。

Congratulations on your silver wedding anniversary.

ご幸福をお祈りします。

I wish you every happiness.

ご結婚おめでとうございます。

I wish you good luck.

お幸せに。

My best wishes to you.

新年おめでとう。

Happy New Year !

誕生日おめでとう。

Happy birthday to you !

クリスマスおめでとう。

Merry Christmas !

再会を祝して！

May we meet again !

33. 家族の構成 （Family）

父	father	子供	child (children)
母	mother	夫婦	husband and wife; couple
夫	husband	息子	son
妻	wife	娘	daughter
両親	parents	長男	the eldest son
兄	elder brother	次男	the second son
姉	elder sister	長女	the eldest daughter
弟	younger brother	次女	the second daughter
妹	younger sister	婚約者	her fiancé （男）／
兄弟	brother		his fiancée （女）
姉妹	sister	義兄	brother in law
おじ	uncle	義姉	sister in law
おば	aunt	従兄弟／従姉妹　cousin	
いとこ	cousin	甥	nephew
祖父母	grandparents	姪	niece
祖父	grandfather	赤ん坊	baby
祖母	grandmother		
孫（男）	grandson		
孫（女）	granddaughter		

34. 会社の役職名 （Position）

会長	chairman
社長	president (boss〈俗〉)
副社長	vice president
専務	executive director
常務	managing director
取締役	director
重役（幹部）	executive; board of directors

顧問	adviser; councillor
相談役	advisory director
監査役	auditor
支店長	general manager
所長	chief manager
(本)部長	(general) manager; head (chief) of the department
次長	deputy manager
課長	section manager
係長	supervisor; head of a section
社員	staff; member; employee
嘱託	part time employee; employment
上司	supervisor
同僚	colleague; associate; co-worker
役員会	board meeting

35. 機内食のメニュー(例) (Meal in a plane)

－TAIPEI-TOKYO 3 Hours 05 Minutes－

夕食	DINNER
酢入りトマト煮	Tomato Vinaigrette
ショサーソース付き ヒレ肉ステーキ	Pan Fried Fillet Steak w/Chasseur Sauce
ポテト煮	Fondante Potatoes
グリンピースバター 炒め	Buttered Green Peas
にんじんつや煮	Glazed Carrots
マンダリン風チキン	Chicken Mandarin
ご飯バター炒め	Buttered Rice
長豆バター炒め	Buttered Long Beans

ソフトロールパン	Soft Roll
バター	Butter
コーヒー	Coffee
紅茶	Tea
緑茶	Green Tea

36. 華氏 (F.) と摂氏 (C.) 対照表

華氏	摂氏	華氏	摂氏	華氏	摂氏	華氏	摂氏
104.0°	40°	82.4°	28°	60.8°	16°	39.2°	4°
102.2	39	80.6	27	59.0	15	37.4	3
100.4	38	78.8	26	57.2	14	35.6	2
98.6	37	77.0	25	55.4	13	33.8	1
96.8	36	75.2	24	53.6	12	32.0	0
95.0	35	73.4	23	51.8	11	30.2	−1
93.2	34	71.6	22	50.0	10	28.4	−2
91.4	33	69.8	21	48.2	9	26.6	−3
89.6	32	68.0	20	46.4	8	24.8	−4
87.8	31	66.2	19	44.6	7	23.0	−5
86.0	30	64.4	18	42.8	6		
84.2	29	62.6	17	41.0	5		

37. 度量衡 (Weights and Measures)

長さ (length)

1 cm (centimeter〈米〉; −metre〈英〉)	0.393701 インチ
1 m (meter〈米〉; metre〈英〉)	3.28084 フィート
1 km	0.621 マイル
1 μ (micron)	0.00003937 インチ
1 インチ (inch) (=0.0833feet)	2.54 cm
1 フィート (foot)；複数 feet	12 インチ (30 cm)
1 ヤード (yard, 0.91 m)	3 フィート
1 マイル (mile, 1.61 km)	1760 ヤード

面積 (area)

1 アール (are)	100 m²
1 ha (hectare)	100 アール
1 坪	3.305785 m²
1 反	991.736 m²
1 m² (square meter)	0.000247 エーカー
1 平方マイル (square mile)	640 エーカー
1 エーカー (acre)	4046.855 m²

体積 (volume)／容積 (capacity)

1 リットル (liter〈米〉; litre〈英〉)	61.024 立方インチ
1 クォート 1qt. (quart)	0.95 l
1 cm³ (cubic centimeter)	0.001 リットル
1 m³ (cubic meter)	252 ガロン〈米〉
1 立方インチ (cubic inch)	0.01639 リットル
1 バーレル (barrel)	158.987 リットル
1 ガロン (gallon)〈米〉	3.78541 リットル
1 ガロン (gallon)〈英〉	4.54609 リットル

重さ（weight）

1 g (gram)	0.0022046 ポンド
1 kg (kilogram)	2.02064 ポンド
1 t (ton)〈米〉	2000 ポンド
1 t (ton)〈英〉	1.12 トン〈米〉
1 オンス 1oz. (ounce)	28.3495 g
1 ポンド 1lb. (pound)	453.5924 g

38. 曜日・月の表示（Days and months）

曜日	日曜日	Sunday (Sun.)
	月曜日	Monday (Mon.)
	火曜日	Tuesday (Tue.)
	水曜日	Wednesday (Wed.)
	木曜日	Thursday (Thu.)
	金曜日	Friday (Fri.)
	土用日	Saturday (Sat.)
	平日	weekday
	週末	weekend
月	1 月	January (Jan.)
	2 月	February (Feb.)
	3 月	March (Mar.)
	4 月	April (Apr.)
	5 月	May
	6 月	June (Jun.)
	7 月	July (Jul.)
	8 月	August (Aug.)
	9 月	September (Sept.)
	10 月	October (Oct.)
	11 月	November (Nov.)
	12 月	December (Dec.)

39. 数と序数 (Numbers)

	数		
		30	thirty
1	one	40	forty
2	two	50	fifty
3	three	100	one hundred
4	four	150	one hundred and fifty
5	five	1,000	one thousand
6	six	10,000	ten thousand
7	seven	100,000	one hundred thousand
8	eight	1,000,000	one million
9	nine		
10	ten		**序数**
11	eleven	第 1	the first
12	twelve	第 2	the second
13	thirteen	第 3	the third
14	fourteen	第 4	the fourth
15	fifteen	第 5	the fifth
16	sixteen	第 6	the sixth
17	seventeen	第 7	the seventh
18	eighteen	第 8	the eighth
19	nineteen	第 9	the ninth
20	twenty	第 10	the tenth

40. 牛肉・豚肉の名称 (Meat joints)

A. 牛肉 (Beef)

1. neck (くび肉)
2. chuck (肩肉)

8. shank (すね肉)
9. plate (ばら肉)

3．rib（あばら肉）

4．loin（腰肉）

5．fillet（ヒレ）

6．rump（尻肉）

7．brisket（胸肉）

10．flank（わき腹肉）

11．round（もも肉）

12．leg（足）

13．tail（尾）

14．tongue（舌）

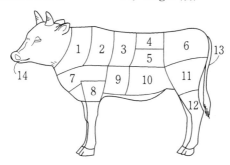

B．豚肉（Pork）

1．ham; fillet; leg（ハム; もも; とっくり）

2．tenderloin（ヒレ）

3．fat back; loin（背ロース）

4．shoulder butt（肩ロース）

5．bacon; belly（ベーコン; バラ; 腹肉）

6．picnic shoulder（肩肉）

7．head（頭）

8．tail（尾）

9．ear（耳）

10．knuckle（膝関節）

11．teats（乳頭）

12．trotter（足）

13．snout（鼻づら）

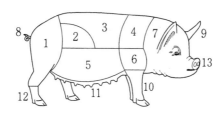

41. 魚の名称 (Fish)

1. snout (口部；口先)
2. mouth (口)
3. eye (眼)
4. gill cover (えらぶた)
5. dorsal fin (背びれ)
6. scales (うろこ)
7. lateral line (側線)
8. tail fin (尾びれ)
9. pectoral fin (胸びれ)
10. pelvic fin (腹びれ)
11. anal fin (尻びれ)

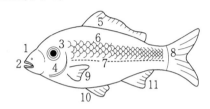

42. 時の表現に関する重要語句 (Time)

あ	朝	morning
	あさって	the day after tomorrow
	明日	tomorrow
	明日の晩	tomorrow night
	あの日に	on that day
	以前に	once
	1時間	one hour
	1時です	It is one o'clock.
	1日中	all day long
	1年間	for a year
	1年前	one year ago
	1ケ月後	one month later; in one month
	1ケ月前	one month ago

	1週間以内に	within a week
	1週間前	one week ago
	いつも	always
	今	now
	おととい(1昨日)	the day before yesterday
か	過去	past
	休暇	vacation
	休日	holiday
	今日	today
	去年、昨年	last year
	9時ちょうどに	at exactly nine o'clock
	曇った日に	on a cloudy day
	今朝	this morning
	現在	present
	5月2日に	on May 2
	午後	afternoon; P.M.
	午後に	in the afternoon
	午後4時	four o'clock in the afternoon
	5時20分	five twenty
	午前	morning; A.M.
	午前3時	three o'clock in the morning
	午前中に	in the morning
	今年(本年)	this year
	今年に	in this year
	ごはん時に	at mealtimes
	今月	this month
	今週	this week
	今日では	nowadays
	今晩	this evening
さ	祭日	national holiday
	さきおととい	three days ago
	昨日	yesterday

	昨日の朝	yesterday morning
	昨晩	yesterday evening
	さっき	some time ago
	3時です	It is three o'clock.
	しあさって	two days after tomorrow
	4月に	in April
	時間	time
	7時半に	at half past seven; at seven thirty
	10時5分	five past ten; ten five
	10時30分	half past ten; ten thirty
	10時15分	a quarter past ten; ten fifteen
	10時15分前	a quarter to ten
	正午	noon; midday
	将来に	in the future
	深夜	midnight
	ずっと以前	long ago
	先月	last month
	先週	last week
	その前日	the day before
た	たった今	just now
	次の月曜日	next Monday
	同時に	at the same time
	時々	sometimes
な	夏に	in summer
	夏休みの間	during summer vacation
	何時ですか	What time is it ?
	2〜3日	a few days
	2時に	at two o'clock
	日没	sunset
	日曜日に	on Sunday
	年始	the beginning of the year
	年度	business year

	年末	the end of the year
は	初めに	at the beginning
	日が暮れる	It's getting dark.
	日付	date
	日の出	sunrise
	昼間	daytime
	秒	second
	分	minute
ま	毎日	every day
	真夜中	midnight
	明後日	the day after tomorrow
	明朝	tomorrow morning
	明晩	tomorrow evening
	未来には	in the future
	昔(かつて)	in the past
や	夕方に	in the evening
	翌日	the next day
	夜が明ける	It's getting lightdown.
	夜が明け始める	It's beginning to get light.
	夜に	at night
	夜になる	The night falls.
ら	来月	next month
	来週	next week
	来年	next year
	6月2日火曜日	(on) Tuesday, the 2nd of June
	6時15分過ぎ	a quarter past six

43. 数値などに関する重要語句 (Quantity)

あ 厚く切った豚肉(あばら骨 1 rib pork chop
　　付き)一枚

1度	a degree
1日当たりのパーセント値	% daily value
1パイントのビール(約0.5リットル)	a pint of beer
1枚	a sheet(紙); leaf(葉)
1個のロールパン	a roll
一対	a pair
一滴	a drop
1杯のコーヒー	a cup of coffee
1片	a piece
1本のワイン	a bottle of wine
インチ	inch; in
牛ひき肉 4/3 ポンド	3/4 1b uncooked ground-beef
うすいホワイトソース 1/3 カップ	1/3 C thin white sauce
ウスターソース小さじ 1/2 杯	1/2 t Worcestershire sauce
大さじ 1 杯	a tablespoonful; 1 T
大さじ 1 杯のバター	1 T butter
大さじ 1 杯のレモン汁	1 T lemon juice
大さじ 2 杯の小麦粉	two tablespoons flour
お酒 1 杯	a cup of *sake*
オンス(約 28.35 g、約 29.6 cc)	ounce; oz
か カップ	cup; C
殻つきの小海老	small whole shrimp
乾燥缶詰とうもろこし 1 カップ	1 cup canned dried whole kernel corn
切り刻んだ固ゆで卵 1 個	1 chopped hard boiled egg
キログラム	kilogram; kg

	グラニュー糖を混ぜたゼリー	jelly and powdered sugar
	グラム	gram; g
	ケーキ1切れ	a piece of cake
	ごく少量	a little
	小さじ1杯	a teaspoonful; 1 t
	こしょうの実2、3粒	a few grains of pepper
	個数	number
	コップ1杯	a glassful
	粉チーズ	grated cheese
	粉チーズ1/2カップ	1/2 C grated cheese
	細かく刻んだ調理済ハム	minced cooked ham
	細かくさいの目に切った生のトマト	diced fresh tomatoes
	小麦粉小さじ1杯	1 t flour
さ	砂糖をもう2さじばかり入れて下さい	Please put two more spoonfuls of sugar in it.
	30度以下です	It's under thirty degrees.
	3分の1	a third; one third
	3分の2	two thirds
	塩小さじ1/2杯	1/2 t salt
	塩小さじ1/4杯	1/4 t salt
	塩、こしょうごく少量	a pinch each of salt and pepper
	塩少々	a pinch [dash] of salt
	12分の1	a twelfth; one twelfth
	食パン1個	a loaf of bread
	酢大さじ1杯	1 T white vinegar
	正確には29.3度です	It's exactly twenty nine point three degrees.
	センチメートル	centimeter; cm
た	高さ2フィートです	It's two feet high.

	高さはどれくらいなの？	How high is it?
	卵 (小) 1 個	1 small egg
	卵の黄身 1 個を軽く泡立てたもの	1 slightly beaten egg yolk
	玉ねぎみじん切小さじ 1 杯	1 t finely chopped onion
	チーズ 3 切れ	three slices of cheese
	茶さじ 1 杯の塩	1 t salt
	茶さじ 2 杯の砂糖	2 t of sugar
	直径はいくつですか？	What's the diameter?
	直径 6 インチです	It's six inches in diameter.
	チリ・パウダー小さじ 1 杯	1 t chili powder
	ティースプーン (小さじ)	teaspoon; t, tsp
	テーブルスプーン (大さじ)	tablespoon; T, tbsp
	豆腐 1 丁	a block of *tofu*
	等分	equal share; equal amount
	トースト 1 枚	a piece of toast
	トマトソース 1 カップ	1 C tomato sauce
な	長さ 5 センチです	It's five cm long.
	長さはどれくらいある？	How long is it?
	生米 1 カップ	1 C uncooked rice
	29 度ちょっと越えるくらい	It's just over twenty-nine degrees.
	煮たキャベツ 1/3 カップ	1/3 C boiled cabbage
	2 分の 1	a half; one half
は	はかり	balance; scale
	パーセント	percent
	バターあるいはマーガリン小さじ 1 杯	1 t butter or margarine
	八分目	eight tenths
	幅 3 インチです	It's three inches wide.
	幅はどれくらい？	How wide is it?
	ハム 2 枚	two slices of ham

	パン粉 1 カップ	1 C bread crumbs
	パン粉 1/2 カップ	1/2 C bread crumbs
	パン 1 かたまり	a loaf of bread
	パン 1 切れ	a piece of bread
	半分に切ったベーコン 8 枚	8 strips of bacon, cut in half
	ひき肉 1/2 ポンド	1/2 lb ground beef
	1 かたまりの砂糖	a lump of sugar
	1 缶のビール	a can of beer
	1 切れ	a slice
	1 粒	a grain
	1 箱	a box
	1 盛［山］	a pile
	1 人分	one helping [portion]
	ピーマンのみじん切り 1/2 カップ	1/2 C finely chopped green pepper
	～袋入	～packets enclosed
	プラス	plus
	ポンド	pound; lb
ま	マイナス	minus
	水 1 杯	a glass of water
	水 1/2 カップ	1/2 C water
	ミディアム・ホワイトソース 1/3 カップ	1/3 C medium white sauce
	ミルク 1/4 カップ	1/4 C milk
	メートル	meter; m
	目分量	eye measure
や	4 分の 1	one fourth; a quarter
	4 分の 3	three fourths; three quarters
ら	りんごの絞り汁 1/4 カップ	1/4 C apple juice

44. お金などに関する重要語句 (Money)

あ	赤字	red figures; in the red
	受け取り手形	bill receivable
か	会計	accounts
	会費	membership fees [dues]
	価格	price; value
	格安	low in price
	格安品	low price goods
	勘定書	check; bill
	給料	pay
	勤労所得	earned income
	クラブの会費	club dues
	月給(俸給)	salary
	決算	reckoning
	原価	cost; price
	現金	cash
	減奉	pay cut
	高価	high price
	高給	high (big) salary
	光熱費	heating and lighting expenses
	小売価格	retail price
さ	採算価格	break even price
	財布	wallet
	先払い(前払い)	payment in advance
	サービス料	service charge
	時給	payment by the hour
	自給自足	self sufficiency
	資金(特定の目的の)	funds
	支出	expenses; outgoings
	実収	net actual income
	実費	actual expenses
	支払	payment
	私費で(自費で)	at one's own expense

	借金	debt; loan
	謝礼	thanks
	収益	proceeds; profits
	集金する	collect money [bill]
	収入	income; earnings
	酒税	liquor tax
	昇給	rise in salary; pay raise
	諸経費	sundry expenses
	生活費	living expenses
	請求	demand
	請求書	bill
	税込み収入	before-tax income
	精算する	clear up (one's debts)
	餞別(せんべつ)	good-bye present
た	代金後払い	deferred payment
	代金前払い	advance payment
	単価	unit price [cost]
	追加予算	supplementary budget
	手当(金銭の)	allowance
	手頃な値段	reasonable price
	手取り給	take-home pay
	倒産する	belly up
な	日給	daily wages [pay]
	入金	receipt of money
	値上げ	raising the price; raising; price hike〈米〉
	値下げ	cut in price
	値段	price
	値引き	reduction in price
	年収	annual income
は	配当金	dividend
	薄利	small profits
	薄利多売	small profits and quick returns
	パーティーの会費	contribution fee

ま	無料	free (of charge)
	明細	details
ら	料金（一般的な）	charge
わ	割り勘	share the expenses; split the cost

45. 料理で使われるカタカナ用語
(English cooking terms)

あ **アッド・オールタニットリイ** (add alternately)

　２つのものを交互に加え混ぜ合わせる。

か **カットアップ** (cut up)

　切り刻む、細かく切る。

カットイン (cut in)

　バターやショートニングを細かく分割してから、小麦粉など乾燥した材料によく混ぜる。ブレンダーか２本のナイフを用いる。

ガーニッシュ (garnish)

　できあがった料理に、刻んだパセリとかパプリカなどを散らす。つまをあしらう。

キューブ (cube)

　一辺が１cm ぐらいの立方体のもの。立方体に切る。ステーキにさいの目を入れる。

クリーム (cream)

　ショートニング（パン、パイなどに用いるバターやラード）あるいはショートニングと砂糖を、スプーンでボールにこすりつけるようにしてかきわまし、クリーム状にする。

グリル (grill)

魚や肉をじか火で網焼きする。あぶり焼きする。

グレイズ (glaze)

風味あるいは装飾のために、シロップやたれをかける。照りをつける。

グレイト (grate)

グレイター(おろし金)でおろす。

さ シア (sear)

肉の表面を素早くあぶりこがす。

シマー (simmer)

たぎらない程度に熱した液でグツグツ煮る。とろ火で煮る。

ジュリエン (julienne)

千切りにする。

シュレッド (shred)

包丁あるいは器具を用いて細長く乱切りにする。

スクレイプ (scrape)

野菜や果物の皮を刃物でひっかくようにそぎ取る。

スコア (score)

網目状の切り目を浅く斜めに入れる。

スコールド (scald)

牛乳など液体を沸騰寸前まで温める。野菜などを湯通しししてあく抜きする。湯がく。

スター (stir)

こげつかないようにスプーンかフォークでかき回す。

スチュー (stew)

とろ火でとろとろ煮る。

スティープ (steep)

色や風味を取り出すために、熱いが煮立っていない液体に浸す。

スティーム (steam)

　蒸気で蒸す、ふかす。

スライス (slice)

　パン、ハムなどを薄くそぐ。

ソテイ (saute)

　少量の油であまり動かさずに揚げる(いためる)。

た ダイス (dice)

　"キューブ"の半分ほどの大きさの立方体に刻む。さいの目に切る。

チョップ (chop)

　包丁あるいは器具を用いて、肉や野菜を大まかに切る。あばら骨付きの厚切り肉片などを切る。

ディープフライ (deep fry)

　油を十分に使って揚げる。

トス (toss)

　軽く持ち上げたりひっくり返したりして混ぜ合わせる。(サラダとドレッシングなど)

トースト (toast)

　パンなどをキツネ色に焼く。

ドット (dot)

　バターやチーズなどの細かいかたまりを料理の表面にばらまく。

ドレッジ (dredge)

　粉をまぶす。小麦粉などを振りかける。

な ニード (knead)

　手を使って強く練り混ぜる。

パウンド (pound)

　肉を柔らかくするために料理用のつちや皿の角などで肉をたたく。

パーボイル (parboil)

　少しの間ゆでる。準備段階の調理で、このあと本格的に調理する。

パンフライ (panfry)

　フライパンを使って少量の油で揚げる。

パンブロイル (panbroil)

　油を塗らないフライパンで蓋をしないで肉を焼く。

ピット (pit)

　果物の種を取り除く。

ビート (beat)

　混ぜ器を使って強くかき混ぜる。泡立てる。

ピューレイ (puree)

　野菜や果物などをつぶし裏ごしにしてどろどろにする。

フォールド (fold)

　泡立てた卵白やクリームなどをほかのものに静かに混ぜ合わす。泡をつぶさないように注意しながら、スプーンかゴムベラを用いてさっくり混ぜ合わす。

フラワー (flour)

　小麦粉をまぶす。

ブランチ (blanch)

　短時間煮沸する。熱湯に通す。アーモンドなどの皮をむきやすくしたり、できあがった食品を冷凍したり缶詰にするときにする。

プリヒート (preheat)

　焼き始める前に鍋やオーブンをあらかじめ適正な温度

に熱しておく。

フレイク (flake)

　魚などの身をフォークを使って細かくほぐす。

ブレイズ (braise)

　しっかりと蓋をした平鍋あるいはオーブンを使って、少量の液体でとろとろ煮込む。

ブレッド (bread)

　パン粉をまぶす。

ブレンド (blend)

　二つ以上のものを十分にかき混ぜる。

ブロイル (broil)

　ブロイラーを使ってオーブンあるいは炭火でじか焼きする。

ペア (pare)

　ナイフなどを使って果物や野菜の皮をむく。

ベイク (bake)

　パンケーキ、じゃがいもなどをオーブンで焼く。

ベイスト (baste)

　肉やケーキを焼いている間に風味をつけるためにバターやたれなどをかける。

ホイップ (whip)

　速く強くかき混ぜ泡立たせる。

ボイル (boil)

　煮る。煮沸する。

ポーチ (poach)

　とろ火でゆるやかに煮る。

ま　マリネイド (marinade)

　酢、ぶどう酒、油、香料、野菜などを混ぜ合わせたつ

け汁に一定時間つける。

ミンス (mince)
肉や野菜をみじん切りにする。

ら レベルオフ (level off)
計量容器に入っているものの上を、ナイフかへらで平らにし余分なものを落とす。

ロースト (roast)
特にオーブンで水を使わずに直接焼く。とうもろこしやじゃがいもなどをアルミホイルなどに包んで、熱い灰や燃えさしの中で焼く。

46. 食に関する用語ひとこと（Terms on cooking）

あ アイソトニック飲料 (isotonic drink)
ミネラル等を含むスポーツ飲料の一種。体に吸収しやすく体液に近い性質を持つ。

アイランドキッチン (island kitchen)
流し・ガス台・調理台を部屋の中央にまとめた台所。

アクアビット (aquavit)
じゃがいもが原料のスカンジナビア産の蒸留酒。

アセロラ (acerola〈西〉; Barbados cherry〈英〉)
熱帯果実。西インド諸島原産。ビタミンCの含有量が特に高い。

アニマルフリー (animal free)
菜食主義者やダイエット中の人向に動物性の食材が含まれない食品。

アペリチフ (apéritif〈仏〉)
ワインなどの食前酒

アボカド (avocado)
熱帯アメリカ原産で脂肪分が多く「森のバター」と呼

ばれ、80％は不飽和脂肪酸。繊維とビタミンＡが多
く14種のビタミンと17種のミネラルを含み栄養価が
高い。

アルマニャック (armagnac)
　フランス産の上等ブランデー。

栄養素 (nutrive elements)
　ビタミン、ミネラル、繊維など栄養のためにとる物
質。

栄養のバランス (balance of nutrition)
　蛋白質、脂肪、糖質などのバランス。

エスニック料理 (ethnic cooking)
　民族的な料理。

エディブルフラワー (edible flower)
　低農薬で栽培する食用花。

FAO (Food and Agriculture Organization of the
United Nations)
　国連食糧農業機関(国連専門機関)。本部はローマ。
1945年に設立。

エンリッチドフード (enriched food)
　ビタミン・ミネラルを加えた栄養価の高い強化食品。

オイル・アンド・ヴィネガー・ドレッシング (oil and
vinegar dressing)
　酢と油をミックスしたシンプルなドレッシング。

オクラ (okra)
　アオイ科の一年草。エジプト原産。煮て食べ、種子は
コーヒー豆の代用になる。強壮効果があるとされる。

か　加圧食品 (pressurized food)
　数千気圧の圧力をかけ殺菌した食品。

海草 (seaweed)
　とくにわかめは、コレステロール値を改善する。

カスタード (custard)
　クリーム状の菓子料理。牛乳・卵・砂糖を煮つめる。

ガストロノミー (gastronomy)
　美食、美食法。

カタドロマス (catadromous)
　降河性魚類。海で生まれて川や湖で育つ魚。

カット野菜 (cut vegetables)
　切り刻んで売られている野菜。

カナッペ (canapé〈仏〉)
　チーズ・魚・卵をパンやクラッカーにのせた食品。

カバーチャージ (cover charge)
　レストランなどでの席料やサービス料。

ガーリック (garlic)
　にんにく。

キュイジーヌモデルヌ (cuisine moderne〈仏〉)
　新傾向のフランス料理の一つで、伝統的料理をさっぱ
　りと仕上げる。

キール (Kir〈仏〉)
　白ワインにクレームドカシスを混ぜたカクテル。

クラブ・サンドイッチ (club sandwich)
　パン三枚に具をはさみ二層になっているもの。

クルトン［クルートン］(croûton〈仏〉)
　スープに浮かべる揚げパン。

ケイターリングサービス (catering service)
　出張料理サービス。その場で料理を提供する。

コキーユ (coquille〈仏〉)
　肉・貝・魚などを貝殻などに似た形の容器に詰め、蒸
　し焼きしたフランス料理。

コテージチーズ (cottage cheese)
　柔らかな白色チーズ。脱脂乳等から作る。

コニャック (cognac〈仏〉)
　高級ブランデー。フランスのコニャック地方の原産。

コラーゲン (collagen)
　皮膚や骨、歯、関節、血管など結合組織を構成する蛋

白質の一種で、素肌を潤す効果があると言われ、人体の蛋白質の 3 分の 1 を占める。

コンソメ (consommé〈仏〉)
　一般的には澄んだスープの総称。肉と野菜を長時間煮込んでこした澄ましスープ。

コーン・ビーフ (corned beef)
　塩漬けビーフのように処理した胸部の肉の薄切り。

コーンフレーク (cornflakes)
　とうもろこしの粉から作る薄片状の食品。

さ　サウザンドアイランド・ドレッシング (Thousand Island dressing)
　マヨネーズがベースのこってりしたドレッシング。

サパークラブ (supper club)
　軽い食事も一緒にできるナイトクラブ。

サングリア (sangria)
　赤ワインに果汁を絞り込み、シロップやソーダで割ったスペインの飲み物。

参鶏湯[さんげたん] (sangetan)
　朝鮮料理で朝鮮人参と鶏肉を煮込んだスープ。強壮、疲労回復、冷え症などによい。

GRAS リスト (generally recognized as safe list)
　米国の食品医薬品局で安全性を認めた食品リスト。

ジェラール (Gerard〈仏〉)
　フランス・ヴォージュ地方のトリイ村で 1800 年頃からジェラル家によってはぐくまれてきた正統派ナチュラルチーズ。

シェリー (sherry)
　南部スペイン原産の強いワイン。食前酒。

ジャンクフード (junk food)
　カロリーは高いが栄養価の低い軽食。

ジャンバラヤ (jambalaya)
　アメリカ南部のスペイン料理で炊き込みご飯の一種。

ジュンサイ (water shield)
　スイレン科の多年生水草。若芽・若葉は食用として珍重。強壮効果があるとされる。

シリアル (cereal)
　コーンフレークやオートミールなど、朝食用に加工された穀物のこと。

スコーン (scone)
　丸く小さいパン。バター・ジャムをつけて食べる。

スープストック (soup stock)
　煮込みなどの材料となる煮だし汁。

スライサー (slicer)
　ハムやパンの薄切り機器。

スルメ (dried cuttlefish)
　肉質にタウリンというアミノ酸が含まれ、それが脳の機能向上や血圧の安定、動脈硬化の予防などにも効果的なことが判明してきている。

セントラルキッチン (central kitchen)
　一カ所で集中的に調理する厨房方式。

ソムリエ (sommelier〈仏〉)
　フランス料理店などでワイン酒を専門に扱う給仕人。

ソムリエナイフ (sommelier knife)
　ワインの栓抜き。

た　ダイエタリーファイバー (dietary fiber)
　食物中にある消化されない成分で、便秘を予防し食物中の有害物質を吸着・排出する作用をする食物繊維。

大豆 (soybean)
　成分のイソフラボンは、骨の指標を改善する。蛋白質や脂質に富んでいる。

タコス (tacos〈西〉)
　とうもろこし粉の薄焼きに、炒めたひき肉や生野菜、チーズなどの具をはさんだメキシコ料理の一種。

タベルナ (tavèrna〈伊〉)

小料理店・軽食堂・居酒屋。

タルタルステーキ (tartar steak)
　刻み玉ねぎやパセリ、ピクルスなどを添えて、生の牛肉を細かくたたき卵黄をのせた料理。

タルタルソース (tartar sauce)
　魚肉料理やサラダに用いるソースで、マヨネーズにピクルスや玉ねぎなどを、みじん切りにして加える。

タルト［タート］(tarte〈仏〉)
　果物入りのパイ、あるいはそれに似せたお菓子。

タンドリーチキン (tandoori chicken)
　インド料理で、ヨーグルトと香辛料に漬け込んだ鶏肉を壺形のかまどで焼いたもの。

チェーサー (chaser)
　水や軽い飲み物。強い酒を飲む時に添える。

チェダーチーズ (Cheddar cheese)
　英国チェダー原産。牛乳を原料として作る堅くてきめの細かいチーズ。

チキンナゲット (chicken nugget)
　骨を抜いた鶏肉を固めて揚げたもの。

チーズフォンデュ (cheese fondue)
　スイスの鍋料理。白ぶどう酒などでよく溶かしたチーズをパンにつけ食べる。

チャツネ (chutney)
　酸っぱい香辛料で、果物・にんにく・唐辛子で作る。

チャパティー (chapati)
　ネパールやインド地方の主食で、小麦粉をこね、せんべいのように焼いたもの。

チルドビーフ (chilled beef)
　０℃前後で保存された冷蔵輸送牛肉で、冷蔵中に適度に熟成する。

低温殺菌牛乳 (low temperature long time pasteurization) **(LTLT)**

低温で加熱殺菌処理した牛乳。

ディジェスティフ (digestif〈仏〉)
　食後酒。消化を促すための酒類。

ディナークルーズ (dinner cruise〈日〉
　客船で海辺の夜景を見ながら食事を楽しむこと。

ティラミス (tiramisu〈伊〉)
　イタリアのデザートの一種。

テキーラ (tequila)
　メキシコ特産の蒸留酒。

テークアウト (take out〈米〉)
　料理品や飲食物の持ち帰り方式。

デザイナーフーズ (designer food)
　目的に応じた新機能性食品。調合した栄養補強食品。

テーブルワイン (table wine)
　食事中に手軽に飲めるワイン。

デミグラスソース (demiglace sauce)
　スープ、トマトピューレなどに牛肉と野菜を炒めたものを煮込み、裏ごしした茶色いソース。

デリカテッセン (delicatessen〈英〉; delikatessen〈独〉)
　食料品店で販売する調理済みの食品。美味、美食の意味もある。

トリュフ (truffle〈仏〉)
　フランス特産で地中に育つきのこの一種。

トロピカルフルーツ (tropical fruits)
　熱帯産果物。

な **ナイトキャップ** (nightcap)
　夜寝る前に飲む酒。

ナチュラルチーズ (natural cheese)
　動物の乳に酵素や乳酸菌などを作用させて固め、醸成、発酵させたもの。

納豆 (fermented beans)
　良質な蛋白質を含み、納豆菌は各種ビタミンを作り、

細菌を殺す性質も高く、コレステロールを減らす成分
や、血圧を下げる効果もあり、健康食の王様と言われ
ている。

ナポリタン (Napolitain〈仏〉)
トマトを使いナポリ風の味付けにしたスパゲティ。

ナリッシュメント (nourishment)
滋養物食物。栄養状態。

ヌーベルキュイジーヌ (nouvelle cuisine〈仏〉)
新鮮な材料を生かして、少量で健康的なスタイルを求
めたフランス料理。

ヌーベルシノワ (nouvelle chinois〈仏〉)
新しい食材の組み合わせで、フランス料理風の盛り付
けが特徴の中国料理。

ノンオイル・ドレッシング (oil free dressing)
油を全く含まないドレッシング。

は バイオ食品 (biotechnology food)
遺伝子組み換え、細胞融合などのバイオテクノロジー
を用いて生産された食品。

ハウス・ドレッシング (house dressing)
店の特製ドレッシング。

バウチャー (voucher)
会社などの近くの飲食店で使用できる共通食事券。

パスタ (pasta〈伊〉)
マカロニ、スパゲティ、ペンネなど洋風麺類の総称。

パストラミ (pastrami)
香辛料をきかせたくん製牛肉など。

蜂蜜 (honey)
糖質は低いがビタミンCや鉄分を含む。

バーボンウイスキー (bourbon)
アメリカ、ケンタッキー州バーボン産ウイスキー。と
うもろこし、ライ麦を主原料にしている。

バンケット (banquet)

宴会やパーティー、晩餐会のごちそう。

ピッツェリア (pizzeria〈伊〉)
　ピザ料理専門店。

ビーフジャーキー (beef jerky〈日〉)
　乾燥させた牛肉食品。

ピルスナー［ピルゼンビール］ (pilsner)
　ホップをきかせた軽い貯蔵ビール。

ピロシキ (piroshki)
　肉・野菜などを小麦粉の皮の中に包み、油で揚げたまんじゅう。

ビンテージ (vintage)
　特に限られた地域の高級ぶどう酒。

ビンテージイヤー (vintage year)
　ぶどうの作柄がよいワインの当たり年。

ファインフード (fine food)
　高付加価値食品。

フアット (fat)
　料理用の油。動植物の脂肪。

ブイヤベース (bouillabaisse〈仏〉)
　魚介類に香草を加えて塩味で煮込んだ南フランス、マルセイユの名物料理。

フィルム食品 (film food)
　食品をシート状に加工したもの。またはシート食品。セロハン食品。

フォアグラ (foie gras〈仏〉)
　特別な飼料を与えて人工的に肥育したガチョウやカモの肥大した肝臓。

フーディズム (foodism)
　特に自然食品や無添加物。食品に関心を持つこと。

プディング (pudding)
　柔らかい洋風蒸し菓子。果実・クリーム・牛乳・卵・砂糖・小麦粉などを材料にする。

フード・チェーンストア (food chain store)
　同じ商標の食品を扱うチェーンの食品小売・飲食店。
ブリーチーズ (Brie cheese)
　フランスのブリー原産。白色で柔らかく塩味のついた
　チーズ。
ブリトー (burrito)
　とうもろこし粉製の皮で食材を包んだメキシコ料理。
フルータリアン (fruitarian)
　健康上や倫理上の理由から動物性食品を食べず、植物
　性食品を食べる人。
ブルーチーズ (blue cheese)
　特異なにおいのある青かびチーズ。
プルニエ (prenier〈仏〉)
　魚料理専門店。フランスの魚料理の総称。
ブルワリー[ブルーハウス] (brewery)
　ビールなど酒類の醸造所。
フレーバーコーヒー (flavored coffee)
　バニラなどの香料を入れたコーヒー。
フレンチ・ドレッシング (French dressing)
　サラダオイルと酢をベースにして、塩、香辛料などを
　混ぜ合わせて作る。
プロセスチーズ (process cheese)
　普通のチーズを加熱して発酵を止め、調味加工し成形
　したチーズ。
ベークドポテト (baked potato)
　じゃがいもを皮つきのまま丸ごと焼いたもの。
ベーグル (bagel)
　リング状の丸パン。クリーム、チーズを添える。
ベスト・ビフォア・デート (best before date)
　食品の賞味期限の日付表示。
ベータカロチン (β-carotene)
　緑黄色野菜に多く含まれ、体内に吸収されてビタミン

Aになる。

ベバリッジ[ビバレッジ] (beverage)
　水以外の飲み物。

ヘルシーフード (healthy food)
　健康志向色の強い食品や料理。

ベルモット (vermouth)
　白ワインをベースに香草や薬草を配合した蒸留酒を加えたもの。

ポアソン (poisson〈仏〉)
　魚介料理。魚。

ボジョレーヌーボー (Beaujolais nouveau〈仏〉)
　フランスのブルゴーニュ地方ボジョレー地区産のワインの新酒。出荷解禁日は11月の第三木曜日。

ホースラディッシュ (horseradish)
　調味料として用いる西洋わさび。

ポトフ (pot-au-feu〈仏〉)
　牛肉と野菜類に香草を入れて煮込んだフランスの家庭料理。

ポートワイン (port wine)
　ポルトガル原産の深紅色のワイン。

ホモ牛乳 (homogenized milk)
　消化しやすくした加工牛乳で、脂肪球を均質に分散したもの。

ボンゴレ (vongole〈伊〉)
　スパゲティなどに殻付きのあさりを入れた料理。

ま　マリネ (marine〈仏〉)
　酢に油やワインなどを混ぜたたれに魚や肉を漬ける。

ミクロブリュー (micro brew)
　自家製ビール。brew は beer の俗語。

ミニブルワリー (mini brewery)
　小規模の地ビール醸造所。

ミネラルウオーター (mineral water)

カルシウム・マンガン・鉄分など鉱物質の栄養分を含む水。

ムニエル (meuniere〈仏〉)
フランス風料理。魚に小麦粉をまぶしバターで焼く。

ムール貝 (moule〈仏〉)
食用となる二枚貝の一種。肉は味が良い。

モルトウイスキー (malt whisky)
大麦の麦芽(モルト)だけを原料にしたウイスキー。

モロヘイヤ (mulukhiya)
中東産の高栄養価緑黄色野菜、水溶性食物繊維を含み、血液中の余分な中性脂肪や悪玉コレステロールを除去すると言われている。

や ユーズ・バイ・デート (use by date)
食品などの使用期限の日付表示。

ら ラガービール (lager beer)
大麦の麦芽を用いて熱処理した貯蔵ビール。

羅漢果[らかんか] (rakanka)
中国原産の乾燥果実。甘みは非常に強いがカロリーは極めて低い。煎じて飲むと咳止めや解熱、高血圧などに効果があると言われる。

ラビオリ (ravioli〈伊〉)
トマトソースや粉チーズをかけて食べるぎょうざに似たイタリア料理。

ラム (rum)
砂糖きびを原料とする蒸留酒。

リキュール (liqueur)
醸造酒や蒸留酒などに果実・薬草を浸したり、糖類・香辛料・色素を加えてつくる。カクテル酒の一種。

リゾット (risotto)
米に肉や玉ねぎ、チーズなどを入れるイタリア風炊き込みご飯。

緑黄色野菜 (brightly colored vegetables)

ベーターカロチン含量の多い野菜。

緑茶 (green tea)
　生産地では胃ガン死亡率が全国平均より極端に低く、
　発ガン抑制効果があると言われている。

レシピ (recipe)
　調理・料理の手順、材料、分量など。

レトルト食品 (retort food)
　調理済み食品を特殊な袋に詰め、密封し高温減菌した
　即席食品。

ロックフォールチーズ (Roquefort cheese)
　フランスのロックフォール原産。羊肉を原料にした強
　い香りのある青かびチーズ。

ローファットミルク (low-fat milk)
　普通の牛乳に比べて脂肪分を少なくしてある牛乳。

わ　ワイナリー (winery)
　ワイン酒の醸造所。

ワーキングディナー (working dinner)
　仕事の話をしながら食べる夕食。

ワーキングランチ (working lunch)
　仕事の話をしながら食べる昼食。

47. 各国の料理 (Foods from various countries)

アフリカ料理	African food
イタリア料理	Italian food
インド料理	Indian food
韓国料理	Korean food
郷土料理	local food
ギリシャ料理	Greek food
スペイン料理	Spanish food
タイ料理	Thai food

中華料理	Chinese food
ドイツ料理	German food
日本料理	Japanese food
フランス料理	French food
ベトナム料理	Vietnamese food
ポリネシア料理	Polynesian food
マレーシア料理	Malaysian food
メキシコ料理	Mexican food
ロシア料理	Russian food

48. パーティーあれこれ（Party）

オープンハウス・パーティー(open house party)
家を開放して、たくさんの人を呼ぶ。

カクテル・パーティー(cocktail party)
各自が自由に料理を取りながら、お酒などを楽しむ。

歓迎パーティー(reception)
開会スピーチ、乾杯、食事、閉会スピーチの順に進む。

スタッグパーティー(stag party)
男性だけの社交的な集い。女性を伴わないパーティー。

ディナー・パーティー(dinner party)
カクテルなどを飲み軽い会話を楽しみながら、ディナーへと進む。席順が決まっている。

バーベキュー・パーティー(barbecue party)
野外にパーティを移したら、男性がリードする。あとは好きなものを食べる。

ブラックタイ・パーティー(black-tie party)
タキシード着用が原則。

ホワイトタイ・パーティー(white-tie party)
燕尾服を着用が原則。

49. フルコース用食器 （Tableware and cutlery）

赤ワイングラス	red wine glass
ウオーターグラス	water glass
オードブルナイフ	hors d'oeuvre knife
オードブルフォーク	hors d'oeuvre fork
コーヒースプーン	coffee spoon
ゴブレット	goblet
魚用ナイフ	fish knife
魚用フォーク	fish fork
皿	plate
サラダボール	salad bowl
サラダサーバー	salad servers
シェリーグラス	sherry glass
シャーベットスプーン	sherbet spoon
シャンペングラス	champagne glass
白ワイングラス	white wine glass
スープ皿	soup plate; deep plate
スープスプーン	soup spoon
タンブラー	tumbler
ディナー用の皿	dinner plate
デザートナイフ	dessert knife
デザートフォーク	dessert fork
ナプキン	napkin, table napkin
ナプキン留め	napkin ring
肉用ナイフ	meat knife
肉用フォーク	meat fork
バター入れ	butter dish
バターナイフ	butter knife
パン皿	bread plate
ワイングラス	wine glass

50. 標準体重一覧表 (Desirable ranges of weight for height for adults)

身長	標準体重	肥満度正常値(10%以下)	肥満度異常値(20%以下)
(height)	(average weight)	(overweight)	(obese)
150cm	45.0kg	49.5kg以下	54.0kg以下
151	45.9	50.5	55.1
152	46.8	51.5	56.2
153	47.7	52.5	57.2
154	48.6	53.5	58.3
155	49.5	54.5	59.4
156	50.4	55.5	60.5
157	51.3	56.5	61.6
158	52.2	57.5	62.6
159	53.1	58.5	63.7
160	54.0	59.4	64.8
161	54.9	60.4	65.9
162	55.8	61.4	67.0
163	56.7	62.4	68.0
164	57.6	63.4	69.1
165	58.5	64.4	70.2
166	59.4	65.3	71.3
167	60.3	66.3	72.4
168	61.2	67.3	73.4
169	62.1	68.3	74.5
170	63.0	69.3	75.6
171	63.9	70.3	76.7
172	64.8	71.3	77.8
173	65.7	72.3	79.1
174	66.6	73.3	79.9
175	67.5	74.3	81.0
176	68.4	75.2	82.1
177	69.3	76.2	83.2
178	70.2	77.2	84.2
179	71.1	78.2	85.3
180	72.0	79.2	86.4

(身長－100)×0.9＝標準体重

51. 補遺・世界の酒

アクアビット	aquavit	北欧
アップルジャック	apple jack	アメリカ
アラック	arrack	中近東
アルマニャック	Armagnac	フランス
カルバドス	Calvados	フランス
キャンティ	Chianti	イタリア
キルシュワッサー	Kirchwasser	ドイツ・スイス他
クミス	kumys	中央アジア
ケフィール	kefir	ロシア・ブルガリア
コニャック	Cognac	フランス
シェリー	sherry	スペイン
テキーラ	tequila	メキシコ
トカイワイン	Tokay wine	ハンガリー
トディ	toddy	スリランカ・中近東
ピンガ	pinga	ブラジル
プルケ	pulque	メキシコ
ポートワイン	port wine	ポルトガル
マッカリ（濁酒）		韓国
マディラ	Madeira	ポルトガル
ミード	mead	東欧
ミラベル	mirabelle	フランス
メスカル	mescal	メキシコ
ラム	rum	ジャマイカ・キューバ

52. 補遺・西洋野菜・新野菜

アーティチョーク	artichoke	食用アザミ。
エンダイブ	endive	縮れた葉の洋野菜。
グリーンリーフ	green leaf	レタスの一種。
コールラビ	kohlrabi	カブに似たキャベツの一種。
スクワッシュ	squash	カボチャの一種。
セルリアク	celeriac	根がカブ状のセロリの変種。
チコリ	chicory	特有の香りと苦みがある。
モロヘイヤ	molokheiya	栄養豊富な野菜。
リーキ	leek	ネギの一種。
ルバーブ	rhubarb	フキに似た赤い野菜。

53. 補遺・食に関する用語 (Terms on cooking)

あ アスパルテーム (aspartame)
人工甘味料で白色の結晶性粉末。

アメリカンサイズ (American size)
容量が 350 mℓ ある大型のもの。

遺伝子組み換え食品 (genetically modified food)

HMR (home meal replacement)
家庭用のメーンディッシュをスーパーマーケットなどで
販売。

エンリッチド　フード (enriched food)
ビタミンやミネラルなどを加えた強化食品。

オーベルジュ (auberge〈仏〉)
宿泊施設を備えた郊外レストラン。

か カーパー (caper)
地中海沿岸を原産地とする香辛料。

ガランティーヌ (galantine〈仏〉)
詰物にした鶏肉料理。

ガルニチュール (garniture〈仏〉)
西洋料理の付け合わせ。肉料理にそえる野菜。

カレンズ (currants)
小粒の種なし干しぶどう。

キーシュ (quiche〈仏〉)
エビ、チーズなどをパイ皮に乗せて焼いたパイ。

キャセロール (casserole〈仏〉)
ふたつき蒸し焼きなべ、その料理。

キュアリング (curing)
食物の保存処理。

グレーシング　レストラン (grazing restaurant)
好みの料理を取って食べるバイキング風のレストラン。

グレープナッツ (grapenuts)
穀物でつくった人造の木の実。

グレン　ウイスキー (grain whisky)
穀物などを原料にしたウイスキー。

グローサリー (grocery)
　食料雑貨店。
ケーシング (casing)
　ねり製品を包む羊や豚の腸。箱、枠などの包装材料。
ケーブ (cave)
　地下や洞窟の酒蔵。
コキール (coquille〈仏〉)
　カニ・エビ・肉などを貝がらの上にのせ、天火で蒸し焼きにしたグラタン。
五臓六腑にしみわたる (sink deep into *one's* heart)
ゴールド　カット (gold cut)
　冷肉やチーズをスライスした盛り合わせ。
コールド　ミート (cold meat)
　冷肉、冷肉料理。
コルネ (cornet〈仏〉)
　菓子などでらっぱ状に巻いた形のもの。
コーン　ビーフ　スタイル (corned beef style)
　大豆などから作ったコーンビーフ。
コーン　ミール (corn meal)
　挽き割りトウモロコシ。

さ　シーズウオー (seeds war)
　種子戦争。国家間企業間での新品種開発のための情報収集争い。
シート食品 (sheet food)
　紙状にした食品。
シャトーブリアン (châteaubriant〈仏〉)
　牛のヒレ肉の網焼きステーキ。
　ボルドー地方産のワイン名。
シャンティー (chantilly〈仏〉)
　泡立てたクリームを使った菓子。
ジャンプ　ステーキ (jump steak)
　カンガルー肉の焼き肉料理。
シャンピニオン (champignon〈仏〉)
　西洋キノコの一種。

シュリンクラッピング (shrink wrapping)
　密封収縮包装。

ショートドリンク (short drink)
　水などで割らない量の少ない食前酒。

ショートニング (shortening)
　油脂の一種で菓子などの歯ざわりをよくするのに使う。

スカッシュ (squash)
　果汁と炭酸水を混ぜた飲み物の総称。

スタウト (stout)
　黒ビールの一種。ギネスなどの銘柄。

シネマバー (cinema bar)
　映画鑑賞をしながら食事や飲酒ができる酒場。

スーパーホット (super hot)
　激辛食品。

スープストック (soupstock)
　煮出し汁。

スフレ (soufflé〈仏〉)
　卵白を泡だてて作った料理や菓子。

スプレードライ (spray-dry)
　噴霧乾燥法で瞬間的に乾燥する食品加工法。

スポーツバー (sports bar)
　飲食しながら、テレビのスポーツ実況中継を鑑賞できる
　バー、レストラン。

スモークドライ (smoke-dry)
　肉・魚を薫製にすること。

清浄食品 (kosher)
　ユダヤ教徒からみて。

た　TTT (time temperature tolerance)
　一定温度で新鮮度がどのくらい保たれるかを表す許容温
　度、時間。

テリーヌ (terrine〈仏〉)
　つぶした魚や肉を型に詰め、オーブンで蒸し焼きにする。

ドライフーズ (dry foods)
　乾燥させ水分を少なくした食品。

は　パイ　アンド　マッシュ (pie and mush)
　ロンドンの庶民風料理。

バイキング（料理）(smorgasbord)

ハーシー (Hershey)
　アメリカの菓子の大手メーカー。ブランド名。

はしご酒（をする）(go barhopping)

パーシャルフリージング (partial freezing)
　半冷凍状態のマイナス3℃で食品を保存する。

パスツリゼーション (pasteurization)
　62℃から65℃で30分加熱する低温殺菌方法。

バースツール (barstool)
　座部が高い円形のいす。

B.Y.O.B. (Bring your own bottle (booze).)
　気軽なパーティーの案内状に書いてあるお酒持参のこと。

ビバレッジ（ベバリッジ）(beverage)
　飲料、飲み物。

ファースティング (fasting)
　超低カロリーの食事療法。断食。

ファッション　フード (fashion food)
　味や栄養よりも外見の良さを示した食品。

ファットスプレッド (fat spread)
　低脂肪で肥満防止用のマーガリン。

フォカッチャ (focaccia〈伊〉)
　イタリアの主食で薄くて平らな丸型パン。

フォローアップ　ミルク (follow up milk)
　離乳期の生後9ヵ月以後に使用するミルク。

フリーズドライ (freeze-dry)
　食品を急速に凍結し真空凍結乾燥する。

フルーツ　ビネガー (fruit vinegar)
　果実酢。

フルーティー (fruity)
　果物の甘ったるい風味。

ブルーパブ (brew pub)
　自家製醸造ビールを出す飲食店。

フレッシュベーカリー (fresh bakery)
　手作りのパンを売る店。

プロム (prom)
　公式の舞踏会。卒業記念に行うパーティー。

ホイップクリーム (whipped cream)
　泡立てた生クリーム。

ポークチョップ (porkchop)
　豚のあばら肉を切り身にして焼いた料理。

ホースラディッシュ (horseradish)
　西洋ワサビ。

ポトフー (pot-au-feu〈仏〉)
　野菜類に香草を入れて煮込んだフランスの家庭料理。

ポトラッチディナー (potlatch dinner)
　各自の得意料理を持ち寄って開く夕食会。

ホーム フリージング (home freezing)
　料理の材料などを家庭で冷凍すること。

ま　マイクロウェーバブル (microwavable)
　電子レンジで調理できることを示す用語。

マセドワン (macédoine〈仏〉)
　野菜のごった煮。

マウスユニット (mouse unit)
　フグなどの毒性を表す単位。

マルチパック (multipack)
　缶飲料を6本一組にする包装。販売方法。

マンナン食品 (mannan food)
　コンニャクの球茎に含まれるマンナンを使った低カロ
　リー食品。

ミート　アンド　ポテイトウズ (meat and potatoes)
　料理の基本材料となることから最も重要なもの、基本。

ミネストローネ (minestrone〈伊〉)
　肉や野菜を細かく刻んで煮た具の多いイタリア料理。

ミルクバー (milk bar)
　牛乳、サンドイッチなど軽食用簡易店舗。

や　USDA (United States Department of Agriculture)
　アメリカ農務省。家畜の肉につけられる等級マーク。

ライト食品 (light food)
　塩分・糖分・アルコール・脂肪をおさえた肥満や成人病

予防食品。

ライフスタイル　ディジーズ (life style disease)
　成人病など食生活から生ずる病気。

リハイドレーション (rehydration)
　乾燥食品などを水を加えて元に戻す。補水する。

レイトプレート (late plate)
　レストランなどで夕食時間帯より遅く出される単品料理。

レディーミックス (ready-mix)
　即席食品で食材が調合済みのもの。

ロングドリンクス (large cocktail)
　時間をかけてゆっくり飲む。

わ　ワインテースター (wine taster)
　ブドウ酒鑑定の時に使う杯。ブドウ酒の品質鑑定人。

54. 水分の含有量 （平均）

レタス	lettuce	97%
キュウリ	cucumber	95%
トマト	tomato	94%
卵	egg	74%
牛肉	beer	70%
鶏肉	chicken	55%
パン	bread	42%
ハム	ham	38%
チーズ	cheese	26%
バター	buttar	9%
砂糖	suger	0%
塩	salt	0%

■ **編著者**

中島　恵子（なかじま　けいこ）
　大阪成蹊大学教授

藤平　英一（ふじひら　えいいち）
　英光社社長

■ **協力**

アラン．D．ローゼン
　熊本大学外国人教師

栄沢啓子

食とクッキング英語小事典（第2版）

[検印廃止]

1998年12月19日　初版発行	2003年8月5日　第6刷発行
2006年6月10日　第2版発行	2024年2月20日　第2版第5刷発行

編 著 者　中島恵子／藤平英一

協 力 者　A. D. ローゼン／栄沢啓子

発 行 者　丸小雅臣

〒 162-0065　東京都新宿区住吉 8-9

発 行 所　**開文社出版株式会社**

TEL 03-3358-6288　　FAX 03-3358-6287
URL https://www.kaibunsha.co.jp

ISBN 978-4-87571-774-4　　C2582